Literary, Rhetorical, and Linguistics Terms Index

Literary, Rhetorical, and Linguistics Terms Index

FIRST EDITION

An Alphabetically Arranged List of Words and Phrases Used in the English-speaking World in the Analysis of Language and Literature, Selected from Authoritative and Widely Consulted Sources, Presented in a Format Designed for Quick Reference, and Including a Descriptive Bibliography of the Sources

Laurence Urdang
Editor in Chief

Frank R. Abate
Managing Editor

Gale Research Company
Book Tower · Detroit, Michigan 48226

Editorial Staff:

Laurence Urdang, *Editor in Chief*

Frank R. Abate, *Managing Editor*

David M. Glixon, *Editor*

Peter M. Gross, *Editor*

Edwin E. Williams, *Editor*

Sue H. Grossman, *Editorial Assistant*

Keyboarding, Programming, and Typesetting by
Alexander Typesetting, Inc., Indianapolis, Indiana
Typographic and Systems Design by Laurence Urdang

Copyright © 1983 by Gale Research Company

Library of Congress Cataloging in Publication Data

Urdang, Laurence.
    Literary, rhetorical, and linguistics terms index.

    "An alphabetically arranged list of words and phrases used in the English-speaking world in the analysis of language and literature, selected from authoritative and widely consulted sources, presented in a format designed for quick reference, and including a descriptive bibliography of the sources.
      Bibliography: p.
      Includes index.
      1. Philology--Terminology--Indexes. I. Abate, Frank R. II. Title.
P29.5.U72   1983   410'.14   83-1636
ISBN 0-8103-1198-4

Contents

Preface 7
How To Use This Book 9
Bibliography 11
Literary, Rhetorical, and Linguistics Terms Index 21

Preface

Owing to an increase of scholarly interest and activity in recent decades, the specialized vocabulary that has long been an essential feature of the technical analysis of language and literature has grown enormously. Simultaneous with this growth, the tendency toward specialization in scholarship has seen the development of new approaches to the study of language and linguistics with a resulting burgeoning of terms to describe them. Perceiving a need to document the terminology of the various interrelated fields of the literary critic, the grammarian, and the linguist, we have compiled *Literary, Rhetorical, and Linguistics Terms Index*. The *Index* is based upon more than 17,000 citations of special words and phrases within certain disciplines, essentially those that, while reflecting different viewpoints, are concerned with language in its many forms. The sources selected for the *Index* are English-language reference books that are readily available and regularly consulted and that use and explain terms frequently encountered in several related subject areas. The goal has been to create a handy reference work for the librarian, the scholar, and anyone who is curious about the fields of literary analysis and criticism, rhetoric, prosody, grammar, linguistics, etc., and who has access to a good, up-to-date reference collection.

The subject areas treated in the *Index* have developed through centuries of observation of language and can be traced to antiquity. Terminology made standard in the writings of Plato and Aristotle and by their successors (notably the scholars of ancient Alexandria, as well as Cicero, Horace, Quintilian, and Longinus) is still in use today. Pāṇini codified a tradition of Sanskrit scholarship which, because of his pioneering work, continued to flourish and then exercised great influence on grammarians in the West. The practice and development of literary and linguistic study, already well established by the fall of Rome, was carried on and enhanced by Byzantine and Arabian scholars and by the European monastic societies and universities; rekindled during the Renaissance, it has spread and become more detailed ever since. More recently many new words and phrases (and new connotations for older terms) have become established, having grown out of the revolutionary insights of critics and linguists of this century. The vast and ever-growing lexicon of language, literature,

8 □ Preface

and linguistics comprises terms both long in use and freshly coined which have arisen from widely disparate sources.

The *Index* provides a convenient tool that can help consolidate this mass of terminology, thus easing the task of those who study language in its diverse aspects. By consulting a word or phrase listed in the *Index* the user can at a glance see how many sources have the term, identify which they are, and then determine where to look for detailed information. In addition, the appearance of an item in the *Index* can be indicative not only of the mere existence of the term in a special sense, but also of the universality of treatment in the sources and the depth of coverage of sources relative to one another. Such information is useful in itself and can promote the efficient use of research time.

The sources themselves, listed and briefly described in the Bibliography, have been chosen with the intention of making the *Index* as functional as possible. The sources selected are current, readily available in libraries and through bookstores, and thorough, that is, comprehensive in coverage and sufficiently explanatory of the terms. Referred to a source by the *Index,* the user can expect to find a definition, example, or explanation that will elucidate the term in question. Moreover, references to individual sources have been presented in such a way that needed information can be quickly and easily found in the source, as is explained in How To Use This Book. As regards the comprehensiveness of the sources, the editors have endeavored to provide as complete a coverage of terms in the given fields as possible, without undue reliance upon obscure or highly specialized works. Consultation of the Bibliography will show that the best-known and most useful handbooks in these fields have been indexed, resulting in a compilation of terminology that is unique in its depth yet not unwarranted in extent.

The editors wish to encourage users of the *Index* to offer suggestions aimed at improving its quality, scope, accuracy, and usefulness. While every effort has been made to create a new reference tool that is both valuable and practical, important sources may have been overlooked; the editors would be glad to learn of any such omissions and, indeed, of any other ways in which the *Index* might be improved.

Frank R. Abate

Essex, Connecticut
December 1982

How To Use This Book

Below each term in the *Index* there is an alphabetic symbol, or symbols separated by semicolon. These symbols, in capital letters, represent the sources in which the terms are found. The full list of symbols and the corresponding sources is in the Bibliography.

Frequently a symbol may be followed by a virgule (/), then a number or term in italics. The style is explained as follows:

1. A symbol given alone indicates that the entry can be found as a headword listed alphabetically in the indicated source, e.g.,

    ablative
    FDLP.

    in which **ablative** is the headword and FDLP the source in which it can be found.

2. A symbol followed by a number indicates that the entry can be found on that page number in the source, e.g.,

    abstract noun
    ME/*332.*

    in which **abstract noun** is a term used on page *332* of ME, the source in which it can be found.

3. A symbol followed by a word or phrase indicates that the entry can be found under that particular headword listed alphabetically in the source, e.g.,

    accented
    DLDC/*versification.*

    in which **accented** is a term used in the entry for *versification*, and DLDC the source in which it can be found.

A similar format is used when an entry is taken from the index of a source, e.g.,

    academics
    CR/*Index*

in which **academics** is a term given with page references in the Index of CR, the source in which it can be found.

In all cases the editors have endeavored to represent the individual terms

10 □ How To Use This Book

as they are found in the sources. Thus, if a source has a term in italics, with accents, peculiarly spelled, or in any other form, that style is maintained in the *Index*. As a result, some entries that might differ only in minor typographic respects are shown separately. The exception to this policy is that standard rules of capitalization have been imposed throughout the *Index,* despite the fact that some sources capitalize all headwords, or all letters in headwords.

Bibliography

Listed below are all sources from which terms were taken in the compilation of the *Index*. They are given in alphabetic order by their respective alphabetic symbols, at left, and for each the bibliographic information is followed by a brief description. The description provides information about the content and organization of the source, and indicates how material from the source was selected and presented in the *Index*.

Please note that the alphabetic symbols for the sources are acronymic representations of the titles of the sources and (where necessary) authors.

CODEL	*The Concise Oxford Dictionary of English Literature,* 2nd ed., 628pp., Oxford: Oxford University Press, 1970.

This book is based on Harvey's *The Oxford Companion to English Literature,* which is itself a source for the *Index*. The concise version was included on the grounds that users may have easier access to it; the same criteria were used in indexing both (see below). The arrangement is alphabetic.

CR	*Classical Rhetoric and Its Christian and Secular Tradition from Ancient to Modern Times,* George A. Kennedy, xii + 291pp., Chapel Hill: University of North Carolina Press, 1980.

Intended as a short introduction to the subject of classical rhetoric and its influence, this book outlines and explains the history and important figures in the development of rhetoric. A good deal of terminology is used and explained throughout, and this material was taken from the index of the book. Hence, all terms

12 □ Bibliography

taken from this source refer the user to the source's index for page number.

DLDC *Dictionary of Literary, Dramatic, and Cinematic Terms,* 2nd ed., Sylvan Barnet, Morton Berman, William Burto, eds., 124pp., Boston: Little, Brown and Company, 1971.

This dictionary covers a broad range and thus the definitions are of necessity short and to the point. The entries are limited to the more common terms of literary criticism. Easy to use, this is a small, handy reference book with appealing simplicity. Most terms are covered under general entries such as *novel, tragedy, figurative language,* etc. Although the book has no index, there is extensive use of cross references. The arrangement is alphabetic, but many terms from this source were found within entries, and those are given in the *Index* with the appropriate headword as reference.

DLTC *A Dictionary of Literary Terms,* rev. ed., J. A. Cuddon, 761pp., Garden City, New York: Doubleday & Co., 1976.

This dictionary treats the field of literary terminology, including technical terms, forms, genres, modes and styles, groups and movements, -isms, and motifs. It focuses mainly on Classical, European, and Near Eastern literatures. Ample cross references are provided. All headwords were included in the *Index*. The arrangement is alphabetic.

DLTS *Dictionary of Literary Terms,* Harry Shaw, 402pp., New York: McGraw-Hill, 1972.

Aimed at readers, writers, and students, this book defines terms used in and about literature (including magazines and newspapers), film, television, and speeches. There are more than 2000 entries owing in part to a rather liberal approach to the inclusion of terms; the *Index* covers the majority of headwords given. The arrangement is alphabetic.

DMCT *A Dictionary of Modern Critical Terms,* Roger Fowler, ed., ix + 208pp., London: Routledge & Kegan Paul, 1973.

Not a dictionary in the usual sense, this book offers encyclopedic definitions of important terms and concepts in modern criticism; it is a compilation of entries contributed by "a fairly large and varied gathering of critics and teachers." Cross references and suggested sources for further reading follow many entries. The arrangement is alphabetic.

EDSL *Encyclopedic Dictionary of the Sciences of Language,* Oswald Ducrot and Tzvetan Todorov, tr. by C. Porter, xiii + 380pp., Baltimore: The Johns Hopkins University Press, 1979.

About eight hundred terms are defined within the fifty articles that make up this work, and the explanation of a term may cover several pages. Each article addresses a specific topic such as "Generative Linguistics," "Saussurianism," "Synchrony and Diachrony," or "Time and Modality in Language." Fields covered include poetics, rhetoric, stylistics, psycholinguistics, sociolinguistics, and geolinguistics, semiotics, and philosophy of language. The book is divided into four sections: The first, "Schools," traces the history of modern linguistics; the second, "Fields," describes related disciplines such as sociolinguistics; in the third section, "Methodological Concepts," general concepts such as sign, *langue, parole,* and code are discussed; the fourth section, "Descriptive Concepts," analyzes specific concepts such as phonemes, morphemes, and parts of speech. In short, the *Encyclopedic Dictionary of the Sciences of Language* serves as an introduction to contemporary linguistics and semantics. By virtue of its index of terms defined and an index of authors, it can serve as a dictionary as well as an introductory text. There is considerable bibliographic information provided within and at the end of each article. The usage is American. This book is organized by concepts and chapters rather than an alphabetized list of words.

14 □ Bibliography

FDLP *A First Dictionary of Linguistics and Phonetics,* David Crystal, 390pp., Boulder: Westview Press, 1980.

This is a limited survey, on historical principles, of twentieth-century terminology in linguistics and phonetics. It lists more than one thousand headwords as well as another thousand technical phrases in boldface within the entries. Each explanation is self-contained; although there are numerous cross references, they are not essential to the exposition of any given term. Most entries contain encyclopedic information, including the historical context in which the term was used, examples to illustrate the significance of the term, and specific bibliographical information. Both headwords and terms within entries are included in the *Index*. The arrangement is alphabetic.

GLT *Glossary of Linguistic Terminology,* Mario Pei, xvi + 299pp., New York: Columbia University Press, 1966.

While not pretending to absolute completeness, this glossary does give concise definitions and explanations for "the general terminology used by linguists... historical, descriptive, and geolinguistic, American and European, that has gained a measure of acceptance in the field" (from the Foreword). It documents the terminology that was well established in the field of linguistics at the time of its publication. Synonyms and cross references are amply provided. The arrangement is alphabetic.

HL *A Handbook to Literature,* 4th ed., Hugh Holman, ix + 537pp., Indianapolis: Bobbs-Merrill, 1980.

This carefully revised and expanded handbook contains "comparatively brief explanations of the words and phrases which are peculiar to the study of English and American literature and which a reader or a student may wish to have defined, explained, or illustrated." (from To the User). All of the more than 1560 entries appear in the *Index;* the arrangement is alphabetic.

LGEP *A Linguistic Guide to English Poetry,* Geoffrey N. Leech, xiv + 240pp., London: Longman Group Ltd., 1979.

Not a dictionary, this book is not organized by alphabetical order but by chapters with such headings as "Varieties of Poetic License," "Foregrounding and Interpretation," "Verbal Repetition," etc. It has an adequate index. A small book which concentrates on a linguistic approach to the interpretation of poetry, its objective is to illustrate the use of linguistics as a tool of literary criticism. It is designed as an introductory textbook on English stylistics, "the study of the use of language in literature," and as such has examples for discussion at the end of each chapter. This book is primarily of interest to the linguist, critic, or student interested in an elementary exposition of various aspects of linguistic criticism. The orientation and usage of this book are British. Terms taken from this source are listed in the *Index* followed by the number of the page on which they were cited.

ME *Modern English: A Glossary of Literature and Language,* Arnold Lazarus, Andrew MacLeish, H. Wendell Smith, eds., 462pp., New York: Grosset & Dunlap, 1971.

Presented as a glossary, this book gives full descriptions and plentiful examples for terms used in the study of literature, rhetoric, and linguistics. Bibliography is also provided with some longer entries. The arrangement is alphabetic, in two separate sections: one on literature and composition, another on language. Hence all terms in the *Index* are given with the appropriate page number.

OCAL *The Oxford Companion to American Literature,* 4th ed., James D. Hart, ix + 991pp., New York: Oxford University Press, 1965.

Designed as a reader's companion to important people, places, and institutions likely to be encountered in or to have had influence upon American literature, this source provides concise information on organizations, locations, trends,

16 ▫ Bibliography

religious movements, and pseudonyms. Only headwords appear in the *Index*; names of authors and works were excluded. The arrangement is alphabetic.

OCEL *The Oxford Companion to English Literature,* 4th ed., Sir Paul Harvey, ed., rev. by Dorothy Eagle, x + 961pp., Oxford: Oxford University Press, 1967.

As a reader's companion to English literature, this source provides information on widely encountered expressions, technical terms, and institutional names. Only its headwords are listed in the *Index*; names of authors and works were excluded. The arrangement is alphabetic.

OO "An Onomastic Onomasticon," George H. Scheetz, *American Name Society Bulletin,* No. 65, October 28, 1981, pp. 4-7.

This article collects and defines more than fifty terms with the *-onym* or *-anym* suffix that are used about names. The author consulted standard dictionaries and wordbooks in compiling the list.

PEPP *Princeton Encyclopedia of Poetry and Poetics,* 2nd ed., Alex Preminger, ed., Frank J. Warnke, C. B. Hardison, Jr., assoc. eds., xxiv + 992pp. Princeton: Princeton University Press, 1974.

The editors of this book describe their policy as one of "accuracy, utility, interest," and "thoroughness," in this, the most comprehensive reference book on poetry. Its more than 1000 entries are of sufficient depth to be of value to the scholar as well as the general reader. There are extensive cross references and substantial bibliographies at the end of most entries. All headwords from the text and supplement are in the *Index*. The arrangement is alphabetic; those entries in the *Index* that were taken from the supplement are given with a page number.

PH *Poetry Handbook: A Dictionary of Terms,* 4th ed., Babette Deutsch, xiv + 203pp., New York: Funk & Wagnalls, 1974.

Concentrating exclusively on poetry, this book is oriented toward terms "meaningful for writers and readers of verse in the English language." The author, herself a poet and critic, illustrates the craft of poetry with definitions that are clearly written and supplemented by numerous examples. While not exhaustive, the book treats its subject in a thorough, yet succinct and readable way. Cross references are excellent. The arrangement is alphabetic.

Literary, Rhetorical, and Linguistics Terms Index

A

Abbey Theatre
  HL.
Abecedarian
  DLTS.
abecedarium
  DLTS.
abecedarius
  DLTC; DLTS; HL; PEPP.
Abglitt
  GLT.
ab initio
  DLTS.
ablative
  FDLP.
ablaut
  GLT; ME/*332*.
abnormal vowel
  GLT.
Abolitionist
  OCAL.
ab ovo
  DLTC; DLTS.
abracadabra
  DLTS.
abridged
  DLTS.
abridged edition
  DLTC.
abridgment
  DLTS; HL.

abrupt
  FDLP.
abrupt release
  FDLP/*abrupt*.
Absatz
  GLT.
absolute
  FDLP/*positive*; HL.
absolute construction
  ME/*332*.
absolute form
  GLT.
absolutely arbitrary
  EDSL/*131*.
absolute pitch
  GLT.
absolutism
  DLTC.
absolutism in criticism
  PEPP.
absolutist critic
  DLDC/*criticism*.
absorption
  GLT.
abstract
  DLDC/*concrete*; DLTC; DLTS; HL; PEPP.
abstract diction
  DLTS.

abstraction
DLTS; ME/*4*.
abstraction ladder
ME/*5*.
abstract noun
ME/*332*.
abstract poem
DLTC; PEPP; PH.
abstract poetry
HL.
abstract terms
HL.
abstract units
FDLP/*exponent*.
Abstufung
GLT.
absurd
DMCT.
absurdities
LGEP/*132*.
absurd, the
HL.
Absurd, Theater of the
DLDC; DLTS; HL.
Abtönung
GLT.
Abyssinian poetry
PEPP.
academic
DLTC; DLTS.
academic drama
DLTC; HL.
academician
DLTS.
academics
CR/*Index*.
academies
HL.
Academy
OCEL; CODEL; DLTC.
Academy, The British
CODEL; OCEL.
Academy, The French
CODEL; OCEL.

acatalectic
CODEL; DLTC; DLTS; HL; OCEL; PEPP; PH/*catalectic*.
acatalexis
PH.
accent
DLTC; DLTS; EDSL/*181*; FDLP; GLT; HL; PEPP; PH.
accented
DLDC/*versification*.
accent of intensity
GLT.
accentology
FDLP/*accent*.
accentualism
PEPP.
accentual metre
LGEP/*118*.
accentual pattern
FDLP/*accent*.
accentual-syllabic
LGEP/*114*.
accentual-syllabic verse
HL; PEPP; PH/*metre*.
accentual system
FDLP/*accent*.
accentual unit
GLT.
accentual verse
DLTC; ME/*5*; PH/*metre*.
acceptability
FDLP.
acceptability tests
FDLP/*acceptability*.
acceptable
FDLP/*acceptability*.
acceptable utterance
FDLP/*acceptability*.
accessibility hierarchy
FDLP/*hierarchy*; FDLP/*accessibility*.
accidence
DLTC; DLTS; FDLP/*inflection*; FDLP; GLT; ME/*332*.

accidental gap
GLT.
accismus
DLTS; HL.
acclimatization
GLT.
accommodation
GLT.
accord
PEPP.
accoustic phonetics
FDLP.
accusative
FDLP/*case*; FDLP; ME/*333*.
acephalous
DLTC; PEPP.
achthronym
OO.
acmeism
DLTC; PEPP.
acoustic
FDLP/*abrupt*.
acoustic allophone
GLT.
acoustic analysis
FDLP/*acoustic phonetics*.
acoustic change
GLT.
acoustic cues
FDLP/*acoustic feature*.
acoustic feature
FDLP.
acoustic features
GLT.
acoustic formants
GLT.
acoustic phonetics
FDLP/*phonetics*; GLT.
acoustic phonics
ME/*333*.
acoustic repetition
LGEP/*73*.
acoustics
FDLP/*acoustic phonetics*.

acquisition
FDLP.
acroama
DLTC.
acronym
DLTS; HL; ME/*5*; OO.
acrophony
EDSL/*196*; GLT.
acrostic
DLDC; DLTC; DLTS; HL; PEPP; PH.
acryology
DLTC.
act
DLDC; DLTC; DLTS; EDSL/*340*; HL; ME/*5*.
actant
EDSL/*224*; EDSL/*213*.
action
DLDC/*plot*; DLTC; DLTS; DMCT; EDSL/*340*; HL.
action-actor-goal
FDLP/*actor-action-goal*.
active
FDLP.
active articulators
FDLP/*articulation*.
active voice
ME/*333*.
actor
DMCT/*action*; GLT.
actor-action-goal
FDLP; GLT.
actor-action-goal construction
ME/*333*.
actualisation
FDLP.
actualise
FDLP/*actualisation*.
actualization
GLT.
acute
FDLP.
acute phoneme
GLT.

acyrologia
DLTS.
adage
DLTC; DLTS; HL; ME/6.
Adam's apple
FDLP/*larynx*; FDLP/*vocal cords*.
Adams Papers
OCAL.
adaptation
DLTC; DLTS; HL.
ad astra
DLTS.
ad baculum
DLTC/*argumentum ad*.
ad captandum
ME/6.
ad captandum
DLTS.
ad captandum vulgus
ME/*ad captandum*, 6.
ad crumenam
DLTC/*argumentum ad*.
addendum
DLTC; DLTS.
adding
GLT.
Addisonian
DLTC.
addition
GLT.
additive allomorph
ME/*333*.
address
DLTC; FDLP.
addressee
EDSL/*324*; FDLP/*conative*.
address systems
FDLP/*address*.
adequacy
FDLP.
adequate
EDSL/*41*; EDSL/*39*; FDLP/*adequacy*.

ad hominem
DLTC/*argumentum ad*; ME/*6*.
ad hominem
DLTS.
ad ignorantiam
ME/*7*.
ad ignorantiam
DLTS.
ad infinitum
DLTS.
adjacency pair
FDLP.
adjacent areas
FDLP/*area*.
adjacent sound
FDLP/*assimilation*.
adjectival
FDLP/*adjective*; ME/*334*.
adjectival clause
EDSL/*282*.
adjectival construction
GLT.
adjective
EDSL/*252*; FDLP; ME/*333*.
adjective clause
ME/*334*.
adjective complement
ME/*334*.
adjoin
FDLP/*adjunction*.
adjunct
FDLP; GLT/*word*.
adjunction
FDLP.
ad libitum
DLTS.
ad misericordiam
ME/*7*.
adnominal
FDLP.
adnominatio
PEPP.
adonic
DLTC; PEPP.

25 ☐ affirming the consequent

Adonic verse
  HL.
ad populum
  DLTC/*argumentum ad*; ME/7.
adstratum
  GLT.
adultocentric
  FDLP/*adultomorphic*.
adultomorphic
  FDLP.
adventure story
  DLTS.
adventure story (or film)
  HL.
adverb
  FDLP; ME/334.
adverb clause
  ME/335.
adverb clauses
  FDLP/*adverb*.
adverbial
  FDLP/*adverb*; ME/335.
adverb phrases
  FDLP/*adverb*.
ad verecundiam
  DLTC/*argumentum ad*; ME/7.
adversaria
  DLTC.
adversarius
  HL.
advertiser
  DLTC.
adynaton
  DLTC; PEPP.
Aeolic
  DLTC; DLTS; PEPP.
aerodynamic
  FDLP/*dynamic*.
Aeschylean
  DLTC.
aesthetic distance
  DLDC/*psychical distance*; DLTC; DLTS; HL; ME/7; PEPP; PH.

Aestheticism
  DMCT; DLTC; HL; PEPP.
Aesthetic Movement
  DLDC; CODEL; OCEL.
aesthetics
  DLTS; DMCT; HL.
aet.
  HL.
aetat.
  HL/*aet.*.
affaire d'honneur
  DLTS.
affect
  FDLP/*affective*.
affectation
  DLTC; DLTS.
affective
  FDLP.
affective critic
  DLDC/*criticism*.
affective fallacy
  DLTC; DLTS; DMCT; HL; PEPP.
affective language
  GLT.
affective meaning
  FDLP/*affective*.
affectus
  CR/*Index*.
affiliation
  GLT.
affinities
  EDSL/60.
affinity
  GLT.
affirmative
  FDLP.
affirmed
  EDSL/272.
affirming an alternative
  ME/7.
affirming the consequent
  ME/7.

affix ☐ 26

affix
  DLTS; EDSL/*200*; FDLP; GLT; ME/*335*.
affixation
  FDLP/*affix*; GLT; LGEP/*43*.
affix clipping
  GLT.
affix-hopping
  FDLP/*affix*.
affixing index
  FDLP/*affix*.
affixing languages
  FDLP/*affix*.
affix transformation
  ME/*335*.
afflatus
  DLTC; DLTS; PEPP.
affricate
  FDLP; GLT; ME/*336*.
affrication
  FDLP/*affricate*.
aficionado
  DLTS.
a fortiori
  DLTS.
a fortiori **argument**
  CR/*Index*.
Africa
  FDLP/*ejective*.
African Negro poetry
  PEPP.
African poetry
  PEPP/*909*.
Afrikaans poetry
  PEPP.
Afro-American literature
  HL.
agape
  DLTS.
age-area theory
  GLT.
agenda
  DLTS.

agent
  FDLP/*agentive*; ME/*7*.
agentive
  FDLP.
agentive passive
  FDLP/*passive*.
agentless passive
  FDLP/*passive*.
agent provocateur
  DLTS.
Age of Johnson in English literature
  HL.
Age of Reason
  DLTC; DLTS; HL.
Age of Sensibility
  HL.
Age of the Romantic Triumph in England, 1798-1832
  HL.
agglomeration
  GLT.
agglutinating
  EDSL/*12*.
agglutinating languages
  FDLP/*agglutinative*.
agglutination
  FDLP/*agglutinative*; GLT.
agglutinative
  FDLP.
agglutinative (agglutinating) language
  GLT.
agglutinative language
  ME/*336*.
agitprop
  DLTS.
agnate
  ME/*336*.
Agnus Dei
  DLTS.
agon
  DLDC; DLTC; DLTS; HL.
agrarianism
  DLTS.

27 □ allegro forms

agrarian movement
DLTC.
Agrarians
PEPP/*916*; HL.
agreement
EDSL/*51*; FDLP; GLT; ME/*336*.
agroikos
HL.
aiodos [*sic*]
DLTC.
air
DLTC; PEPP.
air-flow
FDLP/*consonant*.
air-stream mechanism
FDLP.
akhyana
DLTC.
akousma
GLT.
Aktionsart
EDSL/*311*.
Alamo, The
OCAL.
Alarodian
GLT.
alarum
DLTS.
alazon
DLDC/*braggart soldier*; DLTC; DLTS; HL.
alba
DLTC; DLTS; HL.
alba
ME/*aubade, 26*; PEPP; PH/*troubadour*.
Albanian poetry
PEPP.
Alcaic
PEPP; CODEL.
alcaic metre
OCEL.
alcaics
DLTC; DLTS; HL; PH.

Alcmanic verse
PEPP; DLTC.
alethic
FDLP.
alethic modality
FDLP/*alethic*.
Alexandria
CR/*Index*.
Alexandrianism
DLTC; PEPP.
Alexandrine
DLDC/*versification*; CODEL; DLTC; DLTS; HL; ME/*8*; OCEL; PEPP; PH.
alexia
EDSL/*164*.
alexia, literal
EDSL/*164*.
alexia, verbal
EDSL/*164*.
algorithm
FDLP.
alias
DLTS.
alienable
FDLP.
alienable possession
FDLP/*alienable*.
alienation
DLTS.
alienation effect
DLTC.
alien word
GLT.
aljamiado
DLTC.
allegory
CODEL; CR/*Index*; DLDC; DLTC; DLTS; DMCT; EDSL/*258*; HL; LGEP/*163*; ME/*9*; OCEL; PEPP; PH/*metaphor*.
allegro
DLTC; DLTS.
allegro forms
GLT.

alliteration ☐ 28

alliteration
  DLDC/*versification*; DLTC;
  DLTS; DMCT; EDSL/*277*; GLT;
  HL; LGEP/*93*; ME/*9*; OCEL;
  PEPP; PH/*rhyme*.
alliterative meter
  PEPP.
alliterative romance
  HL.
alliterative verse
  DLTC; HL; ME/*10*.
allo-
  FDLP; GLT.
allochrone
  FDLP/*allo-*.
alloeostropha
  PEPP.
allograph
  GLT.
allographs
  FDLP/*allo-*.
allokine
  FDLP/*allo-*; GLT.
allokinemorph
  GLT.
allomorph
  EDSL/*201*; GLT; ME/*336*.
allomorph morpheme
  FDLP/*allo-*.
allomorphs
  FDLP/*morpheme*.
allonym
  DLTC; DLTS; HL; OO.
allophone
  DLTS; EDSL/*172*; GLT; ME/*336*.
allophones
  FDLP/*phoneme*; FDLP/*allo-*.
allophonic
  GLT.
allophonic analogy
  GLT.
allophonic change
  GLT.

allophonic confusion
  GLT.
allophonic extension
  GLT.
allophonic variant
  FDLP/*allo-*.
alloseme
  FDLP/*allo-*; GLT.
allœostrophe
  DLTC.
allotagma
  FDLP/*tagmemics*.
allotax
  GLT.
allotone
  GLT.
allusion
  DLDC; DLTC; DLTS; HL; ME/*10*; PEPP.
almanac
  DLTC; DLTS; HL; OCAL.
alphabet
  EDSL/*195*; GLT.
alphabet poem
  PH.
alphabet verse
  DLTS.
alpha notation
  FDLP.
als ob
  DLTC.
altar poem
  DLTC; HL.
altercatio
  DLTC.
alter ego
  DLTS.
alternance vocalique
  GLT.
alternant
  FDLP/*alternation*; GLT.
alternate rhyme
  DLTC.

29 □ American Party

alternation
EDSL/*17*; FDLP; FDLP/*morphophoneme*; GLT.
alternation change
GLT.
altruism
DLTS.
alveolar
FDLP; GLT.
alveolar ridge
FDLP/*alveolar*.
alveolar stop
ME/*337*.
alveolo-palatal
FDLP.
alveolum
FDLP/*alveolar*.
amalgam
GLT.
amalgamated
EDSL/*202*.
amalgamating language
GLT.
ambages
HL.
ambassadors
CR/*Index*.
ambience
DLTS.
ambiguity
DLDC/*figurative language*; DLTC; DLTS; DMCT; EDSL/*236*; FDLP; HL; LGEP/*205*; ME/*11*; ME/*337*; PEPP; PH.
ambiguous
FDLP/*ambiguity*.
ambiguous sentence
FDLP/*ambiguity*.
ambisyllabic
GLT.
ambivalence
DLTS; HL.
amblysia
DLTC.

ambrosia
DLTS.
amelioration
GLT.
America
OCAL.
America: classical rhetoric in
CR/*Index*.
American Academy of
OCAL.
American Academy of Arts and Letters
HL.
American Anti-Slavery Society
OCAL/*Abolitionist*.
American Dream
DLTS.
American Folk-Lore Society
OCAL.
American Geographical Society
OCAL.
American Guide Series
OCAL/*Federal Writers' Project*.
American Historical Association
OCAL.
American Indian
FDLP/*incorporating*.
American Indian literature
HL.
American Indian poetry
PEPP.
Americanism
DLTS.
American language
HL.
American literature, periods of
HL.
American Men of Letters Series
OCAL.
American Negro poetry
PEPP.
American Party
OCAL/*Know-Nothing movement*.

American Philosophical Society
OCAL.
American poetics
PEPP.
American poetic schools and techniques
PEPP/*916*.
American poetry
PEPP.
American Revolution
OCAL/*Revolutionary War*.
American Sign Language
FDLP/*sign*.
Americas
FDLP/*ejective*.
Amerind
DLTS; PEPP/*920*.
Amerind literature
HL.
Amharic
FDLP/*ejective*.
amicus curiae
DLTS.
amoebean
DLTC.
amoebean verses
PEPP.
amorality
DLTS.
amorphous change
GLT.
amorphous language
GLT.
amour propre
DLTS.
ampersand
DLTC; DLTS.
amphibole
ME/*13*.
amphibology
CODEL; DLTS; HL; OCEL.
amphiboly
CODEL; DLTC; HL; OCEL/*amphibology*.

amphibrach
CODEL; DLDC/*versification*; DLTC; DLTS; EDSL/*187*; HL; ME/*13*; OCEL; PEPP; PH.
amphigory
DLTC; DLTS; HL.
amphimacer
DLDC/*versification*; DLTC; DLTS; PEPP; PH.
amphimacher [*sic*]
HL.
amphisbaenic
PH/*rhyme*.
amphisbaenic rhyme
DLTC; HL.
amplification
CR/*Index*; DLTC; HL; PEPP.
amplificative
GLT.
amplitude
FDLP/*acoustic feature*.
-ana
DLTC.
ana
HL.
Anabaptists
OCAL.
anabasis
DLTC; DLTS; OCEL.
anachorism
DLTC.
anachronism
CODEL; DLDC; DLTC; DLTS; HL; ME/*13*.
anachronism, linguistic
LGEP/*52*.
anaclasis
DLTC; PEPP.
anacoluthon
CODEL; DLTC; DLTS; FDLP; HL; ME/*14*; OCEL; PEPP.
Anacreontic
PEPP.
anacreóntica
DLTC.

31 □ anaphor

Anacreontic poetry
DLDC; HL.
anacreontics
DLTS; PH.
anacreontic verse
DLTC.
anacrusis
CODEL; DLDC/*versification*;
DLTC; DLTS; HL; ME/*14*;
OCEL; PEPP; PH.
anadiplosis
DLTC; DLTS; HL; ME/*14*;
PEPP.
anagnorisis
DLDC/*plot*; DLDC/*tragedy*.
anagnorisis
DLTC; DLTS; HL.
anagoge
DLTS; HL.
anagogical interpretation of scripture
CR/*Index*.
anagram
DLDC; DLTC; DLTS; EDSL/*190*; HL.
analecta
HL.
analects
DLTC; DLTS; HL.
analicity
FDLP/*analytic*.
analogical extension
GLT.
analogue
DLDC; DLTC; DLTS; GLT; HL.
analogy
CR/*Index*; DLTS; EDSL/*13*;
EDSL/*131*; EDSL/*125*; FDLP;
GLT/*analogical change*; HL; ME/*337*; ME/*14*; PEPP.
analysable
FDLP; FDLP/*composition*.
analysed rhyme
DLTC.

analysis
DLTC; DLTS; DMCT; GLT; HL;
PEPP.
analysis-by-synthesis
FDLP.
analysis critic
DLDC/*criticism*.
analysis, discourse
EDSL/*295*.
analysis, propositional
EDSL/*296*.
analytic
FDLP.
analytical criticism
HL.
analytical language
GLT.
analytic editing
HL.
analytic language
ME/*337*.
analytic philosophy
EDSL/*94*.
analytic proposition/sentence
FDLP/*analytic*.
analyzability
EDSL/*231*.
analyzed rhyme
HL; PEPP; PH/*rhyme*.
anamnesis
DLTC.
anantapodoton
PEPP.
ananym
DLTC; OO.
anapaest
CODEL; DLTC; LGEP/*112*;
OCEL; PEPP.
anapest
DLDC/*versification*; DLTS;
EDSL/*187*; HL; ME/*15*; PH.
anapestic
DLDC/*versification*; PH/*metre*.
anaphor
EDSL/*281*.

anaphora
CODEL; CR/*Index*; DLDC; DLTC; DLTS; FDLP; GLT; HL; LGEP/*80*; ME/*15*; OCEL; PEPP.

anaphoric
FDLP/*anaphora*.

anaphoric reference
FDLP/*anaphora*.

anaphoric substitutes
FDLP/*anaphora*.

anaphoric words
FDLP/*anaphora*.

anapodoton
PEPP.

anaptyctic vowel
GLT.

anaptyxis
FDLP/*intrusion*; GLT.

anarchy
DLTS.

anarthria
EDSL/*161*.

anarthric
EDSL/*157*.

anastrophe
DLTC; DLTS; HL; PEPP.

anathema
DLTS; HL.

anatomical parallels
FDLP/*biolinguistics*.

anatomy
DLDC/*satire*; DLTC; HL.

anatonym
OO.

ancestor
FDLP/*family*.

ancestor language
FDLP/*comparative*.

ancien régime
DLTS.

ancients and moderns
CR/*Index*; DLTC.

ancients and moderns, quarrel of
PEPP.

ancients and moderns, quarrel of the
HL.

anecdote
DLDC; DLTC; DLTS; HL; ME/*15*.

anger
FDLP/*intonation*; FDLP/*attitudinal*.

angled brackets notation
FDLP/*bracketing*.

Anglican Church
OCAL/*Protestant Episcopal Church*.

Anglicism
DLTS.

Anglo-Catholic revival
HL.

Anglo-French
HL.

Anglo-Irish literature
HL.

Anglo-Latin
HL.

Anglo-Norman
CODEL; OCEL.

Anglo-Norman language
HL.

Anglo-Norman period
HL.

Anglo-Saxon
CODEL; DLTS; HL; ME/*337*; OCEL.

Anglo-Saxon literature
CODEL.

Anglo-Saxon prosody
PEPP; PH.

Anglo-Saxon versification
HL.

angogy
HL.

angry young man
DLTC.

Angry Young Men
HL.

33 □ anticipation

angst
DLTS; HL.
animadversion
DLTS.
animal communication
FDLP/*creativity*.
animal epic
HL; PEPP/*920*.
animal systems of communication
FDLP/*cultural transmission*.
animate
FDLP.
animateness
FDLP/*animate*.
animate noun
ME/*337*.
animation
DLTS.
animism
DLTS; HL.
anisometric
DLTC; DLTS.
Anlaut
GLT.
annalist
DLTS.
annals
DLTC; DLTS; HL.
anno Domini
DLTS.
annotation
DLTC; DLTS; HL.
annual
OCAL/*gift book*.
annuals
DLTS; HL.
anomalous
FDLP/*nonsense*.
anomaly
CR/*Index*; EDSL/*131*.
anomoiosis
DLTC.
anomolous verbs
ME/*337*.

anonym
OO.
anonymous
DLTC; DLTS.
anonymuncule
DLTC.
anopisthograph
HL.
antagonist
DLDC/*plot*; DLTC; DLTS; HL; ME/*16*.
antanaclasis
EDSL/*277*; PEPP.
antecedent
EDSL/*281*; FDLP; GLT; ME/*338*.
antediluvian
DLTS.
Ante-Nicene Fathers
OCEL.
anterior
FDLP.
anthem
DLTS; HL.
anthology
DLTC; DLTS; HL; ME/*16*; PEPP; PH.
Anthology Club
OCAL.
anthropological linguistics
FDLP; FDLP/*linguistics*.
anthropomorphism
DLTS; HL.
anthroponym
OO.
anthroposemiotic
FDLP/*zoösemiotics*.
anthypophora
DLTC.
antibacchius
DLTC; DLTS; HL; ME/*16*; PEPP.
anticipation
FDLP; GLT.

anticipatory
    FDLP/*regressive*; FDLP.

anticipatory assimilation
    FDLP/*assimilation*; FDLP/*anticipatory*.

anticipatory coarticulation
    FDLP/*anticipatory*.

anticipatory expansion
    GLT.

anticlimax
    CODEL; DLDC; DLTC; DLTS; DMCT; HL; ME/*16*; PEPP.

antidosis
    CR/*Index*.

anti-hero
    DLTC; DLTS; DMCT; HL.

anti-intellectualism
    HL.

antilogy
    DLTC.

anti-masque
    DLDC/*drama*.

antimasque
    DLTC; DLTS; HL; ME/*16*; PEPP/*920*.

antimentalism
    EDSL/*31*.

antimeria
    HL.

antimetabole
    DLTC; HL; PEPP.

Antinomianism
    OCAL.

antinomy
    DLTC.

anti-novel
    DLTC; HL; ME/*16*.

Antioch
    CR/*Index*.

antiphon
    DLTC; DLTS; HL.

antiphrasis
    DLTC; DLTS; EDSL/*338*; HL; ME/*17*.

anti-play
    DLTC.

antiquarianism
    DLTS; HL.

antirealistic novel
    HL.

Anti-Rent War
    OCAL.

antispast
    DLTC; HL; PEPP.

antistoichon
    DLTC.

antistrophe
    CR/*Index*.

antistrophe
    CODEL; DLDC/*ode*; DLTC; DLTS; HL; ME/*17*; OCEL; PEPP; PH/*ode*.

antisyzygy
    DLTC.

antithesis
    CR/*Index*.

antithesis
    DLDC/*form*; DLTC; DLTS; EDSL/*277*; HL; LGEP/*67*; ME/*17*; PEPP.

antode
    DLTC; PEPP.

antonomasia
    DLTC; DLTS; HL; ME/*17*; PEPP.

antonym
    DLTC; DLTS; FDLP; GLT; OO.

antonymy
    FDLP/*antonym*.

aorist
    GLT.

A-over-A
    FDLP.

A-over-A condition
    FDLP.

A-over-A principle
    FDLP.

aperçu
    DLTS.

apex
  FDLP.
aphaeresis
  CODEL; DLTC; DLTS; HL; OCEL; PEPP.
aphasia
  FDLP/*neurolinguistics*; GLT.
aphasia, agrammatical
  EDSL/*162*.
aphasia, amnesic
  EDSL/*163*.
aphasia, conduction
  EDSL/*162*.
aphasia, motor and graphic
  EDSL/*162*.
aphasia of phonic programming
  EDSL/*162*.
aphasia of phrastic programming
  EDSL/*162*.
aphasia, receptive
  EDSL/*163*.
aphasias
  EDSL/*161*.
aphasia, sensory
  EDSL/*163*.
aphasias, expressive
  EDSL/*162*.
aphasias, schizophrenic
  EDSL/*161*.
aphasic grammars
  EDSL/*164*.
aphasics, polyglot
  EDSL/*165*.
apheresis
  GLT.
aphesis
  DLTC; FDLP/*elision*; GLT; LGEP/*18*.
aphigouri
  HL.
aphorism
  CODEL; DLDC; DLTC; DLTS; HL; ME/*17*; OCEL.
aphoristic clause
  GLT.

apical
  FDLP/*apex*; GLT.
apico-alveolar
  GLT.
apico-alveolar lateral
  GLT.
apico-dental
  GLT.
apico-dental lateral
  GLT.
apico-dental sounds
  FDLP/*apex*.
apocalypse
  ME/*18*.
apocalyptic
  DLTS; HL.
apocalyptic literature
  DLTC; DMCT.
apocopated rhyme
  HL; PEPP; PH/*rhyme*.
apocope
  DLTC; DLTS; FDLP/*elision*; GLT/*apocopation*; HL; LGEP/*18*; ME/*19*; ME/*338*; PEPP.
apocrypha
  DLDC/*canon*; DLTC; HL; ME/*19*.
apocryphal
  DLTS.
apodeixis
  CR/*Index*.
apodosis
  CODEL; DLTS.
Apollonian
  DLDC; DLTC; DLTS; HL.
Apollonian-Dionysian
  PEPP.
apologists: Christian
  CR/*Index*.
apologue
  CODEL; DLTC; DLTS; HL; OCEL.
apology
  DLDC; DLTC; DLTS; HL.

apophasis
DLTC; DLTS; HL; ME/*19*.
apophthegm
CODEL; DLTC; HL; OCEL.
aporia
DLTS.
aposiopesis
CODEL; DLTC; DLTS; GLT; HL; ME/*19*; OCEL; PEPP.
apostasy
DLTS.
a posteriori
DLTS.
a posteriori language
GLT.
a posteriori reasoning
ME/*19*.
apostrophe
CR/*Index*.
apostrophe
DLDC/*figurative language*; DLTC; DLTS; HL; LGEP/*185*; ME/*19*; PEPP.
apothegm
DLTS; HL; ME/*21*.
apparition
DLTS.
appelative function
EDSL/*341*.
Appell
EDSL/*341*.
appellative
GLT.
appendix
DLTS.
applicable
FDLP/*application*.
application
FDLP.
applicational grammar
FDLP/*application*.
applied linguistics
FDLP/*linguistics*; FDLP; GLT.
apposition
FDLP; HL; ME/*338*.

appositional
FDLP.
appositive
ME/*338*.
appreciation
DMCT.
apprenticeship novel
HL.
appropriate
FDLP.
appropriateness
DLTS; FDLP/*appropriate*.
appropriateness of illustration
ME/*21*.
approximant
FDLP.
approximate rhyme
DLTS.
approximate-rhyme
DLDC/*versification*.
a priori
DLTS.
a priori judgment
HL.
a priori language
GLT.
a priori reasoning
ME/*22*.
apron
DLTS.
apron stage
HL.
aptronym
DLTC; OO.
aqua vitae
DLTS.
ara
HL.
arabesque
HL.
Arabic
FDLP/*fricative*; FDLP/*length*; FDLP/*diglossia*; FDLP/*discontinuous*.

37 □ *argumentum ad*

Arabic poetry
PEPP.
Arabic rhetoric
CR/*Index*.
Araucanian poetry
PEPP.
arbitrariness
FDLP.
arbitrary
FDLP/*arbitrariness*.
arc
FDLP.
Arcadia
DLDC/*Golden Age*; DLTC; DLTS.
Arcadian
HL.
Arcadian Academy
PEPP.
arcane
DLTS.
archaic
GLT.
archaism
DLDC/*diction*; DLTC; DLTS; DMCT; GLT; HL; LGEP/*13*; LGEP/*52*; ME/*338*; ME/*22*; PEPP.
archetype
DLDC; DLTC; DLTS; DMCT; HL; ME/*22*; PEPP.
Archilochian
PEPP.
Archilochian verse
DLTC.
archimorpheme
EDSL/*112*.
archiphoneme
EDSL/*112*; FDLP; GLT.
archistratum
GLT.
architectonics
DLTS; HL; ME/*22*.
architecture
CR/*Index*.

archive
DLTC; HL.
archives
DLTS.
archiwriting
EDSL/*350*.
arc pair grammar
FDLP/*arc*.
area
FDLP.
area and language studies
GLT.
area (areal) linguistics
GLT.
area language
GLT.
areal classification
FDLP/*area*.
areal linguistics
FDLP/*area*.
areal types or groups
FDLP/*area*.
arena stage
HL.
arena theater
DLTS.
Areopagus
CR/*Index*; DLTS; HL; PEPP.
Argentine poetry
PEPP.
argot
DLTC; DLTS; GLT; ME/*338*.
argument
DLTC; DLTS; EDSL/*270*; FDLP; HL; ME/*22*; PEPP; PH.
argument against the man
ME/*22*.
argumentation
CR/*Index*; DLTS; HL; ME/*23*.
argument from authority
ME/*23*.
argumentum ad
DLTC.

Arianism ☐ 38

Arianism
HL.
Aristotelian
DLTS.
Aristotelian criticism
DMCT; HL.
Aristotelian tradition in rhetoric
CR/*Index*.
Armenian poetry
PEPP.
Arminianism
HL; OCAL.
Armory Show
OCAL.
arrangement
CR/*Index*; FDLP.
ars arengandi
CR/*Index*.
ars dictaminis
CR/*Index*.
ars est celare artem
DLTC.
ars gratia artis
DLTS.
Arsis
OCEL; CODEL; DLTC; DLTS; HL; PH/*thesis*.
arsis and thesis
PEPP.
ars poetriae
CR/*Index*.
art
DMCT.
art ballad
DLTS; HL.
art ballads
DLDC/*ballad*.
arte mayor
DLTC; PEPP.
arte menor
DLTC; PEPP.
Artemus Ward
OCAL.

art epic
DLTS; HL.
art for art's sake
DLDC/*Aesthetic Movement*; DLTC; HL; PEPP.
Arthurian
DLTS.
Arthurian legend
HL.
Arthurian romance
ME/*23*.
article
DLTS; FDLP; HL; ME/*338*; ME/*24*.
articulate
FDLP/*articulation*.
articulation
FDLP; GLT.
articulation test
GLT.
articulative intrusion
ME/*338*.
articulator
FDLP/*articulation*; GLT.
articulatory phonetics
FDLP/*phonetics*; FDLP; GLT; ME/*338*.
articulatory setting
FDLP.
articulatory variables
FDLP/*articulatory phonetics*.
artifact
DLTS.
artificial comedy
DLTC; HL.
artificiality
DLTS; HL.
artificial language
GLT.
artificially constructed language
FDLP/*auxiliary*.
art lyric
DLTS; HL.
Arts and Letters
OCAL.

39 □ Astoria

arts and sciences
 CR/*Index.*
arts, the seven liberal
 DLTC.
Aryan
 OCEL.
arytenoid cartilages
 FDLP/*vocal cords.*
Arzamas
 PEPP.
ascending rhythm
 DLTC; PEPP.
Asclepiad
 DLTC; PEPP.
Asclepiadean
 DLTS.
ascriptive
 FDLP.
Asianism
 CR/*Index.*
aside
 DLDC/*soliloquy*; DLTC; DLTS; HL; LGEP/*186*; ME/*24.*
aspect
 EDSL/*307*; FDLP; GLT; ME/*339.*
Aspects model
 FDLP/*model*; FDLP.
aspects of sound
 GLT.
Aspects theory
 FDLP/*Aspects model.*
Aspects-type models
 FDLP/*Aspects model.*
aspectual
 FDLP/*aspect.*
aspirate
 GLT.
aspirated
 FDLP/*aspiration.*
aspiration
 FDLP; GLT; ME/*339.*
Assamese poetry
 PEPP.

assertion
 EDSL/*314*; ME/*24.*
assibilant (assibilate)
 GLT.
assibilation
 GLT.
assign
 FDLP.
assimilation
 DLTS; EDSL/*175*; FDLP; FDLP/*coalescence*; GLT; ME/*339.*
assimilatory phoneme
 GLT.
association
 DLTC; EDSL/*68*; FDLP.
association group
 FDLP/*association.*
associative etymology
 GLT.
associative field
 FDLP/*association*; GLT.
associative groups
 EDSL/*108.*
associative relations
 FDLP/*association.*
assonance
 CODEL; DLDC/*versification*; DLTC; DLTS; DMCT; EDSL/*190*; GLT; HL; LGEP/*93*; ME/*24*; OCEL; PEPP; PH/*rhyme.*
assumption
 DLTS.
assumptions
 ME/*24.*
Assyro-Babylonian poetry
 PEPP.
asteismus
 PEPP.
asterisk
 FDLP; GLT.
asterisked form
 FDLP/*asterisk.*
Astoria
 OCAL.

Astor Place riot
OCAL.
astrophic
PEPP.
asyllabic
GLT.
asymmetry
DLTS.
asynartete
DLTC; PEPP.
asyndetic co-ordination
FDLP/*co-ordination*.
asyndeton
DLTC; DLTS; HL; ME/*25*; PEPP.
asyntactic
DLTC.
asyntactic compound
GLT.
atavism
DLTS.
Atellana fabula
DLTS.
Atellan fables
DLTC.
athematic
GLT.
Atlanta
OCAL.
Atlantic States
OCAL/*Eastern States*.
atlas
GLT.
atlases, linguistic
EDSL/*58*.
atmosphere
DLDC; DLTC; DLTS; DMCT; HL.
atmosphere of the mind
DLTC.
atomic language
GLT.
atomistic approach
GLT.

atonic
DLTC; GLT; PEPP.
Attelan comedy
ME/*26*.
attenuation
DLTS.
attested
FDLP.
attested form
GLT.
attested forms
FDLP/*attested*.
Attic
CODEL; DLTS; HL; OCEL.
Attic Greek
CR/*Index*.
Atticism
CR/*Index*; DLTC.
Attic orators
CR/*Index*.
Attic salt
CODEL; HL; OCEL.
Attic sentence
DLDC/*style*.
attitude
DLTS; FDLP/*affective*; ME/*26*; PEPP/*920*.
attitudinal
FDLP.
attitudinal element
FDLP/*affective*.
attraction
GLT.
attribute
FDLP/*assign*; FDLP; GLT; ME/*340*.
attributive
FDLP/*attribute*; ME/*340*.
attributive construction
GLT.
attributive identity
FDLP/*ascriptive*.
attrition
GLT.

aubade
DLDC; DLTC; DLTS; HL; ME/26; PEPP; PH/*troubadour*.
aube
DLDC; HL.
au courant
DLTS.
audacity, linguistic
LGEP/29.
audible breath
FDLP/*aspiration*.
audible friction
FDLP/*friction*.
audience
CR/*Index*; DLTS; ME/27.
audio-lingual
GLT.
audiology
FDLP/*auditory phonetics*.
audiometry
FDLP/*auditory phonetics*.
audition colorée
DLTC; PEPP.
auditory
FDLP/*accent*.
auditory discrimination
GLT.
auditory feedback
GLT.
auditory-motor coordination
EDSL/157.
auditory perception
FDLP/*attribute*.
auditory phonetics
FDLP/*phonetics*; FDLP.
auditory target
FDLP/*target*.
Aufhebung
GLT.
Aufklärung
DLTC; DLTS.
augment
GLT.

augmentative
GLT.
augury
DLTS.
Augustan
DLTS; HL.
Augustan Age
DLDC; DLTC; ME/28; OCEL.
Augustinianism
HL.
Auguustan Age
CODEL.
Aunt Edna
DLTC.
aural discrimination
GLT.
aural-oral
GLT.
aureate language
DLTC; PEPP.
Aurora Community
OCAL/*Bethel*.
Ausdruck
EDSL/341.
Auslaut
GLT.
Australian poetry
PEPP.
Austrian poetry
PEPP.
autantonym
OO.
auteur theory
HL.
author
DMCT.
authority
CR/*Index*.
authorized
DLTS.
Author's Club
OCAL.
Author's League of America
OCAL.

autobiography
  CODEL; DLDC/*biography*;
  DLTC; DLTS; DMCT; HL; ME/*28*.
autoclesis
  DLTC.
auto-da-fé
  DLTS.
automatic alternation
  GLT.
automatic writing
  DLTC.
autonomous
  EDSL/*109*; FDLP.
autonomous moneme
  GLT.
autonomous phoneme
  FDLP/*autonomous*.
autonomous sound-change
  GLT.
autonomous syntagm
  GLT.
autonomous syntax
  FDLP/*autonomous*.
autonomy
  DLTS.
autonym
  DLTS; OO.
auto sacramental
  DLTS.
auto sacramental
  PEPP.
autos sacramentales
  DLTC.
autotelic
  DLTC; DLTS; HL; PEPP.
Aux
  FDLP/*analysable*; FDLP.

auxesis
  DLTC.
auxiliary
  FDLP/*terminal*; FDLP; GLT.
auxiliary language
  FDLP/*auxiliary*; GLT.
auxiliary numeral
  GLT.
auxiliary verb
  FDLP/*verb*; ME/*340*.
avant-garde
  HL.
avant-garde
  DLTC; DLTS.
avatar
  CODEL; DLTS; OCEL.
avulsive
  GLT.
Awakening, The Great
  HL; OCAL/*Great Awakening*.
awdl
  DLTC; PEPP.
axiom
  DLTS; EDSL/*226*; HL.
axiomatic
  FDLP.
axiomatics
  FDLP/*axiomatic*.
axis
  FDLP; GLT.
axis of simultaneities
  FDLP/*axis*.
axis of successions
  FDLP/*axis*.

B

babbittry
ME/*29*.

babbling
FDLP/*discontinuous*.

babel
DLTS.

baby-talk
FDLP.

Bacchic
DLTS.

bacchius
DLTC; DLTS; HL; ME/*29*; PEPP.

back
FDLP.

Back Bay
OCAL.

backed
FDLP/*front*.

back formation
GLT; ME/*341*.

back-formation
DLTC; FDLP.

background
HL.

backing
FDLP/*front*.

backlooping
FDLP; FDLP/*loopback*.

back-reference
FDLP/*referent*.

back slang
DLTC.

back sound
GLT.

back vowel
GLT; ME/*341*.

backward rhyme
PH/*rhyme*.

backwards-referring functions
FDLP/*anaphora*.

Baconian
DLTS.

Baconian theory
HL.

Bacon's Rebellion
OCAL.

bad language
FDLP/*language*.

bagatelle
DLTS.

balada
DLTC; PEPP.

balance
DLTS; HL; ME/*29*.

balanced sentence
DLTS.

Bali
CR/*Index*.

ballad ☐ 44

ballad
CODEL; DLDC; DLTC; DLTS; DMCT; EDSL/*192*; HL; ME/*29*; OCAL; OCEL; PEPP; PH.
ballade
HL.
ballade
CODEL; DLTC; DLTS; ME/*31*; OCEL; PEPP; PH.
ballad meter
DLTC; PEPP.
ballad opera
DLTC.
ballad-opera
HL.
ballad stanza
DLDC/*versification*; DLTS; HL; PH.
ballata
DLTS.
Baltimore
OCAL.
banality
DLTS; HL; LGEP/*23*.
Baptists
OCAL.
barbara
OCEL.
barbarism
CR/*Index*; DLTC; DLTS; HL; ME/*32*.
Barbary Wars
OCAL/*Tripolitan War*.
barcarole
DLTC.
bard
DLDC; DLTC; DLTS; HL; ME/*32*; PEPP; PH.
bardic verse
PEPP/*920*.
bardolatry
PEPP.
baroque
CODEL; DLDC; DLTC; DLTS; DMCT; HL; ME/*32*; PEPP; PH.

baroque poetics
PEPP.
baroque sentence
DLDC/*style*.
barzelletta
DLTC; PEPP.
base
FDLP; GLT; ME/*341*.
base component
FDLP/*component*; FDLP/*base*.
base compound
GLT.
base form
GLT; ME/*341*.
base of comparison
GLT.
base of inflection
GLT.
base rules
ME/*341*.
basic alternant
GLT.
Basic English
DLTS; HL; DLTC.
basic form
FDLP/*base*.
basic language
GLT.
basilect
FDLP.
basilisk
DLTS.
basis of articulation
GLT.
Basque
FDLP/*ergative*.
batch
DLTC.
bathos
CODEL; DLDC/*pathos*; DLTC; DLTS; HL; ME/*33*; OCEL; PEPP.
battledore-book
CODEL; OCEL.

45 □ *bergerette*

battle of the ancients and moderns
PEPP.
battle of the books
DLTC.
Battle of the Books, The
HL.
BBC English
FDLP/*received pronunciation*;
FDLP/*accent*.
Beacon Hill
OCAL.
beast epic
DLDC; DLTC; DLTS; HL;
PEPP.
beast fable
HL; PEPP/*920*.
beat
DLTC; PEPP; PH.
Beat Generation
DLDC; DLTS; HL.
Beat movement
OCAL.
beatnik
DLTS.
beat poets
DLTC; ME/*34*; PEPP.
beats
FDLP/*accent*.
beau monde
DLTS.
Beaver, Tony
OCAL.
Bec, monastery of
CR/*Index*.
Bedeutung
EDSL/*249*.
Bedeutungslaute
EDSL/*200*.
begging the question
DLTS; ME/*34*.
beginning rhyme
DLTC; HL; PEPP.
behaviorism
DLTS.

behavioural analysis
FDLP/*allo-*.
behavioural rules
FDLP/*domain*.
behaviourism
FDLP.
behaviourist
FDLP/*semantics*.
Beirut
CR/*Index*.
bel esprit
DLTS.
Belgian poetry
PEPP.
belief
DLTS; DMCT.
belief, problem of
PEPP.
belief, the problem of
HL.
belles lettres
DLTS.
belles lettres
CR/*Index*.
belles lettres
DLTC; ME/*35*.
belles-lettres
HL.
bends
FDLP/*locus*.
Benedictines
CR/*Index*.
benefactive
FDLP.
benefit of clergy
DLTS.
Bengali poetry
PEPP.
Benthamism
HL.
Bent's Fort
OCAL.
bergerette
PEPP.

bergette □ 46

bergette
DLTC.
bestiaries
CODEL; OCEL.
bestiary
DLDC/*beast epic*; DLTC; DLTS; HL; ME/*35*; PEPP.
best seller
DLTC; DLTS.
best sellers
OCAL.
bête noire
DLTS.
Bethel Community
OCAL.
be-verb
ME/*343*.
Beziehungslaute
EDSL/*200*.
bias
DLTS.
bibelot
DLTC; DLTS.
bibelot
HL.
Bible
CODEL; DLTS; HL; OCEL.
Bible as literature
HL.
Bible, English translations of
HL.
Bible, influence on literature
HL.
Bible, the English
OCEL.
Biblical poetry
PEPP/*920*.
biblio-
DLTC.
biblioclasm
DLTS.
Bibliographical Society of America
OCAL.

bibliography
DLDC; DLTC; DLTS; HL; ME/*36*.
bibliolatry
DLTS.
bibliomancy
DLTS.
bibliomania
DLTS.
bibliophile
DLTS.
bibliophobe
DLTS.
bidialect
FDLP.
bidialectal
FDLP/*bidialect*.
bidialectalism
FDLP/*bidialect*.
bidirectional
FDLP/*co-occur*; GLT.
Biedermeier
PEPP.
Biedermeier
DLTC; DLTS.
bienséances, les
DLTC.
bilabial
FDLP; GLT.
bilabial stop
ME/*344*.
bilateral
FDLP/*opposition*; FDLP/*lateral*; FDLP.
bilateral opposition
GLT.
Bildungsroman
DLDC/*novel*; DLTC; DLTS; HL; ME/*36*.
bilingual
EDSL/*60*; FDLP.
bilingualism
FDLP/*bilingual*; GLT.
bilinguals, compound
FDLP/*compound*.

bilingual text
GLT.
billingsgate
DLTS; HL.
Bill of Rights
OCAL.
bimorphemic
FDLP/*mono-*.
binarism
FDLP/*binary feature*.
binarity
FDLP/*binary feature*.
binary
EDSL/*173*.
binary choices
FDLP/*binary feature*.
binary coding
FDLP/*binary feature*.
binary construction
ME/*344*.
binary feature
FDLP.
binary principle
GLT.
binit
GLT.
biographical criticism
PEPP.
biographical fallacy
HL; ME/*36*.
biography
CODEL; DLDC; DLTC; DLTS; DMCT; HL; ME/*36*.
biolinguistics
FDLP/*linguistics*; FDLP; GLT.
biological linguistics
FDLP/*biolinguistics*.
bipartite system
GLT.
bit
GLT.
biuniqueness
FDLP.

black comedy
DLTC; DLTS.
Black English
FDLP/*vernacular*.
black humor
HL; ME/*38*.
black letter
HL.
Black literature
HL; ME/*38*.
blackmail
DLTS.
Black Mountain Poets
DLTC.
Black Mountain School
HL.
Black Mountain School of Poets
PEPP/*920*.
Black poetry
PEPP/*920*.
blade
FDLP.
blade of the tongue
GLT.
blank verse
OCEL; CODEL; DLDC/*versification*; DLTC; DLTS; HL; ME/*40*; PEPP; PH.
blason
PEPP.
blazon
DLTC.
bleed
DLTS; HL.
bleeding
FDLP.
bleeding order
FDLP/*bleeding*.
bleeding rule
FDLP/*bleeding*.
blend
FDLP.
blending
FDLP/*blend*; GLT; ME/*344*.

block ☐ **48**

block
  FDLP.
block-books
  HL.
blocked syllable
  FDLP/*closed*; GLT.
blocked vowel
  GLT.
blocking
  FDLP/*block*.
block printing
  DLTS.
Bloomfieldianism
  FDLP.
Bloomsbury Group
  CODEL; DLTC; HL; OCEL.
Blue and the Gray, The
  OCAL.
blue book
  DLTC.
blue laws
  OCAL.
Blues
  OCAL; DLTC; DLTS; HL; PEPP.
Bluestocking
  CODEL; DLTC; DLTS; ME/*42*; OCEL.
bluestockings
  HL.
blurb
  DLTC; DLTS; HL.
boasting poem
  DLTC; HL.
bob and wheel
  CODEL; DLTC; OCEL; PEPP.
Bobbio, monastery of
  CR/*Index*.
body language
  FDLP/*language*; FDLP/*kinesics*.
Boerde
  DLTC.
Bollingen Poetry Translation Prize
  OCAL.

Bollingen Prize in Poetry
  OCAL.
Bologna
  CR/*Index*.
bombast
  DLDC; DLTC; DLTS; HL; ME/*42*.
bona fide
  DLTS.
bonding
  GLT.
boner
  DLTS.
bonhomie
  DLTS.
bon mot
  ME/*42*.
bon mot
  DLTS; HL.
bon vivant
  DLTS.
book
  DLTC; DLTS.
book clubs
  OCAL.
book of hours
  DLTC.
book review
  DLTS; ME/*42*.
book sizes
  HL.
book word
  GLT.
bootlegging
  OCAL.
border
  GLT.
Border Romances
  OCAL.
borrow
  FDLP.
borrowed word
  GLT.

49 □ breaking

borrowing
  EDSL/7; FDLP/*borrow*; GLT.
Boston
  OCAL.
Boston Athenaeum
  OCAL.
Boston Public Library
  OCAL.
boulevard drama
  DLTC; HL.
bound
  FDLP.
bound accent
  GLT.
boundary
  GLT.
boundary-marker
  FDLP/*boundary-symbol*.
boundary-symbol
  FDLP.
bounded noun
  GLT.
bound form
  FDLP/*bound*; GLT.
bound forms
  FDLP/*morpheme*.
bound morpheme
  FDLP/*bound*; GLT; ME/*344*.
bound stress
  GLT.
Bourbon
  DLTS.
bourgeois
  DLTS.
bourgeois drama
  DLDC; DLTC; DLTS; HL.
bourgeois literature
  HL.
bourgeois tragedy
  HL.
boustrophedon
  DLTC; GLT; OCEL.
bouts-rimés
  DLTC; HL; PEPP.

bouts-rimés
  CODEL; OCEL; PH.
bowdlerize
  DLDC; DLTC; DLTS; HL.
bowdlerized
  ME/*43*.
Bowery, The
  OCAL.
bow-wow theory
  GLT.
box set
  HL.
brace notation
  FDLP/*bracketing*.
brachiology
  DLTC.
brachycatalectic
  DLTC; DLTS; HL; PEPP.
bracketing
  FDLP.
bracket notation
  FDLP/*bracketing*.
brackets
  FDLP/*bracketing*.
braggadocio
  DLTC; DLTS; HL.
braggart soldier
  DLDC.
Brahmin
  DLTS.
Brahmins
  HL; OCAL.
Braille
  DLTS.
branching
  FDLP.
branlant
  GLT.
Brazilian poetry
  PEPP.
Bread and Cheese Club
  OCAL.
breaking
  GLT; ME/*345*.

breath group
FDLP; GLT.
breathing
GLT.
breathy
FDLP.
breathy voice
GLT.
Brechung
GLT.
Breton lay
HL.
Breton lays
CODEL; OCEL.
Breton poetry
PEPP.
Breton romance
HL.
breve
PEPP.
breve
DLTC; DLTS; GLT; HL.
breviary
DLTC; DLTS; HL.
brief
DLTC; DLTS; HL; ME/*43*.
bright vowel
GLT.
Briticism
DLTS.
British Museum
CODEL; HL; OCEL.
British Sign Language
FDLP/*sign*.
broad accent
FDLP/*accent*.
broad consonant
GLT.
broad reference
ME/*43*.
broadside
CODEL; DLTC; DLTS; OCEL.
broadside ballad
DLDC/*ballad*; HL; PEPP.
broadside ballads
ME/*43*.
broad transcription
FDLP/*transcription*; GLT.
broad vowel
GLT.
brochure
DLTC; HL.
broken plural
GLT.
broken rhyme
DLTC; HL; PEPP; PH/*rhyme*.
bromide
DLTS; ME/*44*.
Brook Farm
HL; ME/*44*; OCAL.
Brook Farm Institute
OCEL.
Brooklyn
FDLP/*dialect*; OCAL.
Brother Jonathan
OCAL.
brouhaha
DLTS.
Brownists
OCAL.
brummagem
DLTS.
brut
CODEL; DLTC; OCEL.
BT
FDLP/*baby-talk*.
buccal
FDLP.
buccal cavity
GLT.
buccal sound
GLT.
buccal voice
FDLP/*air-stream mechanism*.
bucolic
CODEL; DLDC/*pastoral*; DLTC; DLTS; HL; OCEL; PEPP; PH/*pastoral*.

51 □ Byzantine poetry

bucolic diaeresis
DLTC; PEPP.
bugarštice
DLTC.
Bulgarian poetry
PEPP.
bull
CODEL; CODEL; DLDC; DLTC; DLTS; OCEL; OCEL.
bululú
DLTC.
bunching
FDLP.
buncombe
CODEL; DLTC; DLTS; OCEL.
bundle
FDLP/*iso-*; FDLP.
bunk
DLTS.
Bunker Hill
OCAL.
bunkum
CODEL; DLTC; DLTS; OCEL.
burden
CODEL; DLTC; HL; OCEL; PEPP; PH/*stanza*.
burlesque
CODEL; DLDC; DLTC; DLTS; DMCT; HL; ME/*44*; OCAL; OCEL; PEPP.
burletta
DLTC.

burletta
DLTS; HL.
Burmese poetry
PEPP.
Burns stanza
DLTC; DLTS; HL; PEPP; PH/*stanza*.
burst
FDLP; GLT.
Burwell Papers
OCAL.
buskin
CODEL; DLTC; DLTS; HL; ME/*45*; OCEL.
Byelorussian poetry
PEPP.
bylina
DLTC; PEPP.
Byronic
CODEL; OCEL.
Byronic hero
DLDC/*classic*.
Byronic stanza
DLTC.
byword
DLTS.
Byzantine Age
DLTC.
Byzantine poetry
PEPP.

C

cabal
DLTS; HL.
cablese
DLTS.
caccia
DLTC; DLTS; PEPP.
cacoëthes
DLTS.
cacoëthes loquendi
DLTS/*cacöethes*.
cacoëthes scribendi
DLTS/*cacöethes*.
cacoethes scribendi
DLTC.
caconym
OO.
cacophony
DLDC/*euphony*; DLTC; DLTS; DMCT; GLT; HL; ME/*46*; PEPP.
cacuminal
GLT.
cadence
DLTC; DLTS; GLT; HL; ME/*46*; PEPP; PH.
cadences
PH/*free verse*.

caesura
CODEL; DLDC/*versification*; DLTC; DLTS; EDSL/*187*; HL; ME/*46*; OCEL; PEPP.
Cajun
OCAL/*Acadia*.
Calderonian honour
DLTC.
calendar
CODEL; DLTC; HL; OCEL.
California gold rush
OCAL/*Forty-niners*.
calligramme
PEPP/*921*; PH.
calligraphy
DLTS; HL.
Calliopean Society
OCAL.
calque
FDLP; GLT.
calumny
DLTS.
Calvinism
DLTS; HL; ME/*46*; OCAL.
calypso
DLTC; DLTS; HL.
Cambridge, Massachusetts
OCAL.
Cambridge Platform
OCAL.

camp
ME/52.
Canadian poetry
PEPP.
canción
DLTC; PEPP.
cancioneiros
DLTC; PEPP.
cancionero
DLTS.
cancrine
DLTC.
canon
DLDC; DLTC; DLTS; HL; ME/52.
canonical
FDLP.
canonical form
GLT.
Canon of Ten Attic Orators
CR/*Index*.
canso
DLTC; HL; PH.
cant
DLTC; DLTS; GLT; HL; ME/346; ME/53.
cantar
DLTC; PEPP.
cantar de gesta
DLTC.
cantar de pandeiro
DLTC.
cante jondo
DLTC; PEPP.
cantica de serrana
DLTC.
canticle
DLTC; DLTS.
canticum
DLTC; PEPP.
cantiga
DLTC; PEPP.
canto
DLTC; DLTS; HL; ME/53; PEPP; PH.

Cantonese
FDLP/*dialect*.
canzo
HL.
canzone
DLTC; HL; PEPP.
canzone
DLTS; PH/*troubadour*.
canzonet
DLTC.
capacity
FDLP.
capa y espada
DLTC; ME/53.
capitalizing
ME/53.
Capitol
OCAL.
capitolo
DLTC; PEPP.
Cappadocian Fathers
CR/*Index*.
caprice
DLTS.
captatio benevolentiae
CR/*Index*.
cardinal
FDLP.
cardinal vowel diagram
FDLP/*cardinal vowels*.
cardinal vowel quadrilateral
FDLP/*cardinal vowels*.
cardinal vowels
FDLP; GLT.
careful
FDLP/*assimilation*.
caricature
DLDC/*burlesque*; DLTC; DLTS; DMCT; HL; ME/56.
Carmel, California
OCAL.
carmen
DLTC; PEPP.

55 □ categorial grammar

carmen figuratem [sic]
ME/56.
carmen figuratum
DLTC; HL.
Carmina Burana
DLTC.
carol
CODEL; DLDC; DLTC; DLTS; HL; ME/56; OCEL; PEPP.
carole
HL/*carol*.
Carolina Playmakers
OCAL.
Caroline
CODEL; DLDC; DLTS; HL; OCEL.
Caroline Drama
CODEL.
Caroline Period
DLTC.
carpe diem
DLDC; DLTC; DLTS; HL; ME/56; PEPP.
carte blanche
DLTS.
Cartesian linguistics
FDLP.
case
FDLP; ME/346.
case frame
FDLP/*frame*.
case grammar
FDLP/*case*.
cases vides
GLT.
Casey Jones
OCAL/*Jones, Casey*.
caste
GLT.
casual speech
FDLP/*bidialect*.
casuistry
DLTS; ME/56.
casus belli
DLTS.

catachrēsis
CODEL.
catachresis
DLTC; DLTS; ME/57; OCEL; PEPP.
catacresis [sic]
GLT.
Catalan poetry
PEPP.
catalectic
CODEL; OCEL; PH.
catalects
DLTC.
catalexis
DLDC/*versification*; DLTC; DLTS/*catalectic*; HL; PEPP; PH/*catalectic*.
catalog
HL.
catalogue raisonné
DLTC; DLTS.
catalogue verse
DLTC; PEPP.
cataphora
FDLP.
cataphoric reference
FDLP/*cataphora*.
catastasis
DLTC; DLTS; HL.
catastrophe
DLDC/*plot*; DLTC; DLTS; DMCT; HL; ME/57.
catch
DLTC; DLTS; GLT; HL.
catch-word
HL.
catchword
DLTS.
catechism
DLTS.
categorial component
FDLP/*category*; FDLP/*base*.
categorial grammar
FDLP/*category*.

categorical syllogism
ME/57.
categories (grammatical)
GLT.
categorisation
FDLP/category.
category
FDLP.
category feature
FDLP/category.
category symbols
FDLP/category.
catenative
FDLP.
catenative verb
FDLP/verb.
catharis
DLDC/tragedy.
catharsis
DLTC; DLTS; DMCT; HL; ME/57; PEPP.
cathedral schools
CR/Index.
Catholicism
OCAL/Roman Catholic Church.
catholicity
DLTS.
Cato
OCAL.
cauda
DLTC; DLTS.
cauda
PEPP.
caudate sonnet
DLTC; PEPP.
causal induction
ME/57.
causal reasoning
ME/57.
causative
FDLP.
cause and effect
DLTS.
causerie
DLTC; HL.
causerie
DLTS.
causes, theory of
CR/Index.
cavalier
DLTS.
Cavalier drama
DLTC.
Cavalier lyric
HL; PEPP.
Cavalier Lyricists
HL.
Cavalier lyrics
CODEL; OCEL.
Cavalier Poets
DLTC; ME/58; DLDC/Caroline; PEPP.
caveat
DLTS.
cavities of speech organs
GLT.
cavity
FDLP.
cavity features
FDLP/cavity.
CD
FDLP/communication.
cedilla
GLT.
Celtic
DLTS.
Celtic literature
HL.
Celtic prosody
PEPP.
Celtic Renaissance
DLDC; HL.
Celtic revival
HL.
Celtic revival, the
HL.

Celtic Twilight
   CODEL; DLTC; OCEL.
cénacle
   DLTC.
cenematics
   FDLP/*ceneme*.
ceneme
   FDLP; GLT.
cenemes
   EDSL/*23*.
cenetics
   FDLP/*ceneme*; GLT.
censorship
   DLTS; PEPP/*922*.
census
   GLT.
center
   GLT.
Center for Editions of American Authors
   HL/*CEAA*.
Center for Scholarly Editions
   HL/*CSE*.
centering
   GLT.
center of Broca
   GLT.
cento
   DLTC; PEPP.
cento
   CODEL; DLTS; HL; PH.
cento(nism)
   DMCT.
central intelligence
   ME/*58*.
centralisation
   FDLP/*centre*.
centralise
   FDLP/*centre*.
Central states
   OCAL/*Middle West*.
central vowel
   GLT; ME/*346*.

centre
   FDLP; FDLP/*syllable*.
centrifugal
   GLT.
centripetal
   GLT.
centroid
   PEPP.
centum languages
   GLT; ME/*346*.
Century Association
   OCAL.
cerebral
   GLT.
certitude
   DLTS.
cesura
   PH.
chacun à son goût
   DLTS.
chain
   FDLP.
chained
   FDLP/*concatenation*.
Chain of Being
   DLDC/*enlightenment*.
chain relationships
   FDLP/*axis*.
chain rhyme
   PEPP.
chain verse
   DLTC; HL.
chair ode
   DLTC.
Chancellorsville, Battle of
   OCAL.
changga
   DLTC.
channel
   FDLP/*medium*.
chanso
   PEPP.
chanson
   DLTC.

chanson ☐ **58**

chanson
 DLTS; HL.
chanson à danser
 DLTC.
chanson à personnages
 DLTC.
chanson de geste
 HL.
chanson de geste
 PH.
chanson de gestes
 DLTC.
chanson de toile
 DLTC; PEPP.
chansonnier
 DLTC.
chansons de geste
 CODEL; OCEL; PEPP.
chant
 DLTC; DLTS; HL; PEPP.
chante fable
 DLTC.
chante-fable
 PEPP.
chantey
 DLTC; DLTS; HL; OCAL.
chant royal
 HL.
chant royal
 DLTC; PEPP; PH/*ballade*.
chaos
 DLTS.
chapbook
 CODEL; DLTC; DLTS; HL;
 ME/*58*; OCEL.
chapbooks
 OCAL.
chapka
 DLTC.
character
 DLDC; DLDC/*plot*; DLDC/*plot*;
 DLTS; DMCT; EDSL/*222*; HL.
characterization
 DLTS; HL.

characterology of speech
 GLT.
characters
 ME/*58*.
character sketch
 DLTS.
characters of style
 CR/*Index*.
character, the
 DLTC.
charactonym
 OO.
charade
 DLTS.
Chardon Street Convention
 OCAL.
charisma
 DLTS.
charivari
 DLTS.
Charleston
 OCAL.
charm
 DLTC; PEPP; PH.
chart
 FDLP.
Chartism
 DLTS; HL.
Chartres
 CR/*Index*.
chastushka
 DLTC; PEPP.
Chaucerian stanza
 DLTC; DLTS; HL.
Chautauqua movement
 OCAL.
chauvinism
 DLTS.
checked
 FDLP.
checked position
 GLT.
checked syllable
 FDLP/*checked*; GLT.

checked vowel
FDLP/*checked*; GLT; ME/*346*.
checking
FDLP.
checking tag
FDLP/*checking*.
cheek
FDLP/*buccal*.
cheeks
FDLP/*air-stream mechanism*.
chef d'œuvre
DLTS.
chest pulse
FDLP; GLT.
cheville
DLTC.
Chevy Chase stanza
DLTC.
chiaroscuro
CODEL; DLTS; HL; ME/*58*; OCEL.
chiasmus
CODEL; DLDC; DLTC; DLTS; EDSL/*277*; HL; ME/*59*; OCEL; PEPP; PH.
Chicago
OCAL.
Chicago Critics
DLTC; HL; DMCT.
Chicago critics, the
PEPP.
child
FDLP/*baby-talk*; FDLP/*'fis' phenomenon*.
child grammars
EDSL/*164*.
child language
FDLP/*complex*.
child language acquisition
FDLP/*acquisition*.
children
FDLP/*analogy*.
children's books
DLTC.

children's language
FDLP/*imitation*.
Children's literature in America
OCAL.
Chilean poetry
PEPP.
chimera
DLTS.
chimerat
DLTC.
chiming
LGEP/*95*.
China
CR/*Index*.
Chinese
FDLP/*class*; FDLP/*isolating*; FDLP/*dialect*; FDLP/*inalienable*.
Chinese poetry
PEPP.
chinoiserie
DLTS.
chironym
OO.
Chisholm Trail
OCAL.
chivalric romance
HL; ME/*59*.
chivalry
DLTS.
chivalry in English literature
HL.
cho
FDLP/*chômeur*.
choice
FDLP.
chōka
PEPP.
choliamb
CODEL; OCEL.
choliambus
DLTC; PEPP.
chômeur
FDLP.

Chomsky-adjunction
FDLP/*adjunction*.

Chomskyan
FDLP.

choral character
HL.

choree
DLTC; PEPP.

choriamb
CODEL; ME/*59*; OCEL; PEPP.

choriambics
PH.

choriambus
DLTC; DLTS; HL.

chorus
DLDC; DLTC; DLTS; DMCT; HL; ME/*59*; PEPP.

chorus character
DLDC/*chorus*.

chrestomathy
DLTC; DLTS; HL.

chria
CR/*Index*.

Christabel meter
DLTC; PEPP.

Christadelphians
OCAL.

Christian humanism
DLDC/*Renaissance*.

Christianity, established in England
HL.

Christian rhetoric
CR/*Index*.

Christian Science
OCAL.

chromatic accent
GLT.

chrone
FDLP/*chroneme*.

chroneme
FDLP; GLT.

chronicle
DLDC; DLTC; DLTS; HL.

chronicle novel
DLTC.

chronicle play
DLDC/*chronicle*; DLTC; DLTS; HL; PEPP.

chronicles
CODEL; OCEL.

chronique scandaleuse
HL.

chronogram
DLTC.

chronological order
DLTS.

chronological primitivism
DLDC/*primitivism*; HL.

chronological theory
GLT.

ch'ü
PEPP.

Ciceronian
DLTC.

Ciceronianism
CR/*Index*.

Ciceronians
HL.

Ciceronian sentence
DLDC/*style*.

Ciceronian style
HL.

ci-devant
DLTS.

Cincinnati, Society of the
OCAL.

cinéma vérité
HL.

cinquain
DLTC; DLTS; HL; PEPP; PH.

cipher
DLTC; DLTS.

circa
DLTS.

circular
DLTS.

61 □ clause terminal

circularity
    FDLP/*counter-intuitive*.
circular reasoning
    ME/*60*.
circumambages
    DLTC.
circumlocution
    DLTC; DLTS; HL; LGEP/*132*; ME/*60*.
circumstance, tragedy of
    DLTC.
circumstant
    EDSL/*213*.
circumstantial evidence
    DLTS.
circus
    OCAL.
citation
    DLTS; FDLP/*citation form*.
citation form
    FDLP.
citation slips
    FDLP/*citation form*.
Civil War
    OCAL.
clairvoyance
    DLTS.
clarity
    CR/*Index*.
class
    FDLP; GLT.
class cleavage
    FDLP/*class*; GLT.
class dialects
    FDLP/*dialect*; FDLP/*class*.
classeme
    FDLP.
classic
    CODEL; DLDC; DLTC; DLTS; DMCT; HL; ME/*60*; OCEL.
classical
    GLT; HL; ME/*60*; PH.
classical hexameter
    PH.

classical meters in modern languages
    PEPP.
classical poetics
    PEPP.
classical prosody
    PEPP; PH/*metre*; PH.
classical tragedy
    HL.
Classicism
    CR/*Index*; CODEL; DLTC; DLTS; HL; ME/*60*; PEPP.
classicism/romanticism
    DLTC.
Classic Revival
    OCAL/*Greek Revival*.
classification
    FDLP/*class*; FDLP/*adjective*.
classification of languages
    GLT.
classificatory language
    GLT.
classifier
    GLT.
classifiers
    FDLP/*class*.
class language
    GLT.
class meaning
    GLT.
class nouns
    FDLP/*class*.
class sign
    GLT.
class word
    GLT.
clause
    FDLP; FDLP/*arc*; ME/*346*.
clause-mate
    FDLP.
clausematiness
    FDLP/*nondiscrete grammar*.
clause terminal
    GLT.

clause-wall
 FDLP.
clausula
 DLTC; DLTS.
clausula
 PEPP.
clear
 FDLP.
clear lateral
 GLT.
clearness
 DLTS.
cleavage
 GLT.
clef
 DLTC.
cleft lip
 FDLP/*palate*.
cleft palate
 FDLP/*palate*.
cleft sentence
 FDLP.
Clements Library
 OCAL.
clench
 DLTC.
clericalism
 DLTS.
clerihew
 CODEL; DLDC/*light verse*; DLTC; DLTS; HL; OCEL; PEPP; PH.
cliché
 CODEL; DLDC; DLTC; DLTS; FDLP/*collocation*; HL; ME/*62*; OCEL; PEPP.
click
 FDLP; GLT.
click displacement
 FDLP/*click*.
clicks
 EDSL/*156*.
cliff-hanger
 DLTS.

climactic order
 DLTS.
climate of opinion
 DLTS.
climax
 CR/*Index*; DLDC/*plot*; DLTC; DLTS; HL; ME/*62*; PEPP.
cline
 FDLP.
clinical linguistics
 FDLP.
clipped
 GLT.
clipped word
 GLT.
clipper ships
 OCAL.
clipping
 GLT; ME/*347*.
clitic
 FDLP.
cloak and dagger
 HL; ME/*63*.
cloak-and-dagger
 DLTS.
cloak and sword
 HL; ME/*63*; PEPP.
clock
 GLT.
close
 FDLP.
close(d)
 GLT; ME/*347*.
closed
 FDLP; ME/*63*.
closed-class words
 GLT.
closed construction
 GLT.
closed corpus
 FDLP/*corpus*.
closed couplet
 DLTC; DLTS; HL.

63 □ cognitive processes

close(d) juncture
GLT.
closed list
GLT.
closed repertory
GLT.
closed syllabification
GLT.
closed syllable
GLT; ME/347.
close(d) vowel
GLT.
close juncture
FDLP/juncture.
close reading
DLDC/explication.
closet drama
DLDC/drama; DLTC; DLTS; HL; PEPP.
close transition
FDLP/juncture; FDLP/transition.
closing sound
GLT.
closure
FDLP; GLT.
closure, poetic
PEPP/923.
clou
DLTC.
clue
DLTS/clew.
cluster
EDSL/267; FDLP; GLT.
coalescence
FDLP; GLT.
coalescent
FDLP/reciprocal.
coalescent assimilation
FDLP/assimilation.
coarticulated stop
GLT.
coarticulation
FDLP; GLT.

cobla
DLTC; PEPP.
cock-and-bull story
CODEL; DLTC; DLTS; HL; OCEL.
Cockney
FDLP/affricate; FDLP/glottal.
Cockney rhymes
DLTC.
Cockney school
DLTS; HL.
Cockney School of Poetry
DLTC; PEPP.
cocktail party phenomenon
FDLP.
coda
DLTS; FDLP/syllable; FDLP; GLT/of syllable; HL.
code
EDSL/104; FDLP.
code-switching
FDLP/code.
codex
CR/Index; DLTC; DLTS; HL.
codicil
DLTS.
coexistence
GLT.
cofradía
DLTC.
cogito, ergo sum
DLTS.
cognate
DLTS; FDLP; ME/347.
cognates
GLT.
cognition
FDLP/developmental linguistics.
cognitive factors
FDLP/comprehension.
cognitive meaning
DLDC/connotation; DLTS; FDLP; LGEP/40.
cognitive processes
EDSL/73.

cognitive psychology
    FDLP/*Chomskyan*.
coherence
    DLTS; HL; ME/*63*.
cohesion
    FDLP.
cohesive
    FDLP/*cohesion*.
co-hyponyms
    FDLP/*hyponym*.
coin
    DLTC.
coinage
    DLTS; GLT.
coincidence
    DLTS; HL.
coined words
    HL.
cola
    DLTC.
collaboration
    DLTS; HL.
collage
    DLTC; DLTS; HL.
collapse
    FDLP.
collate
    DLTS; HL.
collation
    GLT.
collections, unified
    PEPP/*923*.
collective
    FDLP.
collective noun
    ME/*347*.
collective unconscious
    DLDC/*archetype*; DLTS; HL.
colligate
    FDLP/*colligation*.
colligation
    FDLP.
collision
    GLT.

collocability
    FDLP/*collocation*.
collocate
    FDLP/*collocation*.
collocation
    FDLP; GLT.
collocational range
    FDLP/*collocation*.
collocational restrictions
    FDLP/*collocation*.
colloquial
    GLT; ME/*347*.
colloquialism
    DLTC; DLTS; GLT; HL.
colloquial speech
    FDLP/*assimilation*.
colloquy
    DLTC; DLTS; HL.
Colombian poetry
    PEPP.
colon
    DLTC; PEPP.
colonial lag
    GLT.
colonial(colonizing) language
    GLT.
Colonial Period in American Literature, 1607-1765
    HL.
colophon
    CODEL; DLTC; DLTS; HL; OCEL.
color
    DLTS.
colors
    CR/*Index*.
colour terms
    FDLP/*gradience*.
colporteur
    DLTS.
column
    HL.
combination
    EDSL/*109*.

65 □ commonplace book

combinative change
    GLT.
combinatorial
    FDLP.
combinatorial relations
    FDLP/*combinatorial*.
combinatory change
    GLT.
combinatory phonology
    GLT.
combinatory variant
    GLT.
combining form
    DLTS.
comedia de capa y espada
    PEPP.
comédie
    DLTC.
comédie-ballet
    DLTC.
comédie de moeurs
    DLTC.
comédie larmoyante
    DLTC.
comedy
    CODEL; DLDC; DLTC; DLTS;
    DMCT; HL; ME/*65*; OCEL;
    PEPP.
comedy of humors
    DLDC/*comedy*; PEPP.
comedy of humours
    DLTC; HL; ME/*67*.
comedy of ideas
    DLTC.
comedy of intrigue
    DLTC; HL.
comedy of manners
    CODEL; DLDC/*comedy*; DLTC;
    DMCT; HL.
comedy of morals
    DLTC; HL.
comedy of situation
    HL.
come-outers
    OCAL.

comic
    EDSL/*154*.
comic figures
    DLDC/*convention*.
comic opera
    CODEL/*opera*; HL.
comic relief
    DLDC; DLTC; DLTS; HL; ME/
    67.
command
    FDLP.
commedia dell'arte
    DLDC; DLTC; DLTS; HL; ME/
    72; OCEL.
commedia dell'arte
    CODEL.
commedia erudita
    DLTC.
comme il faut
    DLTS.
comment
    EDSL/*271*; FDLP/*topicalisation*;
    FDLP/*comment*; FDLP; GLT.
commissive
    FDLP.
commitment
    DLTC.
common
    FDLP.
common case
    GLT.
common core
    FDLP/*common*; GLT.
common gender
    GLT.
common measure
    DLTC; DLTS; HL; PH.
common meter
    HL.
common noun
    ME/*347*.
common particular measure
    PH/*common measure*.
commonplace book
    DLTC; DLTS; HL.

commonplaces
CR/*Index*.

common rhythm
DLTC; PEPP; PH.

commonwealth
DLTS.

Commonwealth Interregnum
HL.

Commonwealth Period
DLDC/*puritanism*; DLTC.

communicate
FDLP/*communication*.

communication
EDSL/*11*; FDLP; GLT.

communication fallacy
DLTC.

communication heresy
DLTC.

communicative competence
FDLP/*communication*; FDLP/*competence*.

communicative dynamism
FDLP/*functional sentence perspective*; FDLP/*communication*.

commus
DLTC.

commutation
EDSL/*25*; FDLP; GLT.

commutation test
FDLP/*commutation*; GLT.

comp
DLTS.

compact
FDLP.

compact phoneme
GLT.

companion poems
HL; PEPP/*924*.

comparative
FDLP.

comparative clause
FDLP/*comparative*.

comparative criticism
DLTC; PEPP.

comparative degree
ME/*347*.

comparative form
FDLP/*comparative*.

comparative grammar
EDSL/*9*; FDLP/*grammar*; FDLP/*comparative*.

comparative linguistics
DLTC; FDLP/*linguistics*; GLT.

comparative literature
DLTC; DMCT; HL.

comparative method
FDLP/*comparative*; GLT.

comparative philology
FDLP/*comparative*.

comparative reconstruction
FDLP/*reconstruction*.

comparative sentence
FDLP/*comparative*.

comparativism
EDSL/*9*.

comparison
ME/*348*.

comparison and contrast
DLTS.

comparison of languages
GLT.

compassion
DLTS.

compendium
DLTS; HL.

compensation
DLTC; DLTS; HL; PEPP; PH.

compensatory lengthening
GLT; ME/*348*.

compensatory shortening
GLT; ME/*348*.

competence
EDSL/*120*; FDLP; ME/*348*.

competence grammar
FDLP/*grammar*.

complaint
DLDC/*lyric*; DLTC; DLTS; DMCT; HL; PEPP.

complement
EDSL/*210*; FDLP; ME/*348*.
complementarity
FDLP/*complementary*.
complementary
EDSL/*109*; FDLP.
complementary distribution
EDSL/*172*; FDLP/*complementary*; FDLP/*distribution*; GLT; ME/*349*.
complementary infinitive
ME/*349*.
complementary terms
FDLP/*complementary*.
complementation
FDLP/*complement*; GLT.
complementiser
FDLP/*complement*.
complementizer transformation
ME/*349*.
complete assimilation
GLT.
complete closure
FDLP/*closure*.
completed aspect
EDSL/*309*.
complete feedback
FDLP/*feedback*.
completing
FDLP/*complement*.
completive (sentence)
GLT.
complex
EDSL/*114*; FDLP; GLT.
complexio
PEPP.
complexity
FDLP/*complex*.
complex metaphor
DLTC; PH/*metaphor*.
complex-negative
EDSL/*115*.
complex
GLT/*vowel*.

complex nucleus
FDLP/*complex*.
complex peak
GLT.
complex-positive
EDSL/*115*.
complex prepositions
FDLP/*preposition*.
complex sentence
FDLP/*complex*; ME/*350*.
complex stop
FDLP/*complex*.
complex symbol
FDLP.
complex tone
FDLP/*complex*.
complex transformation
EDSL/*290*; ME/*351*.
complex (vowel) nucleus
GLT.
complex word
FDLP/*complex*; GLT.
complication
DLDC/*plot*; DLTS; HL; ME/*73*.
component
FDLP; GLT.
componential analysis
EDSL/*265*; FDLP/*component*.
composite verbs
FDLP/*composition*.
composite verses
DLTC; PEPP.
composition
CR/*Index*; DLTC; DLTS; FDLP; GLT.
compositional meaning
FDLP/*composition*.
composition in depth
HL.
compos mentis
DLTS.
compound
FDLP; GLT.

compound bilingualism
FDLP/*co-ordination*.

compound-complex sentence
ME/*351*.

compound grapheme
GLT.

compounding
FDLP/*compound*.

compound phoneme
GLT.

Compound Rule
FDLP/*cycle*.

compound sentence
ME/*351*.

compound word
GLT; ME/*351*.

comprehension
FDLP.

comprehensive
DLTS.

compromise language
GLT.

computational linguistics
FDLP/*linguistics*; FDLP.

computer language
FDLP/*language*.

computer poetry
PEPP/*925*.

computer program
FDLP/*algorithm*.

computing
FDLP/*algorithm*.

comstockery
DLTS; HL; ME/*73*.

Comstock Lode
OCAL.

con amore
DLTS.

conative
EDSL/*341*; FDLP; GLT.

con brio
DLTS.

concatenation
FDLP; HL; ME/*351*.

conceit
CODEL; DLDC/*metaphysical poets*; DLTC; DLTS; DMCT; HL; ME/*74*; PEPP; PH.

conceptism
PEPP.

conceptismo
DLTC.

concept signified
FDLP/*sign*.

conceptual
FDLP/*ideational*.

conceptualization
CR/*Index*.

concerte particular
PH.

conciseness
DLTS.

conclusio
CR/*Index*.

conclusion
ME/*74*.

concord
EDSL/*51*; FDLP; ME/*351*.

concord (concordance)
GLT.

concordance
DLTC; DLTS; HL.

concordances
FDLP/*computational linguistics*.

Concord, Massachusetts
OCAL.

concrete
DLDC.

concrete and abstract
PEPP.

concreteness
DLTS.

concrete noun
ME/*352*.

concrete poetry
DMCT; ME/*74*; PEPP/*927*; PH.

concrete terms
HL.

69 □ conjunctive adverb

concrete universal
DLDC/*concrete*; DLTC; HL; ME/*74*; PEPP; PH.
concrete verse
DLTC.
condensation
DLTS; HL.
condition
FDLP.
conditional
FDLP.
conditional sound change
GLT.
conditional syllogism
ME/*74*.
conditional variant
GLT.
conditioned
FDLP/*environment*; FDLP; GLT.
conditioned sound change
GLT.
conditioned variant
FDLP/*variant*.
conditioned variants
FDLP/*context*.
conditioning
FDLP/*conditioned*; GLT.
conduplicatio
PEPP.
Confederacy
OCAL.
confession
DLTS; HL.
confessional literature
DLTC.
confessional novel
DLTC.
confessional poetry
DLTC; HL; PEPP/*928*; PH.
confessional verse
ME/*74*.
confidant
DLDC; DLTC; DLTS; HL.

confidante
DLDC/*confidant*; HL.
configuration
EDSL/*267*; FDLP; GLT.
configurational
FDLP/*configuration*.
confirmatio
CR/*Index*.
conflict
DLDC/*plot*; DLTC; DLTS; HL; ME/*75*.
conformal language
EDSL/*23*.
conformity to genre
EDSL/*261*.
conformity to type
EDSL/*261*.
congeneric groups
GLT.
Congregationalism
OCAL.
congruence
FDLP; GLT.
conjoin
FDLP.
conjoined
FDLP/*conjoin*.
conjoining processes
FDLP/*conjoin*.
conjoining transformation
ME/*352*.
conjugation
DLTS; GLT; ME/*352*.
conjunct
FDLP/*conjunction*.
conjunct form
GLT.
conjunction
FDLP; ME/*352*.
conjunctive
FDLP; GLT.
conjunctive adverb
ME/*352*.

connected speech
FDLP.
Connecticut Wits
HL; OCAL; PEPP.
connection
FDLP.
connective
FDLP.
connective construction
GLT.
connectivity
FDLP/*connective*.
connector
FDLP/*connective*; GLT.
connoiseur
DLTS.
connotation
DLDC; DLTC; DLTS; FDLP; GLT; HL; LGEP/*41*; ME/*75*; PH.
connotation and denotation
PEPP.
connotative
FDLP/*connotation*.
connotative language
EDSL/*23*.
conquestio
CR/*Index*.
consciousness, stream of
DLTC.
consistency
DLTC.
consonance
DLDC/*versification*; DLTC; DLTS; DMCT; EDSL/*190*; GLT; HL; LGEP/*93*; ME/*75*; PEPP; PH/*rhyme*.
consonant
FDLP; GLT; ME/*352*.
consonantal
FDLP/*consonant*.
consonantal alphabet
EDSL/*195*.
consonantal dissonance
PH/*rhyme*.

consonant cluster
GLT.
consonantism
GLT.
consonant shift
GLT; ME/*353*.
conspectus
DLTS.
conspiracy
FDLP.
constant
FDLP/*opposition*; FDLP; GLT.
Constantinople
CR/*Index*.
Constantinople, patriarchal school
CR/*Index*.
Constantinople, University of
CR/*Index*.
constative
EDSL/*342*; FDLP.
constellation
GLT.
constituency
FDLP/*constituent*.
constituency grammar
FDLP/*constituent*.
constituent
EDSL/*231*; FDLP; GLT; ME/*353*.
constituent analysis
FDLP/*immediate constituent*; FDLP/*constituent*.
constituent boundaries
FDLP/*click*.
constituent class
GLT.
constituent sentence
ME/*353*.
constituent structure
FDLP/*constituent*.
constituent structure grammar
FDLP/*constituent*.
constitutio
CR/*Index*.

71 □ contextual features

constitutive rule
EDSL/*343.*
constraint
FDLP.
constrastive stress
FDLP/*accent.*
constricted
FDLP/*constriction.*
constriction
FDLP.
constrictive
GLT.
construct
DLTS; FDLP/*construction*; GLT.
constructed language
GLT.
construction
EDSL/*214*; EDSL/*210*; FDLP;
GLT; ME/*353.*
constructional homonymity
FDLP/*construction.*
constructivism
DLTC.
constructivists
PEPP.
consumer sentence
ME/*353.*
contact
FDLP.
contact assimilation
FDLP/*assimilation.*
contact clauses
ME/*353.*
contact vernacular
FDLP/*vernacular*; GLT.
contamination
DLTC; GLT.
conte
DLTC; DLTS; HL.
conte dévot
DLTC; PEPP.
content
DLDC/*form*; EDSL/*20*; FDLP;
GLT; LGEP/*73.*

content analysis
EDSL/*241.*
content elements
GLT.
contentive
GLT.
content plane
FDLP/*content.*
contents
DLTS.
content word
GLT.
content words
FDLP/*content.*
contests
DLTC.
contests, poetic
PEPP.
context
DLTS; DMCT; EDSL/*333*;
FDLP; ME/*75.*
context-free
FDLP/*phrase-structure.*
context-free grammar
FDLP/*context.*
context-free rules
EDSL/*227*; FDLP/*context.*
context of situation
FDLP/*situation*; FDLP/*context.*
context of utterance
FDLP/*context.*
context-sensitive
FDLP/*phrase-structure*; FDLP/
context.
context-sensitive rules
EDSL/*227.*
contextual
FDLP/*context.*
contextual analysis
FDLP/*context.*
contextual determination
EDSL/*236.*
contextual features
FDLP/*context.*

contextualisation ☐ **72**

contextualisation
   FDLP/*context*.
Contextualism
   PEPP/*929*; DLTC; HL.
contextual meaning
   FDLP/*meaning*; FDLP/*context*.
contextual semantic feature
   EDSL/*266*.
contextual variant
   GLT.
contextual variants
   EDSL/*171*; FDLP/*free*; FDLP/*context*.
contiguous
   FDLP/*homorganic*.
contiguous assimilation
   FDLP/*assimilation*; GLT.
contiguous dissimilation
   GLT.
Continental Congress
   OCAL.
continuant
   FDLP/*frictionless*; FDLP; GLT; ME/*353*.
continuative
   EDSL/*311*.
continuity
   DLTS.
continuity hypothesis
   FDLP/*discontinuous*.
continuous
   FDLP/*progressive*; FDLP.
continuous constituents
   GLT.
continuous tense
   FDLP/*continuous*.
continuum
   FDLP/*cline*.
contoid
   FDLP; GLT.
contour
   FDLP; GLT.
contracted
   FDLP/*contraction*.

contraction
   DLTS; FDLP; ME/*353*.
contractions
   DLTC; PEPP.
contradiction
   LGEP/*132*.
contradictory
   FDLP.
contra-factive
   FDLP/*factive*.
contraposition
   ME/*76*.
contrapuntal
   DLTS; HL.
contrary
   FDLP.
contrast
   DLTC; FDLP/*cline*; FDLP; GLT; HL; ME/*76*.
contrast and comparison
   DLTS.
contrastive
   FDLP/*contrast*.
contrastive accent
   FDLP/*accent*.
contrastive analysis
   FDLP/*contrast*; GLT.
contrastive function
   GLT.
contrastive grammar
   GLT.
contrastive linguistics
   FDLP/*linguistics*; GLT.
contrastive phrasal doublets
   GLT.
contrastive stress
   FDLP/*stress*.
contretemps
   DLTS.
control
   DLTS.
controlling image
   DLTS; HL.

controlling question
ME/76.
controlling statement
ME/76.
control of phonation
EDSL/157.
contronym
OO.
controversiae
CR/Index.
conundrum
DLTC; DLTS.
convention
DLDC; DLTC; DLTS; DMCT; FDLP; HL; ME/76; PEPP.
conventional
FDLP/convention.
conventional symbol
DLDC/symbolism.
convergence
FDLP; GLT.
convergence area
GLT.
conversational implicatures
FDLP/implicature; FDLP/co-operative principle.
conversational situations
FDLP/appropriate.
conversational speech
FDLP/anacoluthon.
conversational structure
FDLP/co-operative principle.
conversational turn
FDLP/turn.
conversation fillers
FDLP/comment.
conversation piece
DLTC; DLTS.
conversation pieces
PEPP.
conversation poem
DLDC/lyric.
converse
FDLP.

converseness
FDLP/converse.
conversion
FDLP; GLT.
Conway Cabal
OCAL.
co-occur
FDLP.
co-occurrence
FDLP/collocation; FDLP/co-occur; ME/354.
co-operative principle
FDLP.
Cooperstown, New York
OCAL.
co-ordinate
FDLP/co-ordination.
co-ordinate bilinguals
FDLP/co-ordination.
coordinate clause
ME/354.
co-ordinate clauses
FDLP/co-ordination.
co-ordinate coarticulation
FDLP/articulation.
co-ordination
FDLP.
coordination
GLT; ME/355; ME/76.
coordinative construction
GLT.
coordinator
GLT.
coordinators
ME/355.
Copenhagen Linguistic Circle
FDLP/Copenhagen School.
Copenhagen School
FDLP.
copia
CR/Index.
copla
DLTC; PEPP.

Copperheads
OCAL.

copulative
FDLP.

copulative verb
ME/*355.*

copy
DLTS; FDLP/*copying*; HL.

copying
FDLP.

copyright
CODEL; DLTC; DLTS; HL; ME/*77*; OCEL.

copy tags
FDLP/*copying*; FDLP/*checking.*

copy text
HL.

copywriting
DLTS.

coq-à-l'âne
DLTC; PEPP.

coranto
DLTC.

core (common)
GLT.

co-referential
FDLP.

Corinth
CR/*Index.*

Cornish poetry
PEPP.

coronach
DLTC; OCEL.

coronach
DLTS; HL; PEPP.

coronal
FDLP; GLT.

corpora
FDLP/*corpus.*

corpus
EDSL/*32*; FDLP; GLT.

corpus-based
FDLP/*corpus.*

Corpus Christi
DLTS.

Corpus Christi plays
HL.

corpus-restricted
FDLP/*corpus.*

correct
FDLP.

correctness
CR/*Index*; DLTC; FDLP/*correct*; GLT.

correlation
EDSL/*109*; FDLP; GLT.

correlatives
ME/*356.*

correlative verse
DLTC; PEPP.

correlative verses
HL.

correlative words
GLT.

correspond
FDLP.

correspondence
GLT.

correspondence fallacy
FDLP/*correspond.*

correspondence hypothesis
FDLP/*correspond.*

correspondence of the arts
DLTC.

correspondence theory
FDLP/*correspond.*

corrigendum
DLTS.

cosmic
DLTS.

cosmic irony
DLDC/*irony.*

cossante
DLTC.

cost
FDLP.

costumbrismo
 DLTC.
costume piece
 DLTS.
coterie
 DLTS.
co-text
 FDLP.
cothurnus
 DLTC; DLTS; HL.
countability
 FDLP/*countable*.
countable
 FDLP/*mass*; FDLP.
countable noun
 GLT.
countable nouns
 FDLP/*countable*.
counter-example
 FDLP.
counter-intuitive
 FDLP.
counterplayers
 HL.
counterplot
 DLTC; DLTS; HL.
counterpoint
 DLTC; DLTS; PEPP; PH.
counterpoint rhythm
 HL.
counter-turn
 DLTC.
counter word
 GLT.
counter-word
 ME/*356*.
counterword
 DLTS.
counter words
 ME/*78*.
count noun
 GLT; ME/*356*.
coup de grace
 DLTS.

coup de théâtre
 HL; OCEL.
coup de théâtre
 CODEL; DLTC; DLTS.
couplet
 DLDC/*versification*; DLTC; DLTS; DMCT; EDSL/*191*; HL; ME/*78*; PEPP; PH.
couplet, heroic
 CODEL.
court comedy
 HL.
courtesy book
 DLTC; DLTS.
courtesy books
 HL; ME/*78*.
courtly love
 CODEL; DLDC; DLTC; DLTS; HL; ME/*78*; OCEL; PEPP.
courtly makers
 DLTC; HL; PEPP.
courts of love
 HL.
covenant speech
 CR/*Index*.
Covenant Theology
 OCAL; HL.
Coventry
 DLTS.
covered
 FDLP.
covered wagon
 OCAL.
covert
 FDLP.
covert meaning
 LGEP/*172*.
covowel
 GLT.
cowboy
 OCAL.
Cowleyan ode
 DLDC/*ode*; DLTC; DLTS; HL.
cps
 FDLP/*pitch*.

cracker
   OCAL.
cracker barrel humor
   OCAL.
cradle book
   DLTS.
cradle books
   DLTC.
craft cycle
   DLTC.
craft cycle plays
   ME/79.
craftsmanship
   DLTS.
crambe
   DLTC.
crambo
   DLTC.
crasis
   PEPP.
creak
   FDLP.
creaky
   FDLP/*creak*.
creationism
   DLTC; PEPP.
creative
   DMCT.
creative licence
   LGEP/36.
creativity
   FDLP.
creativity (by shortening)
   GLT.
creativity, linguistic
   LGEP/24.
credibility
   DLTS.
credo
   DLTS.
Creole
   EDSL/60; OCAL.
creole language
   ME/356.
creolise
   FDLP/*creole*.
crest (of sonority)
   GLT.
cretic
   DLTC; ME/80; PEPP.
cri de coeur
   DLTS.
crisis
   DLDC/*plot*; DLTC; DLTS; HL;
   ME/80; PEPP.
criteria
   FDLP.
criterion
   DLTS.
critic
   HL; ME/80.
critical edition
   GLT.
critical realism
   HL.
criticism
   CODEL; DLDC; DLTC; DLTS;
   DMCT; HL; PEPP.
criticism, types of
   HL.
critique
   DLTS; HL.
Crockett almanacs
   OCAL.
cross-cutting
   HL.
crossed rhyme
   DLTC; HL; PH/*rhyme*.
crossing
   GLT.
cross-over
   FDLP.
cross reference
   GLT.
cross-rhyme
   PH/*Welsh forms*.
crown of sonnets
   DLTC; HL; PEPP; PH/*sonnet*.

77 □ cycles

crown poem
DLTC.
cruelty, theater of
HL.
cruelty, theatre of
DLTC.
cryptonym
OO.
cuaderna vía
DLTC; PEPP.
Cuban poetry
PEPP.
cubism
DLTS; PEPP.
Cubist poetry
HL; PH.
cubo-futurism
DLTC; PEPP.
cue
DLTS.
cueca chilena
PEPP.
culminative function
EDSL/*179*; GLT.
culteranism
PEPP.
culteranismo
DLTC.
cultism
PEPP.
cultural
EDSL/*254*.
cultural language
GLT.
cultural level of usage
ME/*356*.
cultural primitivism
DLDC/*primitivism*; HL.
cultural transmission
FDLP; GLT.
culture
DLTS; DMCT; GLT.
culture circle
GLT.

culture shock
ME/*81*.
cultures, the two
DLTC.
cumul
GLT.
cuneiform
GLT.
cuneiform writing
DLTS.
curiosa
DLTS.
curse
DLTS; HL.
cursive
DLTS; GLT.
cursus
CR/*Index*.
cursus
DLTC; PEPP.
curtain
DLTS; HL.
curtain raiser
DLTC; HL.
curtal sonnet
DLTC; HL.
cut
DLTS; HL.
cutback
DLTS.
cut-off point
FDLP/*cost*.
CV
FDLP.
CVC
FDLP/*CV*.
cybernetics
FDLP/*algorithm*; GLT.
cycle
DLTC; DLTS; FDLP; HL.
cycle plays
ME/*81*.
cycles
FDLP/*incompatibility*.

cycles per second
   FDLP/*fundamental*; GLT/*c.p.s.*.
cyclic
   FDLP/*cycle*.
cyclical sets
   FDLP/*cycle*.
cyclic drama
   HL.
cyclic foot
   PEPP.
cynghanedd
   DLTC; PEPP.
cynghanedd
   PH/*Welsh forms*.

cynicism
   DLTS; HL.
Cynics
   CR/*Index*.
Cyrillic alphabet
   GLT.
cywydd
   DLTC; PEPP.
Czech poetry
   PEPP.
Czech prosody
   PEPP.

D

dactyl
CODEL; DLDC/*versification*;
DLTC; DLTS; EDSL/*187*; HL;
LGEP/*112*; ME/*82*; OCEL;
PEPP; PH.

dactylic
DLDC/*versification*; FDLP/*foot*;
PH/*metre*.

dactylo-epitrite
PEPP.

Dada
DMCT.

Dadaism
DLDC; DLTC; DLTS; HL;
PEPP.

DAF
FDLP; FDLP/*feedback*.

daimon
DLTS.

daina
DLTC; PEPP.

damped sound
GLT.

damping
GLT.

dance
FDLP/*allo-*.

dance of death
DLTS.

dandyism
HL.

dangling modifier
ME/*357*.

Danish
FDLP/*dialect*.

Danish poetry
PEPP.

Danites
OCAL.

danse macabre
DLTC.

danza prima
DLTC.

dark
FDLP/*cycle*.

Dark Ages
CODEL; DLTS; HL; OCEL.

dark lateral
GLT.

dark vowel
GLT.

data
FDLP.

dative
FDLP.

dative case
ME/*357*.

daughter-adjunction
FDLP/*adjunction*.

daughter node ☐ 80

daughter node
FDLP/*node*.
dB
FDLP/*loudness*.
dead metaphor
DLDC/*figurative language*;
DLTC; DLTS; HL; ME/*84*;
PEPP; PH/*metaphor*.
Dead Sea scrolls
HL.
deadwood
DLTS.
Deadwood Dick
OCAL.
deaf sign languages
FDLP/*sign*.
debacle
DLTS.
débat
DLDC; DLTC; HL; PEPP.
débat
DLTS.
debate
CR/*Index*.
decadence
DLDC/*Aesthetic Movement*;
DLTC; DLTS; HL; ME/*86*;
PEPP.
Decadents
HL; ME/*86*.
Decalogue
DLTS.
decastich
PEPP.
decastich
DLTC.
decasyllabic
HL.
decasyllabic verse
PH.
decasyllable
DLTC; DLTS; PEPP.
deceptive cognates
GLT.

decibel
FDLP/*loudness*; GLT.
décima
DLTC; PEPP.
decima
DLTS.
decir
PEPP.
decision procedure
FDLP/*procedure*.
declamation
CR/*Index*.
declaration
FDLP.
declarative
FDLP/*indicative*; FDLP.
declarative sentence
ME/*358*.
declension
DLTS; GLT; ME/*358*.
decoder
EDSL/*341*.
decoding
FDLP/*code*; GLT.
decomposable
FDLP/*composition*.
decomposed
FDLP/*composition*.
décor
DLTS.
decorum
DLTC; DLTS; DMCT; HL;
LGEP/*16*; PEPP; PH.
decretals
CODEL; OCEL.
dedialectalization
GLT.
dedication
DLTS.
dediphthongization
GLT.
deduction
CR/*Index*; DLTS.

deductive reasoning
ME/*86.*
deep focus
HL.
deep grammar
FDLP/*deep structure*; GLT; ME/*358.*
deep image
HL; ME/*86.*
deep object
FDLP/*deep structure.*
deep structure
EDSL/*244*; FDLP; LGEP/*45*; ME/*358.*
deep subject
FDLP/*deep structure.*
deep vowel
GLT.
de facto
DLTS.
defeated expectancy
LGEP/*119.*
defective
GLT.
defective foot
DLTC; PEPP.
deferred preposition
GLT.
deficiency
EDSL/*113.*
definite description
EDSL/*250.*
definite meaning
LGEP/*193.*
definite types
FDLP/*article.*
definition
DLTS; GLT; HL; LGEP/*134.*
definitive
DLTS.
definitive edition
DLTC; HL.
deflection (deflexion)
GLT.

degeneracy
DLTS.
degeneration
GLT.
degree
FDLP; ME/*359.*
degree of boundness
GLT/*morpheme.*
de gustibus non est disputandum
DLTS.
deictic
FDLP/*deixis.*
deictics
EDSL/*252.*
deictic words
LGEP/*191.*
Deism
OCAL; DLDC/*enlightenment*; DLTS; HL.
deixis
FDLP.
déjà vu
DLTS.
de jure
DLTS.
delabialization
GLT.
delayed
FDLP.
delayed auditory feedback
FDLP/*feedback.*
delayed subject
ME/*359.*
deletion
FDLP.
deletion transformation
ME/*359.*
deliberative oratory
CR/*Index.*
delicacy
FDLP.
delicate
FDLP/*Hallidayan*; FDLP/*delicacy.*

delimitation ☐ 82

delimitation
  EDSL/*17.*
delimitative function
  EDSL/*178.*
delineation
  DLTS.
delivery
  CR/*Index.*
delivery instance
  EDSL/*188.*
delivery model
  EDSL/*188.*
Delphian Club
  OCAL.
delta
  FDLP.
delusion
  DLTS.
demarcative function
  EDSL/*178*; GLT.
dementia
  EDSL/*163.*
democracy
  CR/*Index.*
demonstration
  CR/*Index.*
demonstrative
  EDSL/*251*; ME/*359.*
demonstrative pronouns
  FDLP/*pronoun.*
demotic
  GLT.
demotic style
  HL.
denasalised
  FDLP/*nasal.*
denasalization
  GLT.
denotation
  DLDC/*connotation*; DLTC; DLTS; FDLP; GLT; HL; LGEP/*40*; ME/*87*; PEPP; PH/*connotation.*
denotative
  FDLP/*denotation.*

denotative language
  EDSL/*23.*
dénouement
  HL.
dénouement
  CODEL; DLDC/*plot*; DLTC; DLTS; DMCT; ME/*88*; OCEL; PEPP.
density of communication
  GLT.
dental
  FDLP; GLT.
dental consonant
  ME/*359.*
dentolabial
  GLT.
deontic
  EDSL/*315*; FDLP.
deontic modality
  FDLP/*deontic.*
dependency
  EDSL/*212*; FDLP.
dependency grammar
  FDLP/*dependency.*
dependency tree
  FDLP/*govern.*
dependency trees
  FDLP/*dependency.*
dependent
  FDLP/*govern*; FDLP.
dependent clause
  ME/*359.*
dependent clauses
  FDLP/*clause.*
dependent rules
  FDLP/*context.*
dependent sound change
  GLT.
depth hypothesis
  FDLP.
depth reading
  ME/*88.*
de rigueur
  DLTS.

83 ☐ determinatum

derivation
EDSL/*13*; EDSL/*140*; EDSL/*228*; FDLP; GLT; ME/*360*.
derivational affix
GLT.
derivational affixes
FDLP/*derivation*.
derivational pattern
FDLP/*back-formation*.
derivational suffix
ME/*360*.
derivative
DLTS; GLT.
derived
FDLP/*derivation*.
derived medium
FDLP/*medium*.
derived primary word
GLT.
derived structure
FDLP/*derivation*.
dernier cri, le
DLTS.
descending
FDLP/*diphthong*.
descending rhythm
DLTC; PEPP.
descort
DLTC; PEPP.
description
DLTS; EDSL/*322*; FDLP; HL; LGEP/*134*; ME/*88*.
description, linguistic
FDLP/*corpus*.
descriptive
FDLP/*description*; GLT.
descriptive adequacy
FDLP/*adequacy*; FDLP/*description*.
descriptive grammar
FDLP/*grammar*; FDLP/*description*; GLT; ME/*360*.
descriptive linguistics
FDLP/*linguistics*; FDLP/*description*; GLT; LGEP/*40*.

descriptively adequate
EDSL/*40*; FDLP/*grammar*.
descriptivism
FDLP/*description*.
descriptivist
FDLP/*description*.
desenlace
DLTC.
Deseret
OCAL.
desert island fiction
DLTC.
desiderative
FDLP.
design feature
FDLP/*feedback*.
design features
FDLP/*language*.
desires
FDLP/*desiderative*.
destinataire
EDSL/*341*.
destinateur
EDSL/*341*.
det
FDLP.
details
DLTS.
detective story
DLTC; DLTS; HL; OCAL.
détente
GLT.
determinant
GLT.
determination
GLT.
determinative
GLT.
determinative complement
EDSL/*211*.
determinative compound
GLT.
determinatum
GLT.

determiner □ 84

determiner
DLTS; FDLP; GLT; ME/*361*.
determiners
EDSL/*253*.
determinism
DLTS; HL; ME/*89*.
detritus
DLTS.
de trop
DLTS.
deus ex machina
OCEL.
deus ex machina
DLDC; DLTC; DLTS; HL; ME/*90*.
deus ex machina
CODEL.
deuteragonist
DLTC; DLTS; HL.
Devanagari
GLT.
development
FDLP/*acquisition*.
developmental linguistics
FDLP.
developmental psycholinguistics
FDLP/*developmental linguistics*.
deviance
FDLP.
deviant
FDLP/*deviance*.
deviation
DMCT; LGEP/*42*.
deviation, dialectal
LGEP/*49*.
deviation, grammatical
LGEP/*44*.
deviation, graphological
LGEP/*47*.
deviation, lexical
LGEP/*42*.
deviation of historical period
LGEP/*51*.
deviation of register
LGEP/*49*.
deviation, orthographic
LGEP/*47*.
deviation, phonological
LGEP/*46*.
deviation, semantic
LGEP/*48*.
device
FDLP.
devil's advocate
DLTS; HL; OCEL.
devil's disciple
DLTS.
devoice
GLT.
devoiced
FDLP/*voice*.
devoicing
FDLP/*diacritic*.
dia-
FDLP.
diachronic
EDSL/*137*; FDLP; GLT; ME/*361*.
diachronic grammar
GLT.
diachronic linguistics
FDLP/*linguistics*; GLT.
diachronic phonetics
GLT.
diacope
DLTC.
diacritic
DLTC; FDLP; GLT.
diacritical
DLTS.
diacritic, diacritical mark
ME/*361*.
diaeresis
CODEL; DLTC; DLTS; GLT; OCEL; PEPP.
diagram
ME/*361*.

85 □ didacticism

dialect
DLTC; DLTS; EDSL/58; FDLP; GLT; ME/363.
dialectalisation
FDLP/*divergence*.
dialectalization
GLT.
dialect atlas
FDLP/*dialect*; GLT.
dialect boundary
FDLP/*dialect*.
dialect geography
FDLP/*dialect*; GLT.
dialectic
CR/*Index*; DLTC; HL; ME/90.
dialectic, Aristotelian
CR/*Index*.
dialectic, Platonic
CR/*Index*.
dialectics
DLTS.
dialect in poetry
PEPP.
dialectism
LGEP/49.
dialectology
EDSL/58; FDLP/*dialect*; GLT; LGEP/41; ME/363.
dialects
HL; LGEP/8.
dialinguistics
FDLP/*dia-*.
dialogue
CR/*Index*; DLDC; DLTC; DLTS; EDSL/303; HL; ME/90; PEPP.
Dial, The
HL.
Dial, The
OCEL.
dialysis
DLTC.
diamorphe
FDLP/*dia-*.
diaphone
FDLP/*dia-*; GLT.

diaphoneme
GLT.
diary
DLTS; HL; ME/91.
diary and journal
DLTC.
dia-system
GLT.
diasystem
FDLP/*dia-*.
diasystems
FDLP/*dialect*.
diatribe
CR/*Index*; DLTC; DLTS; HL.
diatype
FDLP/*dia-*.
dibrach
DLTC; DLTS; HL; PEPP.
dicatalectic
DLTC.
dicho
ME/91.
dichoree
PEPP.
dichronous
PEPP.
dictamen
CR/*Index*.
diction
CR/*Index*; DLDC; DLTC; DLTS; DMCT; HL; ME/91.
dictionaries
HL.
dictionary
DLTC; DLTS; EDSL/51; GLT; ME/363.
diction, poetic
PEPP.
dictum
EDSL/313.
didactic
DLTC.
didacticism
DLTS; HL; ME/92.

didactic literature
DLDC.
didactic novel
HL; ME/*91*.
didactic poetry
DLDC/*didactic literature*; HL; PEPP.
didactic verse
PH.
diegesis
CR/*Index*.
dieresis
HL; ME/*93*.
dies irae
DLTS.
differential meaning
GLT.
differentiation
GLT; LGEP/*38*.
diffuse
DLTS; FDLP.
diffuse phoneme
GLT.
diffusion
GLT.
diffusion and migration theories
GLT.
diffusion concept
GLT.
digest
DLTC; DLTS; HL.
diglossia
FDLP; GLT.
diglossic
FDLP/*diglossia*.
digraph
DLTS; FDLP; GLT; ME/*364*.
digression
CR/*Index*; DLTC; DLTS; HL.
diiamb
DLTC; PEPP.
dilation
GLT.

dilemma
DLTS; ME/*93*.
dilettante
DLTS; HL.
dilogy
DLTC.
dime novel
DLTC; DLTS; HL; OCAL.
dimeter
CODEL; DLDC/*versification*; DLTC; DLTS; HL; ME/*94*; OCEL; PEPP; PH/*metre*.
Diminishing Age in English literature, 1940-1965
HL.
diminishing metaphor
DLTC; PEPP.
diminishing returns
FDLP/*cost*.
diminuendo
DLTS.
diminutive
FDLP; GLT.
ding-dong theory
GLT.
Dinggedicht
DLTC; PEPP.
dionym
OO.
Dionysia
DLTS.
Dionysian
DLDC/*Apollonian*; DLTC; HL; PEPP/*930*.
diphoneme
GLT.
diphthong
DLTS; FDLP; GLT; ME/*364*.
diphthongisation
FDLP/*diphthong*.
diphthongization
GLT.
diplomatic edition
GLT.

diplophonic voice
FDLP/*ventricular.*
dipodic verse
PEPP.
dipodism
GLT.
dipody
DLTC; DLTS; HL; PEPP; PH/*measure.*
dipotic verse
HL.
direct
FDLP.
direct camera
HL.
directive
FDLP; GLT.
directive construction
GLT.
directive functions
FDLP/*conative.*
direct object
FDLP/*indirect*; FDLP/*object*; FDLP/*direct*; ME/*364.*
director
FDLP/*directive*; GLT.
direct question
FDLP/*direct.*
direct speech
FDLP/*indirect*; FDLP/*direct.*
dirge
DLDC/*elegy*; DLTC; DLTS; DMCT; HL; ME/*94*; PEPP; PH/*elegy.*
disambiguate
FDLP.
disbelief
DLTS; DMCT.
disclosure
DLDC/*plot*; DLDC/*tragedy.*
discontinuity
FDLP/*discontinuous.*
discontinuous
FDLP.

discontinuous constituents
GLT; ME/*364.*
discontinuous formant
GLT.
discontinuous morpheme
GLT.
discord
DLTS.
discordia concors
DLTC; HL.
discourse
DLTC; FDLP.
discourse analysis
FDLP/*discourse*; GLT.
discovery
DLDC/*tragedy*; DLDC/*plot*; DLTC; FDLP; HL; ME/*94.*
discovery procedure
EDSL/*34*; FDLP/*procedure*; FDLP/*discovery.*
discrepant correspondence
GLT.
discrete
FDLP.
discreteness
FDLP/*discrete.*
discrete units
GLT.
discrimination
GLT.
discursive
DLTS; EDSL/*319.*
discursive universe
EDSL/*247.*
disemic
DLTC; PEPP.
disguisings
HL.
disinterestedness
DLTC.
disinterestedness in criticism
PEPP.
disjunct
FDLP/*disjunction.*

disjunction □ 88

disjunction
  FDLP; GLT.
disjunctive
  FDLP/*disjunction*.
disjunctive dilemma
  ME/*94*.
disjunctive opposition
  GLT.
disjunctive syllogism
  ME/*94*.
Dismal Swamp
  OCAL.
disparate
  DLTS.
dispersion
  GLT.
displaced
  FDLP/*displacement*.
displaced speech
  FDLP/*displacement*; GLT.
displacement
  FDLP.
dispondee
  DLTC; PEPP.
disputation
  CR/*Index*.
dissertation
  DLTC; DLTS; HL; ME/*94*.
dissimilation
  FDLP; GLT; ME/*364*.
dissimilatory phoneme
  GLT.
dissociation of ideas
  DLTC.
dissociation of sensibility
  DLDC; DLTC; DMCT; HL; ME/*94*; PEPP; PH.
dissonance
  DLTC; DLTS; HL; ME/*94*; PEPP.
dissyllabic
  GLT; PH/*metre*.
distance
  HL.

distance assimilation
  FDLP/*assimilation*.
distant assimilation
  GLT.
distant dissimilation
  GLT.
distich
  DLTC; DLTS; EDSL/*192*; HL; ME/*94*; PEPP; PH.
distinctiones
  CR/*Index*.
distinctive
  EDSL/*171*; FDLP; GLT.
distinctive feature
  FDLP/*feature*; FDLP/*distinctive*.
distinctive features
  EDSL/*173*; ME/*365*.
distinctive function
  GLT.
distinctiveness
  FDLP/*distinctive*.
distinctive oppositions
  FDLP/*opposition*.
distinguisher
  FDLP.
distributed
  FDLP.
distributed stress
  DLTC; HL; PH.
distributed term
  ME/*95*.
distribution
  EDSL/*32*; FDLP; GLT.
distributional analysis
  FDLP/*distribution*.
distributional classes
  EDSL/*33*.
distributionalism
  EDSL/*31*.
distributional structure
  EDSL/*34*.
distribution, law of
  GLT.

89 □ domain

distributive
GLT.
distributive numeral
GLT.
disyllabic
FDLP/*disyllable.*
disyllable
FDLP.
dit
DLTC; PEPP.
dithyramb
CODEL; DLDC; DLTC; DLTS; HL; ME/*95*; OCEL; PEPP; PH.
di-transitive
FDLP.
ditransitive
FDLP/*transitivity.*
ditrochee
DLTC; ME/*95*; PEPP.
dittie
PEPP.
ditty
DLTC; DLTS; HL.
diurnalls
CODEL; OCEL.
divan
DLTC.
diverbium
DLTC; PEPP.
divergence
FDLP; GLT.
divergent change
GLT.
divertissement
DLTC; DLTS.
divine afflatus
DLTS; HL.
divine right
DLTS.
division
DLTS.
divisional pause
DLTC.

dizain
DLTC; PEPP.
do
FDLP/*do-deletion.*
dochmiac
DLTC; PEPP.
Doctor Johnson's Circle
HL/*Literary Club, The.*
doctrinaire
DLTS; HL.
doctrine of usage
GLT/*usage doctrine.*
document
DLTC; DLTS.
documentary
DLTS; DMCT.
documentary novel
DLTC; HL.
documentary theatre
DLTC.
documentation
DLTS.
do-deletion
FDLP.
doggerel
CODEL; DLDC/*versification*; DLTC; DLTS; HL; ME/*101*; OCEL; PEPP; PH.
dog-Latin
DLTC.
dogma
DLTC; DLTS.
doing word
FDLP/*notional.*
do-insertion
FDLP/*do-deletion.*
dolce far niente
DLTS.
dolce stil nuovo
DLTC; PEPP.
Dollar, The Almighty
OCAL.
domain
FDLP.

domal
GLT.
domesticated word
GLT.
domestic comedy
DLTC.
domestic tragedy
DLTC; DLTS; HL.
dominance
EDSL/*150*; FDLP/*domination*.
dominant impression
DLTS.
dominate
FDLP/*domination*.
domination
FDLP.
Dominica
FDLP/*creole*.
Dominicans
CR/*Index*.
Donald Duck
FDLP/*buccal*.
Donald Duck effect
FDLP/*air-stream mechanism*.
donnée
DLTC; ME/*101*.
donnée
HL.
Donner Party
OCAL.
doppelgänger
DLTS.
Doric
DLTC; DLTS; HL.
dorsal
FDLP/*domination*; GLT.
dorso-alveolar
GLT.
dorsum
FDLP/*dorsal*; GLT.
dossier
DLTS.
do-support
FDLP/*do-deletion*.

dot
FDLP/*cardinal vowels*.
do transformation
ME/*367*.
double articulation
EDSL/*53*; FDLP/*articulation*;
FDLP/*articulation*; GLT.
double ballade
PH/*ballade*.
double-bar
FDLP/*juncture*.
double bar juncture
GLT.
double-base
FDLP.
double-base transformation
ME/*367*.
double consonance
PH/*rhyme*.
double consonant
GLT.
double-cross
FDLP/*juncture*.
double cross juncture
GLT.
double dactyl
DLTC; PH.
double dactyls
HL; ME/*101*.
double-decker novel
DLTC; DLTS.
double, duple meter
PEPP.
double entendre
DLTS; HL; ME/*102*.
double entente, un mot à
DLTC.
double irony
DMCT.
double negative
FDLP/*negation*; ME/*367*.
double negatives
FDLP/*grammaticality*.

91 ☐ dream vision

double plot
DLDC/*plot*.
double rhyme
DLTC; DLTS; HL.
double-rhyme
DLDC/*versification*.
doublet
ME/*367*.
double talk
DLTS.
doublets
GLT.
double voice
FDLP/*ventricular*.
doubling
GLT.
down center
DLTS.
Down East
OCAL.
downgraded
FDLP/*downgrading*.
downgrading
FDLP.
downstage
DLTS.
drama
CODEL; DLDC; DLTC; DLTS; DMCT; HL; ME/*102*.
drama of ideas
DLTC.
drama of sensibility
DLTC.
dramatic
EDSL/*153*.
dramatic convention
DLTS.
dramatic conventions
HL.
dramatic illusion
DLDC; DLTS.
dramatic irony
CODEL; DLDC/*irony*; DLTC; DLTS; DMCT; HL; ME/*102*; PEPP.

dramatic lyric
DLTC.
dramatic monologue
DLDC; DLTC; DLTS; HL; ME/*103*; PEPP.
dramatic poetry
DLTS; HL; PEPP.
dramatic propriety
HL.
dramatic proverb
DLTC.
dramatic structure
HL; ME/*103*.
dramatism
HL; ME/*104*.
dramatis personae
DLTC; DLTS; HL; ME/*105*.
Dramatist's Guild
OCAL/*Author's League of America*.
dramatization
DLTC.
dramaturgy
DLTS.
drame
DLTC; HL.
drame
PEPP.
drame romantique
DLTC.
Drang nach Osten
DLTS.
drápa
DLTC; PEPP.
drawing room comedy
HL.
drawing-room comedy
DLTC.
dream-allegory
PEPP.
dream allegory (or vision)
HL.
dream vision
DLDC; DLTC; DLTS.

drift
GLT.

droll
DLTC; HL.

dróttkvætt
LGEP/*90*; PEPP.

dróttkvætt
DLTC.

drowned-in-tears, school of the
DLTC.

dry humor
DLTS.

dual
GLT.

dualism
DLTC; FDLP.

dualist
FDLP/*dualism*.

duality
FDLP.

duality of pattern
GLT.

duality of patterning
FDLP/*duality*.

dual number
ME/*367*.

duan
DLTC.

Dublin
CR/*Index*.

ductus
CR/*Index*.

dulce et decorum
DLTS.

dumb show
DLDC/*drama*; DLTC; DLTS; HL.

dummy
FDLP.

dummy carrier
FDLP/*dummy*.

dummy elements
FDLP/*dummy*.

dummy symbols
FDLP/*dummy*.

dumy
DLTC; PEPP.

Dunkers
OCAL.

duodecimo
DLTC; DLTS; HL.

duologue
DLTC; DLTS; HL.

duple meter
DLTC; HL.

duple rhythm
DLTC; PH.

duplicity
DLTS.

duration
DLTC; EDSL/*177*; FDLP/*length*; FDLP; GLT; PEPP.

duration of activity
FDLP/*aspect*.

durative
GLT.

Dutch poetry
PEPP.

dyfalu
DLTC; PEPP.

dynamic
FDLP.

dynamic accent
GLT.

dynamic character
HL.

dynamic linguistics
FDLP/*dynamic*; GLT.

dynamic middle
GLT.

dynamics
GLT.

dysarthria
EDSL/*161*; FDLP/*neurolinguistics*.

dysgraphia
EDSL/*163*.

dyslexia
  EDSL/*161*.
dyslogias
  EDSL/*163*.
dysphasia
  EDSL/*161*.

dysphemism
  DLTC; DLTS.
dystopia
  HL.

E

ear
   FDLP/*auditory phonetics*.
Early Tudor Age 1500-1557
   HL.
Early Victorian Age 1832-1870
   HL.
ear-training
   FDLP.
East End
   FDLP/*dialect*.
Eastern states
   OCAL.
East Side
   OCAL/*New York City*.
Ebenen
   EDSL/*238*.
ecce homo
   DLTS.
echo
   DLTC; FDLP; PEPP.
echo allusion
   DLTS.
echoic
   LGEP/*73*.
echoic (echo) word
   GLT.
echoism
   GLT.
echolocation
   FDLP/*zoösemiotics*.

echo utterance
   FDLP.
echo verse
   DLTC; DLTS; HL; PEPP.
eclectic
   DLTS; FDLP.
eclipsis
   DLTC; GLT.
eclogue
   CODEL; DLDC/*pastoral*; DLTC; DLTS; HL; ME/*106*; OCEL; PEPP; PH/*pastoral*.
école parnassienne
   DLTC.
economy
   CR/*Index*; DLTS; FDLP; GLT.
economy in writing
   ME/*106*.
ecphonema
   DLTC.
ecphrasis
   CR/*Index*.
edda
   DLTC.
-*ed* form
   FDLP.
Edinburgh
   CR/*Index*.
Edinburgh Review
   CODEL; HL.

Edinburgh Review □ 96

Edinburgh Review
 OCEL.
editing
 HL.
edition
 DLTC; DLTS; HL.
editorial
 HL.
editorializing
 DLTS.
editorial omniscience
 DLDC/*point of view*.
editorial we
 DLTS.
educational linguistics
 FDLP.
educational policy
 FDLP/*bidialect*.
education novel
 HL.
education, rhetorical
 CR/*Index*.
Edwardian
 CODEL; DLTC; DLTS; OCEL.
Edwardian Age
 HL.
effect
 DLTS; DMCT; HL.
effectiveness
 DLTS.
effete
 DLTS.
egalitarian
 DLTS.
ego, egoism
 DLTS.
ego-futurism
 DLTC; PEPP.
egressive
 FDLP; GLT.
Egyptian gold
 CR/*Index*.
Egyptian poetry
 PEPP.

eidyllion
 DLTC.
eight-and-six meter
 DLTC.
Eight, The
 OCAL.
Einfühlung
 DLDC/*empathy*; DLTC; DLTS.
eiron
 DMCT; HL; ME/*106*.
Eisteddfod
 DLTC; CODEL; DLTS; OCEL; PEPP.
ejective
 FDLP; GLT.
elaborated
 FDLP.
elaborated code
 FDLP/*restricted*; FDLP/*elaborated*.
elaboration
 DLTS; HL.
elative
 FDLP/*case*.
El Dorado
 OCAL.
Electra complex
 HL.
electro-areometer
 FDLP/*articulatory phonetics*.
electrodes
 FDLP/*electromyography*.
electrokymogram
 FDLP/*electrokymography*.
electrokymography
 FDLP.
electromyograms
 FDLP/*electromyography*.
electromyography
 FDLP/*articulatory phonetics*; FDLP.
electronics
 FDLP/*acoustic phonetics*.
electropalatograms
 FDLP/*electropalatography*.

97 □ embedment

electro-palatograph
FDLP/*palate.*
electropalatography
FDLP.
elegance
FDLP/*adequacy.*
elegantia
DLTC.
elegant variation
DLTC; DLTS; ME/*106.*
elegiac
CODEL; DLTS; HL; OCEL.
elegiac distich
DLTC; PEPP.
elegiac meter
DLTC.
elegiac pentameter
PH/*pentameter.*
elegiac quatrain
DLDC/*versification.*
elegiacs
PH.
elegiac stanza
DLTC; HL; PEPP.
elegiambus
PEPP.
elegy
DLDC; DLTC; DLTS; DMCT; HL; ME/*106*; PEPP; PH.
element
FDLP; GLT.
elements
HL.
elevation
GLT.
elicit
FDLP/*elicitation.*
elicitation
FDLP.
elide
FDLP/*ellipsis.*
elision
CODEL; DLDC; DLTC; DLTS; FDLP; GLT; HL; ME/*107*; OCEL; PEPP; PH.

elixir of life
DLTS.
Elizabethan
DLDC; DLTS; ME/*107.*
Elizabethan Age
CODEL; HL.
Elizabethan drama
HL.
Elizabethan English
FDLP/*dialect.*
Elizabethan literature
HL; OCEL.
Elizabethan miscellanies
HL.
Elizabethan Period
DLTC.
Elizabethan theaters
HL.
ellipse
PEPP.
ellipsis
CODEL; DLTC; DLTS; EDSL/*277*; FDLP; HL; ME/*107*; OCEL.
ellipsis, elliptical construction
ME/*369.*
ellipted
FDLP/*ellipsis.*
elliptical
FDLP/*ellipsis.*
elocution
DLTS.
elocutionary movement
CR/*Index.*
eloquence
DLTS.
Elysium
DLTS.
embedded parentheses
EDSL/*229.*
embedding
EDSL/*298*; FDLP.
embedment
ME/*369.*

emblem
DLTS; DMCT; EDSL/*225*; PEPP.
emblem book
CODEL; DLDC; DLTC; OCEL.
emblem books
HL.
embrayeurs
EDSL/*252*.
-eme
FDLP/*emic*; GLT.
emendation
DLTC; DLTS; HL.
EMG
FDLP/*electromyography*.
emic
EDSL/*36*; FDLP; GLT.
emotion
PEPP.
emotional appeals
ME/*108*.
emotional effect
FDLP/*emotive*.
emotional element in literature
HL.
emotional element in meaning
FDLP/*attitudinal*.
emotive
FDLP.
emotive accent
GLT.
emotive language
DLTC.
emotive meaning
DLDC/*connotation*; DLTS.
empathy
DLDC; DLTC; DLTS; HL; ME/*108*.
empathy and sympathy
PEPP.
empeiria
CR/*Index*.
emphasis
DLTS; FDLP/*stress*; FDLP/*cleft sentence*; HL; ME/*108*.

emphasized
EDSL/*271*.
emphatic articulation
GLT.
emphatic aspect
ME/*369*.
emphatics
GLT.
emphatic speech
FDLP/*chest pulse*.
empiricism
DLTS; HL.
empty
FDLP; FDLP/*full*.
empty morph
FDLP/*empty*; FDLP/*morpheme*.
empty word
GLT.
empty words
FDLP/*empty*.
enallage
DLTC; DLTS; HL.
encadenamiento
DLTC.
enchiridion
DLTC; DLTS; HL.
enclitic
DLTS; GLT.
enclitics
FDLP/*clitic*.
enclosed rhyme
HL.
encoder
EDSL/*341*.
encoding
EDSL/*254*; FDLP/*code*; GLT.
encomia
CR/*Index*.
encomium
DLDC; DLTC; DLTS; HL; PEPP.
encyclopaedia
DLTC; HL.

encyclopedia
DLTS; HL.
endecha
DLTC; PEPP.
ending
PEPP.
endocentric
EDSL/*214*; FDLP.
endocentric construction
GLT; ME/*369*.
endocentric form
GLT.
endocentric phrase
GLT.
endocentric structure
GLT.
endophasia
GLT.
end-points
FDLP/*cycle*.
end rhyme
DLTC; DLTS; HL; PEPP.
end-rhyme
DLDC/*versification*; PH/*rhyme*.
end-stopped
ME/*108*; PEPP; PH.
end-stopped line
DLDC/*versification*; DLTC; DLTS; LGEP/*123*.
end-stopped lines
HL.
energetics
GLT.
en famille
DLTS.
-*en* form
FDLP.
engagement
DLTC.
English
CODEL; OCEL.
English hexameter
PH/*scansion*.

English language
HL.
English literature, periods of
HL.
English poetics
PEPP.
English poetry
PEPP.
English prosody
PEPP.
English sonnet
DLDC/*versification*; DLTC; DLTS; HL; PH.
English usage
LGEP/*8*.
English vowel shift
GLT.
englyn
DLTC; PEPP.
englyn
PH/*Welsh forms*.
enhancement
GLT.
enigma
DLTS.
enjambement
DLTC; DLTS; HL; ME/*108*.
enjambement
PEPP.
enjambment
OCEL.
enjambment
CODEL; DLDC/*versification*; EDSL/*187*; LGEP/*123*.
Enlightenment
DLDC; DLTS; HL; DLTC.
enoplius
DLTC; PEPP.
en passant
DLTS.
ensalada
DLTC; PEPP.
ensenhamen
DLTC; PEPP.

entailment
FDLP.
entelechy
CODEL; DLTC; OCEL.
entertainment
DLTC.
enthymeme
CR/*Index*; DLTS; HL; ME/*109*.
entr'acte
DLTC; HL.
entr'acte
DLTS.
entremés
DLTC.
entremets
DLTC.
entre nous
DLTS.
entry
FDLP.
entry condition
FDLP/*entry*.
Entwicklungsroman
HL.
enumeratio
CR/*Index*.
enumerative
GLT.
enumerative bibliography
HL.
enunciation
EDSL/*323*.
enunciation disorder
EDSL/*161*.
enunciative context
EDSL/*330*.
envelope
DLTC; HL; PEPP.
envelope stanza
PH/*stanza*.
environment
EDSL/*32*; FDLP; GLT.
environmental conditioning
FDLP/*conditioned*.

envoi
HL/*envoy*; PEPP.
envoi
DLDC/*envoy*; DLTC; DLTS; ME/*envoy, 109*.
envoy
DLDC; ME/*109*; PH/*ballade*.
epanadiplosis
ME/*109*; PEPP.
epanados
DLTC.
epanalepsis
DLTC; HL; PEPP.
epanaphora
DLTC; DLTS; HL; PEPP.
epanodos
HL.
epanorthosis
DLTC.
epenthesis
FDLP; GLT; ME/*369*.
epenthetic
FDLP/*epenthesis*.
ephemeral
DLTS.
epic
CODEL, DLDC; DLTC; DLTS; DMCT; EDSL/*153*; HL; ME/*109*; OCEL; PEPP; PH.
epic caesura
PEPP.
epicede
CODEL; OCEL.
epicedium
CODEL; DLTC; OCEL; PEPP.
epicene
GLT.
epic formula
HL.
epicheireme
CR/*Index*.
epic simile
DLDC/*epic*; DLTC; DLTS; HL; ME/*110*; PEPP.

101 □ *e pluribus unum*

epic theatre
DLTC.
Epicurean
DLTS; HL; ME/*110*.
epideictic
CR/*Index*.
epideictic poetry
DLTC; HL; PEPP.
epidiplosis
DLTS.
epigone
DLTS; HL.
epigram
CODEL; DLDC; DLTC; DLTS; HL; ME/*110*; OCEL; PEPP; PH.
epigraph
DLTC; HL; ME/*111*.
epigraphy
DLTS; GLT.
epilegma
GLT.
epilogue
CR/*Index*; DLDC; DLTC; DLTS; HL; ME/*111*.
epimythium
DLTC.
epinicion
DLTC; PEPP.
epiphany
DLDC; DLTC; DLTS; HL; ME/*111*.
epiphora
DLTS; PEPP.
epiplexis
DLTC.
epiploce
DLTC; PEPP.
epirrhema
DLTC; PEPP.
episememe
GLT.
episode
DLDC; DLTC; DLTS; HL.
episodic
DLTS.

episodic structure
HL.
epistemic
FDLP.
epistemology
DLTS.
epistle
CR/*Index*; DLDC; DLTC; DLTS; DMCT; HL; PEPP; PH.
epistolary
DLTS.
epistolary novel
DLDC/*epistle*; DLTC; HL; ME/*111*.
epistrophe
DLTC; HL; PEPP.
episyntheton
DLTC; PEPP.
epitaph
CODEL; DLDC; DLTC; DLTS; HL; ME/*111*; PEPP; PH.
epitaphios
CR/*Index*.
epitasis
DLTC; DLTS; HL.
epithalamion
DLDC; DLTC; DLTS; HL; ME/*112*; PH.
epithalamium
DLDC/*epithalamion*; HL; PEPP.
epithesis
ME/*369*.
epithet
DLDC; DLTC; DLTS; HL; ME/*112*; PEPP.
epithetologue
GLT.
epitome
DLTC; DLTS; HL.
epitrite
DLTC; ME/*113*; PEPP.
epizeuxis
DLTC; LGEP/*77*; PEPP.
e pluribus unum
DLTS.

epoch
DLTS.

epode
CODEL; DLDC/*ode*; DLTC; DLTS; HL; ME/*113*; OCEL; PEPP; PH/*ode*.

eponym
DLTS; GLT; HL; OO.

eponymous
CODEL; DLTC; OCEL.

epopee
CODEL; DLTC; OCEL.

epos
DLTC.

epyllion
DLDC/*idyll*; DLTC.

epyllion
HL; PEPP.

equalization
GLT.

equational
FDLP/*equative*.

equational verb
FDLP/*equative*.

equative
FDLP/*copulative*; FDLP; FDLP/*degree*.

Equi
FDLP/*equi NP deletion*.

equi NP deletion
FDLP.

equipollent
FDLP/*opposition*; FDLP.

equity
CR/*Index*.

equivalence
DLTC; FDLP; HL; LGEP/*67*; PH/*substitution*.

equivalent
FDLP/*equivalence*.

equivalent sentences
GLT.

equivocation
DLTS; HL; ME/*113*.

equivoque
DLTC; DLTS; HL.

era
DLTS.

Era of Good Feelings
OCAL/*Monroe, James*.

erastianism
HL.

ergative
FDLP.

ergativity
FDLP/*ergative*.

Erie Canal
OCAL.

Eros
DLTS.

erotesis
DLTC.

eroticism
DLTS.

erotic literature
HL.

erotic poetry
DLTC; PEPP.

erratum
DLTS.

error
FDLP.

error analysis
FDLP/*error*.

Erziehungsroman
DLDC/*novel*; DLTC; DLTS; HL.

escape literature
DLDC; DLTC; HL.

escapism
DLTS.

esemplastic
HL; PEPP/*930*.

Eskimo
FDLP/*ergative*.

Eskimo poetry
PEPP.

esophageal
FDLP/*oesophageal*.

esoteric
CODEL; DLTS; OCEL.
Esperanto
DLTC; DLTS; FDLP/*language*; FDLP/*auxiliary*; HL.
espinela
PEPP.
espinella
DLTC.
esprit
DLTS.
essay
CODEL; DLDC; DLTC; DLTS; DMCT; HL; ME/*113*.
essence
DLTS.
essential conditions
FDLP/*felicity conditions*.
establishing shot
HL.
estancia
DLTC.
Estonian poetry
PEPP.
estrambote
DLTC.
estrangement
DLTC.
estribillo
DLTC; PEPP.
estrofa
DLTC.
estrofa mauriqueña
DLTC.
état de langue
FDLP.
eternity
DLTS.
eth
ME/*369*; ME/*369*.
ethical criticism
PEPP.
Ethiopian poetry
PEPP.

ethnic
DLTS.
ethnic groups
FDLP/*bilingual*.
ethnography of communication
FDLP/*ethnolinguistics*.
ethnolinguist
FDLP/*ethnolinguistics*.
ethnolinguistics
EDSL/*63*; FDLP; FDLP/*linguistics*; GLT.
ethnophonemic transcription
GLT.
ethnoscience
EDSL/*62*.
ethopoeia
CR/*Index*.
ethos
CR/*Index*.
ethos
DLTS; HL.
etic
EDSL/*36*; FDLP/*emic*; GLT.
etiquette book
DLTS.
etiquette books
HL/*Renaissance*.
et tu, Brute
DLTS.
etymological fallacy
FDLP/*etymology*.
etymologies
EDSL/*130*.
etymology
DLTS; EDSL/*8*; FDLP; GLT; ME/*369*.
etymology, popular
EDSL/*140*.
etymon
FDLP/*etymology*; GLT.
eulogy
DLDC/*elegy*; DLTS; HL.
euonym
OO.

euphemism ☐ **104**

euphemism
   CODEL; DLDC; DLTC; DLTS; GLT; HL; ME/*114*; OCEL.
euphony
   DLDC; DLTC; DLTS; DMCT; GLT; HL; ME/*115*; PEPP.
euphonym
   OO.
euphoria
   DLTS.
Euphuism
   DLTS; CODEL; CR/*Index*; DLTC; HL; ME/*116*; OCEL; PEPP.
Euphuistic
   DLDC/*style*.
eupolidian
   DLTC.
eureka
   DLTS.
Eutaw Springs, Battle of
   OCAL.
evaluation
   DMCT; PEPP.
evaluation procedure
   FDLP/*procedure*.
"every and all" fallacy
   ME/*116*.
evidence
   CR/*Index*; ME/*116*.
evocation of milieu
   EDSL/*256*.
evolutionary linguistics
   GLT.
exact rhymes
   DLDC/*versification*.
example: as proof
   CR/*Index*.
ex cathedra
   DLTS.
excelsior
   DLTS.
exception
   FDLP/*regular*.

exciting force
   HL.
exclamation
   FDLP.
exclamatory
   FDLP/*exclamation*.
exclusive
   FDLP/*inclusion*; FDLP/*disjunction*.
exclusive first person
   GLT.
excrescent consonant
   GLT.
excrescent sound
   ME/*370*.
excrescent vowel
   GLT.
excursus
   CR/*Index*.
excursus
   DLTC; DLTS; HL.
exegesis
   CR/*Index*; DLDC/*explication*; DLTC; DLTS; HL.
exempli gratia
   DLTS.
exemplum
   DLTC; DLTS; HL.
exemplum
   DLDC; PEPP.
exergasia
   DLTC.
exhaustiveness
   FDLP.
exhibitionism
   DLTS.
exhortation
   DLTS.
existential
   FDLP.
existential criticism
   HL.

105 □ exposition

Existentialism
   HL; OCAL; CODEL; DLDC;
   DLTC; DLTS; DMCT; ME/*117*;
   OCEL.
existential quantification
   FDLP/*quantifier*.
existential sentence
   GLT.
ex libris
   DLTS.
exocentric
   EDSL/*214*; FDLP.
exocentric construction
   GLT; ME/*370*.
exocentric form
   GLT.
exocentric phrase
   GLT.
exocentric structure
   GLT.
exodus
   CR/*Index*; DLTS.
exolinguistics
   GLT.
exophasia
   GLT.
exophora
   FDLP.
exophoric
   FDLP/*exophora*.
exordium
   DLTC; DLTS; HL.
exornationes
   CR/*Index*.
exoteric
   CODEL; OCEL.
exoticism
   PEPP.
expand
   FDLP/*expansion*.
expansion
   EDSL/*32*; EDSL/*213*; FDLP;
   GLT.
expatriate
   HL.

expatriates
   ME/*118*.
expediency
   CR/*Index*.
experiencer
   FDLP/*expansion*.
experiential word
   GLT.
experimental
   DMCT.
experimental phonetics
   FDLP/*phonetics*; GLT.
experimentelen
   DLTC.
expiratory accent
   GLT.
explanatory
   EDSL/*41*; FDLP/*expansion*.
explanatory adequacy
   FDLP/*adequacy*; FDLP/*explanatory*.
expletive
   DLTS; GLT; HL; ME/*370*.
explication
   DLDC; DLTC; DLTS; DMCT;
   PEPP.
explication de texte
   DLTS/*explication*; HL; ME/*118*.
explicative linguistics
   GLT.
explicatory diachronic linguistics
   GLT.
explicit
   DLTS; EDSL/*37*; FDLP.
explosion
   GLT.
explosive
   GLT.
exponence
   FDLP/*exponent*.
exponent
   FDLP.
exposition
   DLDC/*plot*; DLTC; DLTS; HL;
   ME/*119*; PEPP.

ex post facto
DLTS.

expression
EDSL/20; FDLP; LGEP/73; ME/119.

expression element
FDLP/expression.

Expressionism
DMCT; OCAL; DLDC; DLTC; DLTS; HL; ME/120; PEPP.

expression plane
FDLP/content.

expression, theory of
PEPP.

expressive
EDSL/341; FDLP; GLT.

expressive features
GLT.

expressive form, fallacy of
DLTC.

expressive function
EDSL/341; GLT.

expressive theories
EDSL/81.

expressive theory of criticism
HL.

expurgate
DLTS.

extemporaneity
CR/Index.

extempore
DLTS.

extendable corpus
FDLP/corpus.

extended standard theory
FDLP.

extension
EDSL/237; FDLP; GLT.

extensional meaning
FDLP/extension; GLT.

extensive
EDSL/112; FDLP.

external adequacy
FDLP/adequacy.

external hiatus
GLT.

externalization
GLT.

external linguistics
GLT.

external open juncture
GLT.

external proof
CR/Index.

external sandhi
FDLP/sandhi; GLT.

extra-linguistic
FDLP/ethnolinguistics.

extralinguistic
FDLP.

extralinguistic features
FDLP/extralinguistic.

extrametrical
PH/catalectic.

extraneous
DLTS.

extraposition
FDLP.

extrapositive
FDLP/extraposition.

extrasensory
DLTS.

extravaganza
CODEL; DLTC; DLTS; HL; OCEL.

extra-word
GLT.

extrinsic
DLTS; FDLP.

extrinsic meaning (of word or expression)
GLT.

eye dialect
GLT; HL; ME/370; ME/120.

eye language
FDLP/language.

eye rhyme
PEPP.

eye-rhyme
   DLDC/*versification*; DLTC; DLTS; HL; ME/*120.*

F

fable
CR/*Index*; DLDC; DLTC; DLTS; DMCT; HL; ME/*121*; PH.
fable in verse
PEPP.
fabliau
DLTC; HL.
fabliau
CODEL; DLDC; DLTS; OCEL; PEPP.
fabliaux
ME/*121*.
fabula
DLTC; DLTS.
fabulation
DLTC; DMCT.
facetiae
DLTC; DLTS.
facial expressions
FDLP/*communication*.
facial gestures
FDLP/*communication*.
facile
DLTS.
facilitation
FDLP/*transfer*.
factitious
DLTS.
factitive
FDLP.

factitive verbs
ME/*371*.
factive
FDLP.
factive nominal
ME/*371*.
factivity
FDLP/*factive*.
faculty
CR/*Index*.
faded metaphor
ME/*122*.
fading
FDLP/*juncture*.
fairy tale
DLTC; DLTS; HL.
Falkentheorie
DLTC.
falling
FDLP/*diphthong*; FDLP; FDLP/*juncture*.
falling action
DLDC/*plot*; DLTC; DLTS; HL; ME/*123*; PEPP.
falling diphthong
GLT.
falling meter
DLDC/*versification*.

falling rhythm
DLTC; HL; LGEP/*113*; PEPP; PH.
falling-rising
FDLP/*falling*; FDLP/*nucleus*.
false cognates
GLT.
false masque
DLTC.
false starts
FDLP/*error*.
falsetto
FDLP/*phonation*.
familiar essay
DLDC/*essay*; DLTS; HL.
familiar forms
GLT.
familiar verse
DLTC.
families
EDSL/*10*.
family
FDLP; GLT.
family tree
FDLP/*family*.
Family Tree Theory
ME/*371*; GLT.
fancy
DLTS; DMCT; HL; ME/*123*; PEPP; PH.
fancy and imagination
DLTC.
fantastic poets
HL.
fantasy
DLTS; DMCT; HL; ME/*123*; PH/*fancy*.
farce
CODEL; DLDC/*comedy*; DLTC; DLTS; DMCT; HL; ME/*124*; OCEL; PEPP.
farce-comedy
HL.
farrago
DLTS.

fârsa
DLTC.
Far West
OCAL.
fascism
DLTS.
fatalism
DLTS; HL; ME/*124*.
fate
DLTS.
fate drama
DLTC.
Fates
DLTS; HL; ME/*124*.
Fathers of the Church
CR/*Index*.
fatras
PEPP.
fatrasie
DLTC.
fatuous
DLTS.
faucalization
GLT.
faucal plosive
GLT.
faucal sounds
GLT.
Faust theme
DLTC.
favourite
FDLP.
feature
FDLP.
Features of Words
ME/*372*.
Federalist Age in American literature
HL.
Federal Theatre Project
OCAL.
Federal Writers' Project
OCAL.
feedback
FDLP; GLT.

111 ☐ figurative, literal

feeding
FDLP.
feeding order
FDLP/*feeding.*
feeding rule
FDLP/*feeding.*
feeling
DMCT; PEPP.
feelings
FDLP/*expressive.*
feigning
DLTC; PEPP.
Félibrige
PEPP.
felicity conditions
FDLP.
female speech
FDLP/*area.*
feminine caesura
DLTC.
feminine ending
CODEL; DLDC/*versification*;
DLTC; DLTS; HL; PEPP; PH.
feminine rhyme
CODEL; DLDC/*versification*;
DLTC; DLTS; HL; LGEP/*91*;
PEPP; PH.
femininity
FDLP/*class.*
Feminism
OCAL.
fescennine verse
DLTC.
fescennine verses
OCEL; PEPP.
Festnachtsspiel
DLTC.
Festschrift
DLTC; DLTS; ME/*125*; HL.
fetishism
DLTS.
feudalism
DLTS; HL.
feuilleton
DLTS.

ficción
DLTC.
ficelle
HL.
ficelle
ME/*125.*
fiction
CODEL; DLDC; DLTC; DLTS;
DMCT; EDSL/*153*; HL; ME/
125.
fictional
EDSL/*260.*
fictive audience
ME/*125.*
fictive character
ME/*125.*
field
FDLP.
field conditions
GLT.
field of discourse
FDLP/*field.*
field study
FDLP/*field.*
field theory
FDLP/*field.*
field-work
FDLP/*field.*
figura
DLDC/*type.*
figurae
GLT.
figurae causae
DLTC.
figurae system
GLT.
figurate poem
DLTC.
figurative
DLTS/*literal.*
figurative language
DLDC; DLTC; DLTS; HL;
LGEP/*147*; ME/*126*; PH.
figurative, literal
DLTS.

figurativeness
   EDSL/*302*.
figure
   DLDC/*type*; DMCT; EDSL/*265*; EDSL/*273*.
figure of speech
   ME/*126*.
figure-poem
   HL.
figures
   EDSL/*5*.
figures of speech
   CR/*Index*; DLTS; HL; LGEP/*73*; PEPP.
filid
   PEPP/*931*.
filidh
   HL.
filled pause
   FDLP/*pause*; FDLP.
filler
   FDLP.
film
   HL.
film criticism
   HL.
film theory
   HL.
filter
   FDLP.
final (off) glide
   FDLP; GLT.
final position
   GLT.
final state
   FDLP/*finite state grammar*.
final suspense, moment of
   HL.
fin de siècle
   DLTC; ME/*126*; HL; ME/*126*.
fin de siècle
   DLDC/*Aesthetic Movement*; DLTS.
fine arts and poetry
   PEPP.
fine writing
   DLTS.
finida
   PEPP.
finite
   FDLP.
finite automation
   EDSL/*229*.
finite set
   FDLP/*generative*.
finite state grammar
   FDLP.
finite-state grammar
   EDSL/*229*.
finite verb
   ME/*372*.
Finnish
   FDLP/*length*; FDLP/*case*.
Finnish poetry
   PEPP.
first articulation
   FDLP/*articulation*; GLT.
First
   ME/*Great, 372*.
First Folio
   ME/*126*.
first language
   FDLP/*acquisition*; FDLP/*language*.
first names
   FDLP/*address*.
first person
   FDLP/*person*.
first-person observer
   DLDC/*point of view*.
first-person participant
   DLDC/*point of view*.
first rhetoric
   CR/*Index*.
Firthian
   FDLP.
'fis' phenomenon
   FDLP.

fissure
GLT.
fit
DLTC; GLT.
five-act formula
DLTS.
five points of Calvinism
HL.
fixation
GLT.
fixed
FDLP.
fixed form
EDSL/*192*.
fixed poetic forms
HL.
fixed stress
FDLP/*stress*; GLT.
fixed word order
GLT.
flamenca
DLTC; PEPP.
flap
FDLP; GLT.
flapped
FDLP/*flap*.
flapped r [*sic*]
ME/*372*.
flashback
DLDC/*plot*; DLTC; DLTS; HL; ME/*127*.
flat
FDLP.
flat character
DLTC; DLTS; EDSL/*223*; HL.
flat characters
DLDC/*plot*.
flattery
CR/*Index*.
flatting
ME/*127*.
flection
GLT.

flectional endings
GLT.
flectional language
GLT.
Flemish
FDLP/*bilingual*.
Flemish poetry
PEPP.
Fleshly School
ME/*127*.
Fleshly School of Poetry
DLTC; HL.
Fleshly School of poetry, the
PEPP.
flexion, flexional
GLT.
floating element
GLT.
Florence
CR/*Index*.
flow-chart
FDLP/*algorithm*; GLT.
fluctuating spelling
GLT.
fluency
FDLP/*assimilation*.
Flynt, Josiah
OCAL.
flyting
DLDC/*débat*.
flyting
DLTC; HL; PEPP.
focal area
FDLP/*area*; GLT; ME/*372*.
focal word
GLT.
focus
DLTS; EDSL/*271*; FDLP; PEPP.
focus of narration
ME/*127*.
foil
DLDC/*plot*; DLTS; HL; ME/*129*.

Folger Shakespeare Memorial Library
 OCAL.
folia
 DLTC; PEPP.
folio
 CODEL; DLDC; DLTC; DLTS; HL; OCEL.
folios and quartos
 CODEL; OCEL.
folk ballad
 DLTS; HL.
folk drama
 DLTC; DLTS; HL.
folk epic
 DLTS; HL.
folk etymology
 FDLP/*etymology*; GLT; ME/*373*.
folk literature
 DLTC.
folklore
 CODEL; DLDC; DLTS; HL; ME/*129*; OCEL.
Folklore of the U.S.
 OCAL.
folk play
 DLDC/*folklore*.
folk song
 PEPP.
folksong
 DLDC/*ballad*; DLTC; HL; ME/*129*.
folksongs
 DLDC/*folklore*.
folk tale
 DLDC/*folklore*.
folktale
 DLTC; DLTS; HL; ME/*130*.
folly literature
 DLTC.
fool
 DLTS.

foot
 DLDC/*versification*; DLTC; DLTS; DMCT; FDLP; HL; LGEP/*112*; PEPP; PH/*metre*.
Ford Foundation
 OCAL.
foregrounded irregularity
 LGEP/*67*.
foregrounded regularity
 LGEP/*67*.
foregrounding
 DMCT; LGEP/*56*.
foreign language
 FDLP/*acquisition*.
foreign language learning
 FDLP/*contrast*.
foreign languages
 FDLP/*applied linguistics*.
foreign language teaching
 FDLP/*contrast*.
foreign learners
 FDLP/*analogy*.
foreshadowing
 DLDC/*suspense*; DLTC; DLTS; HL; ME/*132*.
forestress
 GLT.
foreword
 DLTC; DLTS; HL; ME/*132*.
forgeries, literary
 HL.
forgery
 DLTC.
forlorn elements
 GLT.
form
 DLDC; DLTC; DLTS; DMCT; EDSL/*20*; FDLP; GLT; HL; LGEP/*37*; PEPP; PH.
formal
 FDLP/*form*.
formal amalgam
 GLT.
formal contrasts
 GLT.

115 □ foul proof

formal criteria
FDLP/*form.*
formal criticism
HL.
formal essay
DLTS; HL.
formal essays
DLDC/*essay.*
formal grammar
FDLP/*grammar.*
formalisation
FDLP/*formalise.*
formalise
FDLP.
Formalism
DMCT; DLTC; FDLP/*formalise.*
formalism, Russian
PEPP/*931.*
formality
FDLP/*form.*
formal satire
DLDC/*satire*; HL.
formal semantics
FDLP/*form.*
formal universals
EDSL/*134*; FDLP/*universal.*
formant
FDLP; GLT.
formants
EDSL/*177.*
format
DLTC; HL.
formation-rule
FDLP.
formative
EDSL/*200*; FDLP; GLT.
formative theory
HL.
form class
GLT.
form-class
FDLP/*form.*
form class word
ME/*373.*

form criticism
CR/*Index.*
formless language
GLT.
forms of address
FDLP/*address.*
forms of discourse
DLTS.
formula
DLTS; HL.
formulae
CR/*Index*; FDLP/*convention.*
formulaic language
FDLP.
formularies
CR/*Index.*
formulas
DLDC/*epic.*
form vs. function
FDLP/*form.*
form vs. meaning
FDLP/*form.*
form vs. substance
FDLP/*form.*
form vs. substance and meaning
FDLP/*form.*
form word
FDLP; GLT.
fornyrðislag
DLTC; PEPP.
fortis
FDLP; GLT; ME/*373.*
Forty-niners
OCAL.
forward reference
FDLP/*referent.*
forwards-referring functions
FDLP/*anaphora.*
fossilised
FDLP.
foul copy
HL.
foul proof
HL.

Four Ages of Poetry
DLTC.

four ages of poetry
PEPP.

Fourier analysis
GLT.

Fourierism
OCAL.

four-level classification
FDLP/*close*.

four levels of meaning
DLTC.

four meanings
DLTC.

four senses of interpretation
HL.

four-syllable metre
LGEP/*117*.

fourteener
DLDC/*versification*; DLTC; DLTS; PEPP; PH/*metre*.

"fourteeners"
HL.

four-term fallacy
ME/*132*.

fourth wall
HL.

fracture
GLT.

fragment
GLT.

frame
FDLP; GLT.

frame features
FDLP/*frame*.

frame story
DLDC; DLTC; DLTS; ME/*133*.

framework-story
HL.

Franciscan Literature
DLTC.

Franciscans
CR/*Index*.

Franco-Norman
HL.

free
FDLP.

free association
DLTC; DLTS.

freedom of speech
CR/*Index*.

free form
FDLP/*free*; GLT; ME/*373*.

free forms
FDLP/*morpheme*.

free meter
DLTC.

free-metre poetry
PEPP.

free morpheme
FDLP/*free*; GLT.

free position
GLT.

Free Religious Association
OCAL.

free repetition
LGEP/*94*.

free stress
FDLP/*free*; GLT.

free syllable
GLT.

free variant
FDLP/*variant*.

free variants
EDSL/*172*; FDLP/*free*; GLT.

free variation
FDLP/*free*; GLT; ME/*373*.

free verse
DLDC/*versification*; DLDC/*versification*; DLTC; DLTS; DMCT; EDSL/*188*; HL; ME/*133*; OCAL/*vers libre*; PEPP; PH.

free word order
FDLP/*free*; GLT.

Freiburg
CR/*Index*.

French
FDLP/*conditional*; FDLP/*borrow*; FDLP/*discontinuous*; FDLP/*clitic*; FDLP/*nasal*; FDLP/*contraction*; FDLP/*liaison*.

French Academy
CR/*Index*.

French and Indian Wars
OCAL.

French forms
DLTC; HL; PH.

French poetics
PEPP.

French poetry
PEPP.

French prosody
PEPP.

frenzy
PEPP.

frequencies
FDLP/*acute*.

frequency
FDLP/*formant*; FDLP/*acoustic feature*; GLT.

frequency, fundamental
FDLP/*fundamental*.

frequentative
FDLP; FDLP/*aspect*.

Freudian critic
DLDC/*criticism*.

Freudianism
DLTS; HL.

Freudian slip
ME/*134*.

Freytag's pyramid
DLTC; HL.

fricative
FDLP; GLT; ME/*374*.

friction
FDLP/*affricate*; FDLP.

frictionless
FDLP.

Friendly Club
OCAL.

Friendly Club of New York
OCAL.

Frisian poetry
PEPP.

front
FDLP.

frontal
GLT.

fronted
FDLP/*front*; GLT.

Frontier
OCAL.

frontier literature
HL.

fronting
FDLP/*theme*; FDLP/*front*; GLT; ME/*374*.

front vowel
GLT; ME/*374*.

frottola
DLTC; PEPP.

Frühromantik
DLTC.

Fruitlands
OCAL.

FSP
FDLP/*functional sentence perspective*.

fu
DLTC; PEPP.

Fugitives, The
DLTC; HL; PEPP.

full
FDLP.

full rhyme
PH.

full voice
GLT.

full word
GLT.

funambulism
HL.

function
FDLP; GLT.

functional ☐ **118**

functional
　GLT.
functional analysis
　FDLP/*function*.
functional and structural theory
　GLT.
functional categories
　FDLP/*category*.
functional change
　GLT.
functional exchange
　EDSL/*239*.
functionalism
　EDSL/*24*; GLT.
functionalists
　EDSL/*24*.
functional linguistics
　FDLP/*function*; GLT.
functional load
　FDLP/*function*; GLT.
functional meaning
　GLT.
functional metaphor
　DLTC; PH/*metaphor*.
functional moneme
　GLT.
functional phonetics
　FDLP/*function*; FDLP/*phonology*.
functional sentence perspective
　FDLP.
functional shift
　GLT; ME/*374*.
functional slot
　FDLP/*tagmemics*.
functional unit
　FDLP/*affricate*.
functional variety of usage
　ME/*374*.
functional word
　GLT.
functional yield
　FDLP/*function*; GLT.
functions
　EDSL/*218*.

functions of duration
　GLT.
functions of pitch
　GLT.
functions of stress
　GLT.
function word
　FDLP; GLT; ME/*375*.
function words
　DLTS.
functives
　GLT.
functor
　FDLP; GLT.
fundamental
　FDLP.
fundamental image
　DLTS; HL.
Fundamentalism
　OCAL.
fundamental pitch
　GLT.
fundamental tone
　GLT.
funeral oratory
　CR/*Index*.
furor poeticus
　PEPP.
fury
　PEPP.
fuse
　FDLP/*fusional*.
fused compound
　GLT.
fusion
　FDLP/*fusional*; GLT.
fusional
　FDLP.
fusional languages
　FDLP/*fusional*.
fustian
　DLTC; DLTS; HL.
future perfect
　FDLP/*perfect*.

future perfect tense
 ME/*376*.
future tense
 ME/*375*.
futurism
 DLTC; DLTS; PEPP.

fuzzy
 FDLP.
fyrtiotalisterna
 DLTC; PEPP.

G

Gaelic
   DLTS.
Gaelic Movement
   HL.
gai saber
   DLTC; OCEL; PEPP.
gai saber
   CODEL.
gaita gallega
   PEPP.
gaita-gallega
   DLTC.
Galician poetry
   PEPP.
Gallegan poetry
   PEPP.
galliambic
   CODEL; DLTC; OCEL.
galliambus
   PEPP.
Gallicism
   DLTS; HL; ME/*135*.
gamelion
   CR/*Index*.
gap
   FDLP; GLT.
gapping
   FDLP.
garland of sonnets
   PH/*sonnet*.

gasconade
   DLTS; HL.
Gastonia Strike
   OCAL.
Gath
   OCAL.
gatha
   DLTC.
gathering
   DLTC; GLT; HL.
gaucho poetry
   PEPP.
gazette
   CODEL; DLTC; DLTS; OCEL.
gazetteer
   CODEL; DLTC; DLTS; OCEL.
geminate
   FDLP.
gemination
   DLTS; GLT; ME/*377*.
gender
   FDLP; GLT; ME/*377*.
gender noun
   GLT.
genemmic phonetics
   GLT.
generación del 1898
   DLTC.
general
   DLDC/*concrete*; FDLP.

general and particular □ 122

general and particular
 DLTC.
general grammar
 FDLP/*general*; GLT.
generalisations
 FDLP/*general*.
generalise
 FDLP/*general*.
generalised transformation
 FDLP/*general*.
generality
 FDLP/*general*.
general linguistics
 FDLP/*linguistics*; FDLP/*general*.
general phonetics
 FDLP/*phonetics*.
general semantics
 FDLP/*general*; GLT.
general stylistics
 FDLP/*stylistics*.
general terms
 HL.
generate
 FDLP/*generative*.
generation
 EDSL/*226*.
generative
 EDSL/*37*; FDLP.
generative grammar
 EDSL/*39*; FDLP/*generative*;
 GLT; ME/*377*.
generative linguistics
 FDLP/*generative*.
generative metrics
 HL; PEPP/*931*.
generative phonology
 FDLP/*alpha notation*; FDLP/
 generative.
generative rule
 FDLP/*rule*.
generative semantics
 EDSL/*56*; FDLP/*generative*.
generative syntax
 FDLP/*generative*.

generativist
 FDLP/*description*.
generic
 FDLP.
generic grammatical category
 GLT.
generic rhyme
 PEPP/*933*.
género chico
 DLTC.
generous plural
 GLT.
genesis
 EDSL/*145*; EDSL/*70*.
genethliac
 CR/*Index*.
genetic classification
 GLT.
genetic fallacy
 ME/*135*.
genetic phonetics
 GLT.
genetic transmission
 FDLP/*biolinguistics*.
Geneva School
 FDLP.
Geneva School of Criticism
 HL.
Geneva School, the
 PEPP/*933*.
genitive
 FDLP/*case*; FDLP.
genitive case
 ME/*377*.
genius
 CR/*Index*; DLTC; PEPP.
geno-text
 EDSL/*360*.
genre
 DLDC; DLTC; DLTS; DMCT;
 HL; ME/*135*.
genre criticism
 HL.

genres
EDSL/*149*; PEPP.
genres: of literature
CR/*Index*.
genteel comedy
HL.
genteelism
DLTS.
genteel tradition
HL.
geographical
FDLP/*dialect*.
geographical classification
GLT.
geographical continuity
FDLP/*contact*.
geographical dialects
FDLP/*geographical linguistics*.
geographical linguistics
FDLP; GLT.
geographical region
FDLP/*area*.
geolinguistics
EDSL/*57*; GLT.
Georgian
DLDC; DLTS; HL.
Georgian Age in English Literature 1914-1940
HL.
Georgianism
PEPP; PH.
Georgian poetry
DLTC; PEPP.
georgic
DLDC/*pastoral*; DLTC; DLTS; HL; PEPP.
Georgics
PH.
German
FDLP/*fricative*; FDLP/*palatalisation*; FDLP/*chroneme*; FDLP/*diglossia*; FDLP/*affricate*.
Germanic sound shifts
GLT.

German poetics
PEPP.
German poetry
PEPP.
German prosody
PEPP.
gerund
FDLP/*-ing* form; FDLP/*particple*; ME/*378*.
Gesellschaftslied
DLTC; PEPP.
gest
DLTS/*geste*.
gest
HL.
gesta
DLTC.
gestalt
DLTS; HL.
gestalt
DLTC.
gestaltist theory
EDSL/*70*.
gestes
ME/*135*.
gestural language
GLT.
gesture
CR/*Index*.
gestures
FDLP/*communication*.
Gettysburg Address
OCAL.
ghasel
PEPP.
ghazel
DLTC.
ghost form
GLT/*ghost word*.
ghost story
DLTC.
ghostword
DLTC.

ghost writer ☐ **124**

ghost writer
 DLTS.
ghost-writer
 DLTC.
ghostwriter
 HL.
Gideon Society
 OCAL.
gierasa
 DLTC.
Gift Books
 OCAL.
gift-books
 HL.
Gilbertian
 CODEL; OCEL.
gingival
 GLT.
given
 FDLP.
given situation
 LGEP/*187*.
Glagolitic alphabet
 GLT.
glee
 DLTC.
gleeman
 DLTS; HL.
glide
 FDLP; GLT; ME/*378*.
gliding vowel
 FDLP/*pure vowel*; FDLP/*vowel*.
gliding vowels
 FDLP/*diphthong*; FDLP/*glide*.
global
 FDLP.
global derivational
 FDLP/*global*.
global rule
 FDLP/*global*.
glosa
 DLTC; PEPP.
gloss
 DLDC; DLTC; DLTS; GLT; HL.

glossary
 DLTC; DLTS; GLT.
glossematics
 EDSL/*20*; FDLP; GLT.
glosseme
 EDSL/*23*; FDLP/*glossematics*; GLT.
glossolalia
 FDLP/*glossematics*; GLT.
glottal
 FDLP; GLT.
glottal catch
 GLT.
glottal constrictions
 FDLP/*glottal*.
glottalic
 FDLP/*ejective*; FDLP/*air-stream mechanism*; FDLP/*glottal*.
glottalisation
 FDLP/*glottal*.
glottalization
 GLT.
glottalized
 GLT.
glottalized timbre
 GLT.
glottal stop
 FDLP/*glottal*; GLT; ME/*378*.
glott-, glotto-
 GLT.
glottis
 FDLP/*air-stream mechanism*; FDLP/*glottal*; GLT.
glottochronology
 FDLP; GLT; ME/*378*.
glottology
 GLT.
glottopolitics
 GLT.
glyconic
 DLTC; PEPP.
gnomai
 CR/*Index*.

gnomic
CODEL; DLTS; HL; ME/*136*; OCEL.
gnomic poetry
DLDC/*aphorism*; PEPP.
gnomic verse
DLTC; PH.
gnostic
DLTS.
gnosticism
HL.
goal
FDLP/*passive*; FDLP; FDLP/*object*.
goat
DLTS.
gobbledegook
DLTC.
gobbledygook
DLTS; ME/*136*.
god from the machine
CODEL; OCEL.
God's truth
FDLP.
Golden Age
DLDC; DLTS.
goliard
PH.
Goliardic verse
DLDC; DLTC; HL; ME/*137*; PEPP.
Gongorism
DLTC; DLTS; PEPP; PH; HL.
Good Gray Poet
OCAL.
good sense
DLTC.
Gotham
OCAL.
Gothic
DLDC; DLTS; HL; ME/*137*; DMCT.
Gothic novel
DLDC/*Gothic*; DLTC; HL; ME/*137*.

Gothic novels
CODEL; OCEL.
Gothic Revival
DLDC/*Gothic*; OCAL.
Gothic romance
OCAL.
Götterdämmerung
DLTS; HL.
Göttinger Dichterbund
DLTC; PEPP.
govern
FDLP; GLT.
governed
FDLP/*govern*.
government
FDLP/*govern*; GLT.
governor
FDLP/*govern*; FDLP/*arc*.
Go West, Young Man
OCAL.
Grabhorn Press
OCAL.
Grace
ME/*138*; DLTC.
Graces, The
HL; ME/*138*.
gracioso
DLTC.
gradability
FDLP.
gradable
FDLP/*gradability*.
gradation
EDSL/*277*; FDLP/*cline*; GLT; ME/*379*.
grade
GLT.
graded antonyms
FDLP/*antonym*.
graded area
GLT.
gradience
FDLP.

gradual
FDLP/*opposition*; FDLP.
gradual opposition
GLT.
graduated
EDSL/*116*.
graffiti
DLTS; ME/*138*.
Grail, Holy
DLTS.
grammar
CR/*Index*; DMCT; EDSL/*51*; EDSL/*54*; FDLP; FDLP/*phrase-structure*; GLT; LGEP/*37*; ME/*379*.
grammar and poetry
PEPP.
grammarian
FDLP/*grammar*.
grammatical
EDSL/*127*; FDLP/*grammar*; FDLP/*grammaticality*; ME/*379*.
grammatical alternation
GLT.
grammatical ambiguity
FDLP/*ambiguity*.
grammatical analysis
GLT.
grammatical borrowing
GLT.
grammatical categories
FDLP/*category*; GLT.
grammatical category
FDLP/*grammar*.
grammatical change
GLT.
grammatical devices
GLT.
grammatical elements
EDSL/*10*.
grammatical equivalents
GLT.
grammatical form
GLT.

grammatical gender
FDLP/*grammar*; FDLP/*gender*; GLT.
grammaticality
FDLP.
grammaticalization
GLT.
grammatically conditioned alternants
FDLP/*alternation*.
grammatical meaning
GLT; ME/*379*.
grammatical mistakes
FDLP/*competence*.
grammatical moneme
GLT.
grammatical morphemes
FDLP/*morpheme*.
grammatical operations
FDLP/*acceptability*.
grammatical stress
GLT.
grammatical structure
GLT.
grammatical subordination
EDSL/*27*.
grammatical system
FDLP/*system*.
grammatical word
FDLP/*grammar*.
grammatology
EDSL/*349*; EDSL/*198*.
Grand Guignol
DLTC.
grands rhêtoriqueurs
CR/*Index*.
grand style
CR/*Index*; DLDC/*style*; DLTC; LGEP/*17*; PEPP.
grand tour
DLTC; ME/*138*.
Grangerize
DLTC; OCEL.
graph
FDLP.

127 □ Grobianism

graphema
GLT.
grapheme
FDLP; FDLP/*allo-*; GLT; ME/*379*.
grapheme analysis
FDLP/*grapheme*.
graphemics
FDLP/*grapheme*; GLT.
graphetics
FDLP.
graphic features
FDLP/*graphetics*.
graphics
FDLP/*graphetics*.
graphic shapes
GLT.
graphic substance
FDLP.
graphological
FDLP/*graphology*.
graphology
FDLP; LGEP/*39*; LGEP/*37*.
graphonomy
GLT.
Grassmann's law
GLT.
Grassman's Law
ME/*380*.
grave
FDLP.
grave phoneme
GLT.
graveyard poetry
PEPP.
Graveyard School
DLDC; DLTS; HL; ME/*139*; OCEL.
Graveyard School of Poetry
DLTC.
Grayson, David
OCAL.
Great Awakening, The
HL; OCAL.

Great Books, the
ME/*139*.
great chain of being
DLTC; ME/*139*.
great chain of being, the
HL.
Great Emancipator, The
OCAL.
great English vowel shift
GLT.
Great Plains
OCAL/*Plains region*.
Great Vowel Shift
FDLP/*sound change*; ME/*380*.
Greek
FDLP/*diglossia*.
Greek grammarians
FDLP/*grammar*.
Greek poetics
PEPP.
Greek poetry
PEPP.
Greek prosody
PEPP.
Greek Revival
OCAL.
Greek romance
DLDC/*novel*.
Greek tragedy
DLDC/*Apollonian*; DLTC.
Green Mountain Boys
OCAL.
Greenwich Village
OCAL.
greeting
FDLP/*adjacency pair*.
greguería
DLTC.
Grenzsignal
GLT.
Grimm's Law
ME/*381*; GLT.
Grobianism
DLTC.

Grolier Club
  OCAL.
groove
  FDLP.
groove fricative
  GLT.
groove fricatives
  FDLP/*groove*.
groove spirant
  GLT.
grotesque
  DLTC; DMCT; HL.
ground
  LGEP/*151*; LGEP/*155*.
group
  FDLP.
group genitive
  FDLP/*group*.
grouping
  FDLP/*realisation*.
Group Theatre
  OCAL.

Grub Street
  DLTC; DLTS; HL.
Grundy, Mrs.
  DLTS; HL.
Guggenheim Fellowships
  OCAL.
guidebook
  DLTC.
Gujarati
  FDLP/*breathy*.
Gujarati poetry
  PEPP.
Gullah
  OCAL.
guslar
  DLTC.
guttural
  GLT.
gymnastic
  CR/*Index*.
gypsy poetry
  PEPP.

H

H
  FDLP/*diglossia*.
habitual collocations
  FDLP/*idiom*.
habitual contrasts
  FDLP/*aspect*.
hack
  DLTS.
hackneyed usage
  ME/*142*.
hadīth
  DLTC.
Haggadah
  OCEL.
hagiography
  DLTC; DLTS; HL.
haiku
  DLTC.
haiku
  DLTS; HL; ME/*142*; PEPP; PH.
Hainbund, Göttinger Hain
  PEPP.
Haiti
  FDLP/*creole*.
Haitian poetry
  PEPP.
half-close
  FDLP/*close*.
half-open
  FDLP/*close*.

half-open vowel
  GLT.
half rhyme
  PEPP.
half-rhyme
  DLDC/*versification*; DLTC; DLTS; HL.
half-rounded vowel
  GLT.
half-truth
  ME/*142*.
half voice
  GLT.
Half-Way Covenant
  OCAL.
hallel
  DLTC.
hallelujah meter
  DLTC.
Hallidayan
  FDLP.
Hall of Fame
  OCAL.
hallucination
  DLTS.
hamartia
  DLDC/*tragedy*; HL.
hamartia
  DLTC; DLTS; ME/*142*.

handbook and manual
DLTC.
handbooks
CR/*Index*; FDLP/*grammar*.
handbooks, prescriptive language in
CR/*Index*.
handwriting
FDLP/*allo-*.
haplography
GLT.
haplology
FDLP; GLT.
happening
DLTC.
harangue
DLTC; DLTS; HL.
hard consonant
FDLP; GLT.
hard palate
FDLP/*palate*.
Harlem
OCAL.
Harlem Renaissance
HL; PEPP/*935*.
harlequin
DLTC; DLTS; OCEL.
harlequinade
HL.
harmonic
GLT.
harmonics
FDLP/*fundamental*.
harmonic structure
FDLP/*acoustic feature*.
harmony
DLTS.
Harmony Society
OCAL.
Hartford Wits
CODEL; HL; OCAL/*Connecticut Wits*; OCEL.
hasty generalization
ME/*142*.

Hausa
FDLP/*flap*; FDLP/*lingua franca*; FDLP/*creak*; FDLP/*glottal*.
Hausa poetry
PEPP/*936*.
H.D.
OCAL.
head
FDLP; FDLP/*tone group*
headless
PH/*catalectic*.
headless line
DLTC; HL; PEPP.
head (of a macrosegment)
GLT.
head (of an intonation)
GLT.
head rhyme
DLTC; DLTS; HL; PEPP; PH/*rhyme*.
head rime
ME/*143*.
head word
GLT.
headword
ME/*382*.
hearer
EDSL/*341*; EDSL/*324*.
hearer's errors
FDLP/*error*.
hearing
FDLP/*auditory phonetics*.
heavy base
GLT.
heavy stress
GLT.
Hebraism
HL; ME/*143*.
Hebraism/Hellenism
DLTC.
Hebraism-Hellenism
PEPP.
Hebrew poetry
PEPP.

131 □ heroic tragedy

Hedge Club
HL.
hedonism
CODEL; DLTS; HL; OCEL.
Hegelianism
HL.
heightened subglottal pressure
FDLP.
heightening of language
LGEP/14.
Helicon Home Colony
OCAL.
Hellenism
DLTS; HL; ME/Hebraism, 143.
Hellenistic
CODEL; OCEL.
Hellenistic poetics
PEPP.
Hell-Fire Club
OCAL.
helper verb
GLT.
helping verbs
ME/382.
hemiepes
DLTC; PEPP.
hemistich
CODEL; DLTC; DLTS; EDSL/187; HL; ME/143; OCEL; PEPP.
hendecasyllabic
CODEL; DLTS; OCEL; PEPP.
hendecasyllabics
PH.
hendecasyllabic verse
HL.
hendecasyllable
DLTC.
hendiadys
CODEL; DLTC; DLTS; HL; ME/143; OCEL; PEPP.
Henry, O.
OCAL.
hephthemimeral
DLTC; PEPP.

heptameter
DLDC/versification; DLTC; DLTS; HL; ME/143; PEPP; PH/metre.
heptastich
DLTC; DLTS; HL; PEPP.
heptasyllabic
DLTC; PEPP.
heresy of paraphrase
DLTC; DMCT; PEPP.
hermeneutics
CR/Index; PEPP/937.
Hermeticism
DLTC; PEPP.
hero
DMCT; EDSL/223; HL.
hero and heroine
DLTC.
hero, heroine
DLTS.
heroic couplet
CODEL; DLDC/versification; DLTC; DLTS; DMCT; HL; ME/143; PEPP; PH/heroic line.
heroic drama
CODEL; DLDC/tragedy; DLTC; DLTS; HL.
heroic line
DLTS; HL; PH.
heroic meter
PEPP.
heroic play
PEPP.
heroic poetry
CODEL; OCEL; PEPP.
heroic quatrain
DLDC/versification; DLTC; HL; PEPP.
heroic simile
PEPP.
heroic stanza
DLTS; HL; PH/heroic line.
heroic tragedy
DLDC/tragedy.

heroic verse
CODEL; DLTC; HL; OCEL; PH/*heroic line*.
heroine
HL/*hero*.
Hertz
FDLP/*fundamental*; FDLP/*pitch*.
hesitation
FDLP.
hesitation form
GLT.
hesitation phenomena
FDLP/*hesitation*.
heterographic
FDLP/*homograph*.
heterographic spelling
GLT.
heterometric
EDSL/*192*.
heteronomous sound change
GLT.
heteronym
FDLP; GLT; OO.
heteronymous
GLT.
heteronymy
FDLP/*homonym*; FDLP/*heteronym*.
heterophemy
GLT.
heterorganic
FDLP/*homorganic*.
heuristic
DLTS; FDLP.
hexameter
CODEL; DLDC/*versification*; DLTC; DLTS; HL; ME/*145*; OCEL; PEPP; PH/*metre*; PH.
hexastich
DLTC; DLTS; HL; PEPP.
H.H.
OCAL.
hiatus
CR/*Index*.

hiatus
DLTC; DLTS; GLT; HL; ME/*145*; PEPP.
hierarchical
FDLP/*hierarchy*.
hierarchical structure
FDLP/*hierarchy*.
hierarchy
FDLP; GLT.
hieratic
GLT.
hieratic style
HL.
hieroglyph
GLT.
hieroglyphic
GLT.
hieroglyphics
EDSL/*195*.
high
EDSL/*155*; FDLP.
high/low falling
FDLP/*falling*.
high burlesque
DLDC/*burlesque*.
high comedy
DLTC; IIL.
higher
FDLP.
higher criticism
DLTC; HL.
high style
DLDC/*style*.
high vowel
FDLP/*close*; GLT.
hilarody
DLTC.
Hindi
FDLP/*heightened subglottal pressure*; FDLP/*aspiration*.
Hindi poetry
PEPP.
hiragana
GLT.

hiss
FDLP/*sibilant*.
historical antecedents
FDLP/*area*.
historical critic
DLDC/*criticism*.
historical criticism
HL.
historical dialect
FDLP/*dialect*.
historical fiction
HL.
historical grammar
GLT.
historical linguistics
FDLP/*linguistics*; FDLP; GLT; LGEP/*41*.
historical morphology
FDLP/*historical linguistics*.
historical novel
DLDC/*novel*; DLTC; DLTS; DMCT; HL; ME/*145*.
historical phonology
FDLP/*historical linguistics*; GLT.
historical play
DLTS.
historical present
DLTS.
historical relationship
FDLP/*comparative*.
historical rhyme
DLTC; PH/*rhyme*.
historical states
FDLP/*comparative*.
historical syntax
FDLP/*historical linguistics*.
historicism
DMCT; HL; PEPP/*937*.
history and poetry
PEPP.
history as literature
ME/*145*.
history of language
FDLP/*biolinguistics*.

history play
DLTC; HL; PEPP.
Hittite poetry
PEPP.
Hochromantik
DLTC.
hocus-pocus
FDLP.
hokku
DLTC; PEPP.
Hokku
ME/*haiku, 142*.
hold
FDLP; GLT; PH.
holding period
GLT.
hole in the pattern
FDLP/*pattern*.
holes in the pattern
GLT.
holidays mentioned in literature
ME/*147*.
holism
DLTS.
Hollywood
OCAL.
holograph
DLTC; DLTS; HL.
holophrase
FDLP; GLT.
holophrasis
DLTC; FDLP/*holophrase*.
holophrastic
FDLP/*holophrase*; GLT.
holosynthetic
GLT.
holy grail
HL.
homeoteleuton
DLTC.
Homeric
DLTS; HL.
Homeric epithet
DLTC; HL; ME/*151*.

Homeric simile
DLDC/*epic*; DLTC; HL.
homiletics
DLTS.
homily
CR/*Index*; DLTC; DLTS; HL;
ME/*151*.
homoantonym
OO.
homoeomeral
PEPP.
homoeoteleuton
CR/*Index*.
homoeoteleuton
PEPP.
homogenous
FDLP/*idealisation*.
homogram
GLT.
homograph
DLTC; DLTS; FDLP; GLT;
LGEP/*208*.
homographic clash
FDLP/*homograph*.
homographs
ME/*151*.
homography
FDLP/*homograph*.
homomorphic
FDLP/*mapping*.
homonym
CODEL; DLTC; DLTS; FDLP;
GLT; LGEP/*207*; ME/*151*;
OCEL; OO.
homonym, homophone
ME/*382*.
homonymic clash
FDLP/*homonym*.
homonymy
EDSL/*236*; FDLP/*homonym*;
LGEP/*206*.
homonymy, grammatical
LGEP/*206*.
homonymy, lexical
LGEP/*206*.

homophone
CODEL; DLTC; DLTS; FDLP;
GLT; LGEP/*208*; ME/*151*;
OCEL.
homophonic clash
FDLP/*homophone*.
homophony
DMCT; FDLP/*homophone*;
LGEP/*38*.
homorganic
FDLP.
homorganic phonemes
GLT.
homostrophic
DLTS; HL.
homotopical
GLT.
honorable
CR/*Index*.
honorific
FDLP; GLT.
hook
FDLP/*cardinal vowels*.
Hoosier
OCAL.
Hopedale Community
OCAL.
Hopi
FDLP/*class*.
hopping
FDLP/*affix*.
Horatian
DLTS.
Horatian ode
DLTC; HL; PEPP; PH/*ode*.
Horatian odes
DLDC/*ode*.
Horatian satire
DLDC/*satire*; HL.
horn book
ME/*152*.
hornbook
CODEL; DLTC; DLTS; HL;
OCEL.

135 □ hyperbole

Hottentot
FDLP/*click*.
hovering accent
DLTC/*hovering stress*; HL/*hovering stress*; PEPP; PH.
hovering stress
DLDC/*versification*; DLTC; HL.
Howadji
OCAL.
howler
DLTC.
hrynhent
DLTC; PEPP.
Hub of the Universe
OCAL.
hubris
DLDC/*tragedy*.
hubris
DLTC; DLTS; HL; ME/*152*.
Hudibrastic
CODEL; DLDC/*versification*; DLTS; OCEL.
Hudibrastic verse
DLTC; HL; PEPP; PH.
Hudson River School
OCAL.
Huguenots
OCAL.
huitain
DLTC; PEPP.
Humanism
ME/*152*; DLDC/*Renaissance*; DLTC; DLTS; HL.
humanisme
DLTC.
humanism, new
PEPP.
Humanism, The New
HL; OCAL.
Humanists
CODEL; CR/*Index*.
humanities
DLTS.
human noun
ME/*382*.

humor
CR/*Index*; DLDC/*comedy*; DLTS; HL; ME/*152*.
humors
DLTS.
humours
DLTC; DMCT; HL; ME/*152*.
humours, comedy of
CODEL; OCEL.
Hungarian poetry
PEPP.
Huntington Library
OCAL.
hyangga
DLTC.
hybrid
DLTC; GLT.
hybrid language
GLT.
hybris
DLDC/*tragedy*.
hybris
HL/*hubris*.
hydronym
OO.
hymn
DLDC; DLTC; DLTS; HL; ME/*153*; PEPP.
hymnal stanza
DLTC; HL; PH/*common measure*.
hymns
OCAL.
hypallage
CODEL; DLTC; DLTS; HL; OCEL; PEPP.
hyperbaton
DLTC; DLTS; HL; LGEP/*18*; PEPP.
hyperbole
CODEL; DLDC/*figurative language*; DLTC; DLTS; DMCT; EDSL/*277*; GLT; HL; LGEP/*166*; LGEP/*170*; LGEP/*167*; ME/*154*; OCEL; PEPP.

hypercatalectic
DLTC; HL; PEPP; PH/*catalectic*.
hyper-correction
GLT.
hypercorrection
FDLP.
hyperdochmiac
DLTC.
hyperform
GLT.
hypermeter
DLDC/*versification*.
hypermetric
PEPP.
hypermetrical
HL; PH/*catalectic*.
hypermetric syllable
DLTC.
hypernasal
FDLP/*nasal*.
hypersememic
FDLP.
hypersemotactics
FDLP/*tactics*.
hyper-urbanism
GLT.
hyphaeresis
DLTC; PEPP.
hypocorism
CODEL; DLTC; DLTS; GLT; OCEL.
hypocorisma
DLTS.
hyponasal
FDLP/*nasal*.
hyponym
FDLP; OO.

hyponymy
FDLP/*hyponym*.
hypophonemic
FDLP.
hypophonotactics
FDLP/*tactics*.
hyporchema
DLTC; PEPP.
hyporrhythmic
PEPP.
hypostatization
DLTC.
hypotactic
FDLP.
hypotaxis
DLTC; FDLP/*hypotactic*; GLT; HL.
hypothesis
CR/*Index*.
hypothesis
DLTS.
hypothetical predictions
FDLP/*attested*.
hypotyposis
DLTC.
hypozeugma
DLTC.
hypsos
CR/*Index*.
hysteron proteron
CODEL; DLTC; DLTS; HL; ME/*155*; OCEL; PEPP.
Hz
FDLP/*pitch*; FDLP/*fundamental*.

I

IA
　FDLP/*item and arrangement*; FDLP.
iamb
　DLDC/*versification*; DLTC; EDSL/*187*; HL; LGEP/*112*; ME/*156*; PEPP; PH.
iambelegus
　DLTC; PEPP.
iambes
　PEPP.
iambes, les
　DLTC.
iambic
　CODEL; DLDC/*versification*; FDLP/*foot*; OCEL; PH/*metre*; PH.
iambic trimeter
　DLTC.
iambus
　DLTS; HL.
ibidem
　DLTC; DLTS.
ibycean
　PEPP.
IC
　FDLP/*immediate constituent*; FDLP; GLT.
IC analysis
　FDLP/*constituent*.

Icelandic poetry
　PEPP.
icon
　DLTC; DLTS; EDSL/*86*.
icon and iconology
　PEPP/*941*.
iconic
　FDLP/*iconicity*; GLT.
iconicity
　FDLP.
iconoclasm
　DLTS.
ictus
　CODEL; DLTC; DLTS; HL; OCEL; PEPP; PH.
id
　DLTS.
ideal
　FDLP/*idealisation*.
idealisation
　FDLP.
ideal reader
　DLTC.
ideal spectator
　DLTC.
ideas of style
　CR/*Index*.
ideational
　FDLP.

idée fixe
   DLTC.
idée fixe
   DLTS.
idée reçue
   DLTC.
idem
   DLTC.
identical rhyme
   DLTC; DLTS; HL; PH/*rhyme*.
identification
   DLTS; EDSL/*18*.
identification of languages
   GLT.
identifying units
   GLT.
identity
   GLT; LGEP/*65*.
identity of the narrator
   EDSL/*330*.
identity operation
   FDLP/*zero*.
ideogram
   EDSL/*194*; GLT.
ideogram, ideograph
   ME/*383*.
ideograph
   DLTC; DLTS; GLT.
ideographic
   GLT.
ideology
   DLTS.
ideophone
   GLT.
idiolect
   DLTC; DLTS; EDSL/*57*; FDLP; GLT; ME/*383*.
idiom
   DLTC; DLTS; FDLP; GLT; HL; ME/*156*.
idiomatic
   FDLP/*idiom*.
idiomatic expression
   GLT.

idiomatic usage
   GLT.
idiophone
   FDLP.
idiophoneme
   GLT.
idiosyncratic connections
   FDLP/*collocation*.
Ido
   DLTC.
idola
   DLTS.
idyl
   PH/*pastoral*.
idyll
   CODEL; DLDC; DLDC/*pastoral*; DLTC; DLTS; HL; OCEL; PEPP.
Igbo
   FDLP/*implosive*.
ignis fatuus
   DLTS.
ignoratio elenchi
   OCEL.
ignoratio elenchi
   CODEL.
Ik Marvel
   OCAL.
illative
   FDLP/*case*.
ill-formed
   FDLP; FDLP/*well-formed*.
ill-formedness
   FDLP/*ill-formed*.
illiteracy
   DLTS.
illocutionary
   FDLP.
illocutionary act
   EDSL/*343*.
illuminated manuscript
   DLTS.
illusion
   DLTC; DLTS.

illusion of reality
ME/*156*.
image
DLTS; DMCT; HL; PH.
imagery
CR/*Index*; DLDC; DLTC; DLTS; HL; ME/*156*; PEPP.
imagination
CR/*Index*; DLTC; DMCT; HL; ME/*157*; PEPP; PH.
imaginative writing
DLTS.
Imagism
DMCT; OCAL; CODEL; DLTS; ME/*158*; OCEL; PEPP; PH.
Imagists
DLDC; DLTC; HL; ME/*158*; PH/*imagism*.
imitation
CR/*Index*; DLDC; DLTC; DMCT; FDLP; HL; PEPP; PH.
imitation label
GLT.
imitative word
GLT.
imitative words
DLTS.
immanence
DLTS.
immanent linguistics
GLT.
immediate constituent
FDLP; GLT/*IC*; ME/*383*.
immediate constituent analysis
FDLP/*immediate constituent*.
immediate constituents
EDSL/*32*; FDLP/*constituent*.
immediate speech
GLT.
immediate theater
ME/*158*.
immigrant language
GLT/*dialect*.
immovable speech organs
GLT.

imparisyllabic
GLT.
imperative
FDLP; FDLP/*command*.
imperative mood
ME/*383*.
imperfect aspect
ME/*384*.
imperfective
FDLP/*perfect*; FDLP/*aspect*; GLT.
imperfective aspect
EDSL/*307*.
imperfect rhyme
DLTS.
impersonal verb
GLT.
impingement (of an immediate situation)
GLT.
implicational universals
FDLP/*universal*.
implicature
FDLP.
implied author
DMCT; EDSL/*329*; HL.
implosion
GLT.
implosive
FDLP; GLT.
imprecation
DLTS; HL.
impression
DLTC; DLTS; HL.
Impressionism
OCAL; CODEL; DLTC; DLTS; HL; ME/*159*; OCEL; PEPP.
Impressionistic critic
DLDC/*criticism*.
impressionistic criticism
HL; PEPP.
imprimatur
DLTC; HL.
imprimatur
DLTS.

imprint
DLTC; DLTS.
improper compound
GLT.
impulsion
GLT.
impure marker
GLT.
inalienable
FDLP/*alienable*; FDLP.
inanimate
FDLP/*animate*.
inanimate noun
ME/*384*.
inanities
LGEP/*132*.
incantation
DLTC; DLTS; HL; PEPP.
Inca poetry
PEPP.
incapsulating language
GLT.
inceptive
FDLP; FDLP/*aspect*.
inchoative
EDSL/*311*; FDLP/*aspect*; FDLP/*inceptive*.
incident
DLTS; HL.
inciting moment
HL.
included
FDLP/*inclusion*.
included position
GLT.
included sentence
GLT/*utterance*.
inclusion
FDLP.
inclusive
FDLP/*disjunction*; FDLP/*inclusion*.
inclusive first person
GLT.

incompatibility
FDLP.
incompatible
FDLP/*incompatibility*.
incomplete closure
FDLP/*closure*.
incongruity
GLT.
incontiguous assimilation
GLT.
incontiguous dissimilation
GLT.
incorporated
FDLP/*incorporating*.
incorporating
FDLP/*polysynthetic*; FDLP.
incorporating language
GLT.
incorporating sounds
GLT.
incorporation
FDLP/*incorporating*; GLT.
incremental repetition
DLDC/*ballad*; DLTC; DLTS; HL; PEPP.
incubus
DLTS.
incunabula
DLTC; DLTS; ME/*160*; OCEL.
incunabulum
HL.
indeclinable
GLT.
indefinite pronoun
FDLP/*pronoun*.
indefinite pronouns
ME/*384*.
indefinite types
FDLP/*article*.
independent clause
ME/*384*.
independent element
GLT.

141 □ inferred situation

indeterminacy
EDSL/*237*; FDLP.
indeterminate
FDLP/*indeterminacy*.
index
DLTC; DLTS; EDSL/*86*; ME/*160*.
Index Expurgatorius
DLTC; HL; ME/*Index librorum prohibitorum, 160*.
Index Expurgatorius
CODEL; OCEL.
indexical
FDLP.
Index Librorum Prohibitorum
DLTC; HL; ME/*160*.
Index Librorum Prohibitorum
OCEL/*Index Expurgatorius*.
India
CR/*Index*.
Indian poetics
PEPP.
Indian poetry
PEPP.
Indian prosody
PEPP.
Indians
OCAL.
indicative
FDLP.
indicative mood
ME/*384*.
indicator
GLT.
indices
EDSL/*218*; FDLP/*indexical*.
indigenous language
GLT.
indignatio
CR/*Index*.
indirect
FDLP.
indirect object
FDLP/*object*; FDLP/*direct*; ME/*385*.

indirect objects
FDLP/*indirect*.
indirect question
FDLP/*direct*; ME/*385*.
indirect requests
FDLP/*felicity conditions*.
indirect satire
DLDC/*satire*; HL.
indirect speech
DLTC; FDLP/*indirect*.
indirect spelling
GLT.
indirect statement
ME/*385*.
Indo-European
DLTS; FDLP/*asterisk*; ME/*385*.
Indonesian poetry
PEPP.
induced
GLT.
inducer
GLT.
induction
CR/*Index*; DLTC; DLTS; HL; ME/*161*.
inductive leap
ME/*161*.
inductive reasoning
ME/*161*.
Industrial Revolution
HL.
inessive
FDLP/*case*.
infantilism
DLTS.
infants
FDLP/*breath group*.
infection
GLT.
inference
DLTS; FDLP/*axiomatic*; ME/*164*.
inferred situation
LGEP/*187*.

infinite set □ 142

infinite set
FDLP/*generative.*
infinitive
FDLP; ME/*385.*
infinitive phrase
ME/*385.*
infix
FDLP; GLT; ME/*385.*
infixation
FDLP/*affix*; FDLP/*infix.*
inflect
FDLP/*inflection.*
inflecting
EDSL/*12.*
inflecting language
FDLP/*inflection.*
inflection
DLTC; EDSL/*200*; FDLP; GLT; ME/*385.*
inflectional affix
GLT.
inflectional ending
GLT.
inflectional formatives
FDLP/*formative.*
inflectional language
GLT; ME/*385.*
inflectional process
FDLP/*derivation.*
inflectional suffix
ME/*386.*
inflexional
FDLP/*inflection.*
inflexion, inflexional
GLT.
influence
HL; ME/*164.*
informal
FDLP/*form.*
informal essay
DLDC/*essay*; DLTS; HL.
informant
FDLP; GLT.

information
EDSL/*255*; FDLP.
information structure
FDLP/*information.*
infra dig
DLTS.
infra-word
GLT.
-*ing* form
FDLP.
ingressive
FDLP; GLT.
ingressive stop
FDLP/*implosive.*
inherent features
FDLP.
inheritance
EDSL/*7.*
initial
FDLP.
initial glide
GLT.
initial mutation
GLT.
initial position
GLT.
initial rhyme
DLTC; PEPP; PH/*rhyme.*
initial-rhyme
DLDC/*versification.*
initial state
FDLP/*finite state grammar.*
initial symbol
FDLP.
initiating action
DLTC; PEPP.
initiation
FDLP/*initiator.*
initiator
FDLP; GLT.
injective
GLT.
inkhornists
HL.

143 □ intensive verbs

inkhorn terms
DLTC; GLT.
inlaut
GLT.
in medias res
DLDC/*epic*; DLTC; DLTS; HL; ME/*165*; PEPP.
In Memoriam stanza
DLTC.
In Memoriam stanza
PEPP; PH/*stanza*.
innate
FDLP.
innateness hypothesis
FDLP/*innate*.
inner closure
GLT.
innocent eye
DLDC/*point of view*.
innovation
GLT.
Inns of Chancery
CODEL/*Inns of Court*; OCEL.
Inns of Court
CODEL; HL; OCEL.
inns-of-court plays
ME/*165*.
innuendo
DLTS; HL; LGEP/*174*; ME/*165*.
inorganic
GLT.
input
GLT.
inscape
HL.
inscape and instress
DLTC; PEPP.
insertion
FDLP.
insert sentence
ME/*386*.
insinuatio
CR/*Index*.

inspiration
CR/*Index*; DLTC; GLT; PEPP.
instantaneous
FDLP.
instantaneous release
FDLP/*instantaneous*.
instinct
FDLP/*cultural transmission*.
instress
DLTC; HL; PEPP.
instrumental
FDLP/*case*; FDLP.
instrumental phonetics
FDLP/*phonetics*.
instrumental techniques
FDLP/*articulation*; FDLP/*acoustic phonetics*.
integration
GLT.
intellectual variations
GLT.
intensifier
FDLP; ME/*386*.
intension
FDLP; FDLP/*extension*; GLT.
intensional definition
FDLP/*intension*.
intensity
EDSL/*177*; GLT; PEPP.
intensity accent
GLT.
intensive
EDSL/*112*; FDLP.
intensive compound
GLT.
intensive constructions
FDLP/*intensive*.
intensive language course
GLT.
intensive pronoun
ME/*386*.
intensive verbs
FDLP/*intensive*.

intention
DLTC; DMCT; ME/*165*.
intentional fallacy
DLDC; DLTC; DLTS; HL; ME/*166*; PEPP.
intentions
PEPP.
interaction, linguistic
FDLP/*baby-talk*.
interchangeability
FDLP.
interdental
FDLP; GLT.
interdependence
GLT.
interference
FDLP; GLT.
interfering factors
FDLP/*communication*.
interior monologue
DLDC/*novel*; DLTC; DLTS; DMCT; HL; ME/*167*.
interjection
FDLP.
interjectional theory
GLT.
inter-laced rhyme
DLTC.
interlaced rhyme
HL; PH.
interlanguage
GLT.
inter-level
FDLP/*scale-and-category grammar*; FDLP; FDLP/*level*.
interlinguistics
GLT.
interlocking rhyme
HL; ME/*167*.
interlocutor
EDSL/*324*.
interlude
DLTC; DLTS; GLT; HL; ME/*167*; PEPP.

interludes
CODEL; OCEL.
intermediate
FDLP.
intermediate structure
ME/*386*.
intermezzi
DLTC.
intermittent closure
FDLP/*closure*.
internal adequacy
FDLP/*adequacy*.
internal change
GLT.
internal evidence
DLTC.
internal flection
GLT.
internalise
FDLP.
internalize
GLT.
internal linguistics
GLT.
internal modification
GLT.
internal open juncture
FDLP/*juncture*; GLT.
internal pressures
GLT.
internal proof
CR/*Index*.
internal reconstruction
FDLP/*reconstruction*; GLT.
internal rhyme
DLTC; DLTS; HL; ME/*168*; PEPP; PH/*rhyme*.
internal-rhyme
DLDC/*versification*.
internal sandhi
FDLP/*sandhi*; GLT.
international language
GLT.

145 □ introduction

International Phonetic Alphabet
FDLP/*International Phonetic Association*; ME/*387*; GLT/*IPA*.

International Phonetic Association
FDLP.

interpersonal
FDLP/*meaning*; FDLP.

interpolation
DLTS.

interpret
FDLP.

interpretant
EDSL/*85*.

interpretation
DMCT; PEPP/*942*.

interpretation, four-fold method
HL.

interpretation of the Scriptures
CR/*Index*.

interpretative capacity
EDSL/*105*.

interpretive
FDLP.

interpretive semantics
FDLP.

interrogation
CR/*Index*.

interrogative
FDLP.

interrogative mood
ME/*387*.

interrogative pronoun
ME/*387*.

interrogative pronouns
FDLP/*pronoun*.

interrogative sentence
ME/*387*.

interrogative word
ME/*387*.

interruptability
FDLP.

interrupted
FDLP.

intersection
FDLP/*overlapping*.

intersection (of acoustic allophones)
GLT.

inter-sentence relationships
FDLP/*focus*.

intertextuality
EDSL/*359*.

intervocalic
FDLP; GLT; ME/*387*.

interweaving
EDSL/*298*.

intonation
EDSL/*179*; FDLP/*command*; FDLP; GLT; ME/*388*.

intonation(al) pattern
GLT.

intonation contour
GLT; ME/*388*.

intonation formant
GLT.

intonation morpheme
GLT.

intralinguistic
FDLP/*feature*.

intransitive
FDLP/*transitivity*.

intransitive verb
ME/*388*.

intrigue comedy
HL.

intrinsic
FDLP.

intrinsic meaning
GLT.

intrinsic ordering
FDLP/*intrinsic*.

intrinsic semantic feature
EDSL/*266*.

introducing quotations
ME/*168*.

introduction
DLTC; DLTS; HL; ME/*168*.

introflection
GLT.
intrusion
FDLP.
intrusive consonant
GLT; ME/*388*.
intrusive narrator
HL.
intrusive vowel
GLT.
intuition
FDLP; PEPP/*947*.
intuitive
FDLP/*intuition*.
invariable
FDLP; GLT.
invariance
FDLP.
invariant
FDLP/*invariable*; GLT.
invariant alternation
GLT.
invective
CR/*Index*; DLDC/*satire*; DLTC; DLTS; HL.
inventio
ME/*168*.
invention
CR/*Index*; DLTC; HL; PEPP.
inventory
FDLP.
inverse derivation
GLT.
inverse spelling
GLT.
inversion
DLDC; DLTC; DLTS; EDSL/*277*; EDSL/*319*; FDLP; HL; ME/*168*; ME/*389*; PEPP; PH.
inverted
GLT.
inverted accent
PH.
inverted foot
PH/*substitution*.

inverted order question
FDLP/*yes-no question*.
inverted stress
PH/*substitution*.
investigative paper
ME/*168*.
invocation
DLDC/*figurative language*; DLTC; DLTS; HL; ME/*169*; PEPP.
Ionic
DLTC; HL; PH; DLTS; ME/*169*; PEPP.
IP
FDLP/*item and process*.
IPA
FDLP/*International Phonetic Association*; GLT.
IPA chart
FDLP/*chart*.
ipse dixit
DLTS; HL; ME/*169*.
Iranian poetry
PEPP.
Irish bull
DLDC/*bull*; DLTS.
Irish Literary Movement
HL.
Irish Literary Renaissance
DLTC; PEPP.
Irish Literary Revival
HL/*Irish Literary Movement*.
Irish literature
HL.
Irish poetry
PEPP.
Irish prosody
PEPP.
Irish Renaissance
HL/*Irish Literary Movement*.
Irish rhyme
PEPP.

irony
  CODEL; CR/*Index*; DLDC; DLTC; DLTS; DMCT; EDSL/*278*; HL; LGEP/*173*; LGEP/*171*; LGEP/*166*; ME/*169*; PEPP; PH.
irony of fate
  DLDC/*irony*.
irony of tone
  LGEP/*176*.
irregular
  FDLP/*regular*; FDLP.
irregular alternation
  GLT.
irregular forms
  FDLP/*analogy*.
irregularities
  FDLP/*irregular*.
irregular ode
  DLTC; HL; PH.
irregular verb
  ME/*389*.
irrelevant
  GLT.
irritated
  FDLP/*tone group*.
iso-
  FDLP; GLT.
isochronism
  DLTC; FDLP/*isochrony*; GLT; LGEP/*105*; PEPP.
isochrony
  FDLP.
isocolon
  CR/*Index*.
Isocratean tradition
  CR/*Index*.
Isocratic
  DLDC/*style*.
isogloss
  FDLP/*iso-*; GLT; ME/*389*.
isoglosses
  FDLP/*dialect*.
isoglottic line
  FDLP/*iso-*.
isogrades
  GLT.
isograph
  FDLP/*iso-*; GLT.
isolate
  GLT.
isolated
  FDLP; FDLP/*opposition*.
isolated opposition
  GLT.
isolating
  EDSL/*12*; FDLP.
isolating language
  GLT; ME/*390*.
isolating languages
  FDLP/*isolating*; FDLP/*analytic*.
isolation
  FDLP/*isolating*.
isolect
  FDLP/*iso-*.
isolex
  FDLP/*iso-*; GLT.
isolexic line
  GLT.
isometric
  EDSL/*192*.
isometrical syllable
  PH.
isomorph
  FDLP/*iso-*; GLT.
isomorphic
  FDLP/*isomorphism*.
isomorphic line
  GLT.
isomorphism
  EDSL/*22*; FDLP.
isonym
  OO.
isophone
  FDLP/*iso-*; GLT.
isophonic line
  GLT.
isopleth
  FDLP/*iso-*; GLT.

isoseme
  FDLP/*iso-*.
isosyllabic verse
  PH/*isometrical syllable*.
isosyllabism
  FDLP/*syllable-timed*; GLT.
isosyntagmic line
  GLT.
isotonic line
  GLT.
isotype
  GLT.
issue
  DLTC; HL.
Italian
  FDLP/*geminate*; FDLP/*diminutive*; FDLP/*clitic*.
Italianate gentleman
  ME/*170*.
Italian poetics
  PEPP.
Italian poetry
  PEPP.
Italian prosody
  PEPP.
Italian sonnet
  DLDC/*versification*; DLTC; DLTS; HL.

item
  FDLP.
item and arrangement
  FDLP.
item-and-arrangement
  GLT.
item and arrangement models
  FDLP/*morphology*.
item and process
  FDLP.
item-and-process
  GLT.
iterative
  FDLP/*aspect*.
iterative numeral
  GLT.
ithyphallic
  PEPP.
ithyphallic verse
  DLTC.
ivory tower
  DLTC; PEPP.
I.W.W.
  OCAL.

J

jabberwocky
DLTC; DLTS.
Jack Downing
OCAL.
Jacobean
DLDC; DLTS; ME/*171*.
Jacobean Age
DLTC; HL.
Jakobsonian
FDLP.
Jakobsonian hypothesis
FDLP/*Jakobsonian*.
Jamaica
FDLP/*creole*.
Jamestown
OCAL.
jamming
GLT.
Japanese
FDLP/*agglutinative*; FDLP/*honorific*.
Japanese poetry
PEPP.
Japhetic
GLT.
Japhetic theory
GLT.
jarcha
DLTC; PEPP.

jargon
DLTC; DLTS; EDSL/*59*; GLT; HL; ME/*391*; ME/*171*.
jargonophasias
EDSL/*163*.
Jarrow
CR/*Index*.
Javanese poetry
PEPP.
jaw
FDLP/*articulation*.
Jazz
OCAL; DLTS.
jazz poetry
DLTC.
je ne sais quoi
DLTS; PEPP.
je ne scai quoi
DLTC.
jeremiad
CODEL; DLTC; DLTS; HL; OCEL.
jest-book
DLTC; DLTS.
jest-books
HL; ME/*171*.
Jesuit drama
DLTC.

Jesuits
CODEL; CR/*Index*; HL; OCAL; OCEL.

jeu d'esprit
HL; ME/*171*.

jeu d'esprit
DLTC; DLTS.

jeu parti
DLTC.

Jewish rhetoric
CR/*Index*.

Jewish rhetoric in the Middle Ages
CR/*Index*.

Jews, in America
OCAL.

jig
HL.

jingle
DLTC; DLTS; PEPP.

jobelyn
GLT.

joc partit
PEPP.

Joe Miller
DLTC.

jogral
DLTC.

John Henry
OCAL.

Johnny Appleseed
OCAL.

John Phoenix
OCAL.

Johnsonian
DLTC.

Johnson's circle
HL.

Jonathan Oldstyle
OCAL.

Jones, Casey
OCAL.

Jones, Major
OCAL.

jongleur
DLTS; HL.

jongleur
DLTC; PEPP; PH/*troubadour*.

joruri
DLTC.

Josiah Allen's Wife
OCAL.

journal
DLTC; HL; ME/*171*.

journalese
DLTC; DLTS.

journalism
DLTC.

judgment
CR/*Index*.

judicial critic
DLDC/*criticism*.

judicial criticism
HL; PEPP.

judicial oratory
CR/*Index*.

Jugendstil
DLTC; PEPP.

junăcke pesme
DLTC.

junction
EDSL/*240*; GLT.

juncture
DLTS; EDSL/*55*; FDLP; GLT; ME/*391*.

Junggrammatiker
GLT.

Jungian
DLTS.

Jungian criticism
HL.

Junto Club
OCAL/*The Junto*.

juries
CR/*Index*.

justice
CR/*Index*.

Juvenalian
 DLTS.
Juvenalian satire
 DLDC/*satire*; HL.
juvenilia
 DLTC; DLTS; HL.

juxtaposing language
 GLT.
juxtaposition
 DLTS.

K

kabuki
  DLTC.
kabuki
  DLTS.
kabuki plays
  HL.
Kailyard School
  CODEL; DLTC; HL; OCEL.
Kamers van Retorica
  CR/*Index*.
kana
  GLT.
kana majiri
  GLT.
kanji
  GLT.
Kannada poetry
  PEPP.
karagöz
  DLTC.
karma
  DLTS.
kasa
  DLTC.
Kashmiri poetry
  PEPP.
katakana
  GLT.
katharevousa
  GLT.

katharsis
  DMCT; ME/*173*; PEPP.
Katz-Postal hypothesis
  FDLP.
keening
  DLTS.
keneme
  DLTC.
kenning
  DLTC; DLTS; HL; LGEP/*138*;
  ME/*173*; PEPP; PH.
kennings
  DLDC/*periphrasis*.
Kentucky Tragedy
  OCAL.
kernel
  FDLP; GLT.
kernel sentence
  FDLP/*kernel*; ME/*392*.
kernel string
  EDSL/*242*; FDLP/*kernel*.
kerygma
  CR/*Index*.
key
  FDLP; GLT.
key novel
  DLTC.
kharja
  DLTC; PEPP.

kinaesthetic methods
FDLP/*articulatory phonetics.*
kind
DLTC; HL; PEPP.
kine
GLT.
kinema
GLT.
kineme
GLT.
kinemes
FDLP/*kinesics.*
kinemic description
GLT.
kinemics
GLT.
kinemorph
GLT.
kinemorpheme
GLT.
kines
FDLP/*kinesics.*
kinesics
FDLP; GLT.
kinesthetic feedback
GLT.
kinetic
DMCT.
kinetic consonant
GLT.
kinetic imagery
ME/*173.*
King Cotton
OCAL.
King George's War
OCAL/*French and Indian War.*
King's English
DLTC; DLTS.
kinships
EDSL/*9.*
kinship vocabulary
FDLP/*component.*
kismet
DLTS.

kiss
FDLP/*bilabial.*
Kit-Cat Club
CODEL; HL; OCEL.
kitchen-sink drama
DLTC.
kitsch
DLTC; ME/*173.*
Kleen's grammar
EDSL/*229.*
Klondike gold rush
OCAL.
klucht
DLTC.
Knickerbocker Group
DLTC; HL; OCAL.
Knights of the Golden Circle
OCAL/*Copperheads.*
Knights of the Round Table
DLTS.
Knights of the White Camelia
OCAL/*Ku Klux Klan.*
Knittelvers
DLTC; PEPP.
knowledge
CR/*Index.*
knowledge and poetry
PEPP.
knowledge, structure of
CR/*Index.*
Know-Nothing movement
OCAL.
koine
GLT.
kommos
DLTC.
Koran
CODEL; HL; OCEL.
Korean poetry
PEPP.
Ku Klux Klan
OCAL.
Kulturkreislehre
GLT.

155 □ *kyrielle*

Künstlerroman
  DLDC/*novel*; DLTC; DLTS; HL.
Kunstlied
  DLTC.
Kunstmärchen
  DLTC.
kviðuháttr
  DLTC.
kvǫuháttr
  PEPP.

kymogram
  GLT.
kymograph
  GLT.
kyŏnggich'aega
  DLTC.
kyrielle
  DLTC.

L

L
   FDLP/*diglossia*.
label
   FDLP.
labeled parentheses
   EDSL/*229*.
labeled-tree diagram
   ME/*393*.
labelled bracketing
   FDLP/*label*; FDLP/*bracketing*.
label names
   DLTC.
labial
   FDLP.
labial consonant
   ME/*393*.
labialisation
   FDLP/*articulation*; FDLP/*labial*.
labialization
   GLT.
labialized velar
   GLT.
labio-dental
   FDLP.
labiodental
   GLT.
labio-dental consonant
   ME/*393*.
labiopalatalization
   GLT.
labio-velar
   FDLP.
labiovelar
   GLT.
laboratory phonetics
   GLT.
laconic
   CODEL; OCEL.
laconic style
   ME/*174*.
lacuna
   DLTS.
LAD
   FDLP/*acquisition*; FDLP.
lag
   FDLP; GLT.
lai
   DLDC; DLTC; HL/*lay*; PEPP.
laisse
   PEPP.
laisse
   DLTC.
Lake Poets
   CODEL; DLTC; OCEL; PEPP.
Lake School
   CODEL/*Lake Poets*; HL.
Lake School, The
   OCEL/*Lake Poets*.
lallations
   EDSL/*156*.

lambdacism
GLT.
Lambs, The
OCAL.
lament
DLTC; DLTS; DMCT; HL; PEPP.
lamina
FDLP/*laminal.*
laminal
FDLP; GLT.
lamino-alveolar
FDLP/*laminal.*
lamino-dental
FDLP/*laminal.*
lampoon
CODEL; DLDC/*satire*; DLTC; DLTS; HL; ME/*174*; OCEL; PEPP.
Landsmål
GLT.
language
DLTS; DMCT; EDSL/*118*; FDLP; FDLP/*accent*; GLT; ME/*393.*
language acquisition device
FDLP/*acquisition.*
language blends
EDSL/*59.*
language boundary
GLT.
language containing formulae
FDLP/*formulaic language.*
language disorder
EDSL/*161.*
language disorders
FDLP/*applied linguistics.*
language engineering
GLT.
language family
GLT.
language groups
FDLP/*comparative.*
language identification
GLT.

language input
FDLP/*baby-talk.*
language laboratory
FDLP/*language.*
language, mixed
EDSL/*59.*
language, national
EDSL/*59.*
language of colonization
GLT.
language of immigration
GLT.
language planning
FDLP/*language.*
language shift
GLT.
languages in contact
GLT.
language-specific mechanism
FDLP/*analysis-by-synthesis.*
language state
EDSL/*137.*
language system
FDLP/*system*; GLT.
language universals
FDLP/*universal.*
langue
EDSL/*118*; FDLP; GLT; ME/*393.*
langue **and** *parole*
DLTC.
larnyx
FDLP/*air-stream mechanism.*
laryng(e)al
GLT.
laryngealisation
FDLP/*larynx.*
laryngealised sounds
FDLP/*creak.*
laryngeal modulation
EDSL/*157.*
laryngeals
FDLP/*larynx.*

laryngeal theory
GLT.
laryngectomy
FDLP/*cavity*.
laryngograph
FDLP/*larynx*.
laryngoscope
FDLP/*larynx*; GLT.
larynx
FDLP.
last-cyclic rules
FDLP/*cycle*.
lateral
FDLP; GLT.
lateral areas
GLT.
lateral sound
ME/*303*.
Late Victorian Age, 1870-1901
HL.
Latin
FDLP/*agreement*; FDLP/*correspond*; FDLP/*govern*; FDLP/*concord*; FDLP/*fusional*.
Latin grammar
FDLP/*case*.
Latinism
DLTC; DLTS.
Latin poetics
PEPP.
Latin poetry
PEPP.
Latin prosody
PEPP.
Latter-Day Saints
OCAL/*Mormons*.
Latvian poetry
PEPP.
lauda
DLTC; PEPP.
laureate
DLTC; DLTS; HL; ME/*174*; PEPP/*951*.
Lautgesetz
GLT.

Lautverschiebung
GLT.
lawcourts and lawyers
CR/*Index*.
law of distribution
GLT.
law, Roman
CR/*Index*.
lax
FDLP/*tension*; FDLP; GLT.
lax vowel
ME/*393*.
lay
CODEL; DLDC/*lai*; DLTC; DLTS; HL; ME/*lai, 174*; OCEL; PEPP/*lai*; PH.
layering
FDLP.
laying bare
EDSL/*263*.
lead
FDLP.
leap
GLT.
learnability
FDLP.
learned word
GLT.
learning
FDLP/*cultural transmission*.
Leather-Stocking Tales
OCAL.
leave-taking
FDLP/*adjacency pair*.
lect
FDLP.
lectio difficilior
DLTC.
lectionary
DLTC.
left-branching
FDLP; FDLP/*depth hypothesis*.
left recursive
FDLP/*left-branching*.

legema
  GLT.
legend
  DLTC; DLTS; HL; ME/*174*.
legitimate theater
  DLTS; HL.
legitimate theatre
  DLTC.
Leich
  DLTC; PEPP.
leitmotif
  HL.
Leitmotif
  EDSL/*220*; DLDC/*motif*; DLTC.
leitmotiv
  DLTS.
lemma
  DLTC.
length
  FDLP; PEPP.
lengthening
  GLT.
lenis
  FDLP; GLT/*lene*; ME/*393*.
lenition
  GLT.
lento forms
  GLT.
Leonine rhyme
  DLTC; HL; PEPP; PH/*rhyme*.
Leonine verse
  CODEL; DLTS; OCEL.
le poète maudit
  DLDC/*classic*.
Lesbian
  DLTS.
letrilla
  DLTC; PEPP.
letter
  DLTC.
letteraturizzazione
  CR/*Index*.
letter in verse
  PEPP.

letterpress
  DLTS; HL.
letters
  DLTS; FDLP/*allo-*; HL.
letter-writing
  CR/*Index*.
level
  FDLP/*nucleus*; FDLP.
leveling
  GLT.
leveling of inflections
  ME/*393*.
levels
  EDSL/*238*.
level-skipping
  FDLP.
levels of articulation
  GLT.
levels of meaning
  ME/*174*.
levels of usage
  ME/*394*.
level stress
  DLTC.
level tone
  FDLP/*level*.
Lewis and Clark Expedition
  OCAL/*Lewis, Meriwether*.
lexeme
  EDSL/*265*; FDLP; GLT; ME/*394*.
lexical
  GLT.
lexical ambiguity
  FDLP/*ambiguity*.
lexical category
  GLT.
lexical change
  GLT.
lexical cluster
  GLT.
lexical collocation
  GLT.

lexical component
FDLP/*base*.
lexical cycles
FDLP/*cycle*.
lexical elements
EDSL/*10*.
lexical entries
FDLP/*entry*; FDLP.
lexical field
FDLP/*field*; FDLP.
lexical form
GLT.
lexical formatives
FDLP/*formative*.
lexical gap
FDLP.
lexicalise
FDLP.
lexicalist
FDLP.
lexical item
FDLP.
lexical meaning
FDLP; GLT; ME/*394*.
lexical moneme
GLT.
lexical morpheme
FDLP/*morpheme*.
lexical properties
ME/*394*.
lexical selection
FDLP.
lexical sets
FDLP.
lexical stress
FDLP/*stress*.
lexical structure
FDLP.
lexical substitution
FDLP.
lexical system
FDLP.
lexical tone
FDLP/*tone*.

lexical transformation
FDLP.
lexical verb
FDLP/*verb*.
lexical verbs
FDLP/*auxiliary*.
lexical word
GLT.
lexical words
FDLP.
lexicographer
DLTC.
lexicography
DLTC; DLTS; FDLP; GLT; HL; ME/*397*.
lexicology
FDLP; GLT.
lexicon
DLTC; DLTS; EDSL/*51*; FDLP; GLT; HL; LGEP/*37*; ME/*397*.
lexicostatistics
FDLP; GLT.
lexie
EDSL/*217*.
lexis
DLTC; DMCT; FDLP; GLT.
lexotactics
FDLP/*tactics*.
liaison
DLTC; FDLP; GLT.
libel
DLTS.
liberal arts
CR/*Index*.
liberal roles
LGEP/*12*.
libido
DLTS.
Library of Congress
OCAL.
library paper
ME/*179*.
libretto
DLTC; DLTS; HL.

Lied
  DLTC.
ligative article
  GLT.
ligature
  DLTS.
light base
  GLT.
light ending
  DLTC; HL; PH/*feminine ending*.
light opera
  CODEL/*opera*; HL.
light rhyme
  DLTC; PH/*rhyme*.
light stress
  DLTC; PH.
light syllable
  GLT.
light verse
  DLDC; DLTC; DLTS; HL; ME/*179*; PEPP; PH.
light vowel
  GLT.
ligne donnée
  DLTC.
limerick
  CODEL; DLDC/*light verse*; DLTC; DLTS; HL; ME/*179*; OCEL; PEPP; PH.
limited edition
  DLTC; DLTS.
limited omniscience
  DLDC/*point of view*.
line
  DLTC; EDSL/*187*; FDLP/*accent*; PEPP.
linear
  EDSL/*234*; FDLP.
linearity
  CR/*Index*; EDSL/*107*; FDLP/*linear*.
linear opposition
  GLT.
linear phoneme
  GLT.

linear writing
  GLT.
line endings
  DLTC; PEPP.
line of verse
  DLTS.
lingo
  DLTC; DLTS.
lingua franca
  DLTS; EDSL/*59*; FDLP; GLT.
lingual
  FDLP.
linguist
  FDLP; ME/*397*.
linguistic
  EDSL/*254*; FDLP.
linguistically significant generalisation
  FDLP.
linguistic analysis
  FDLP/*applied linguistics*; GLT.
linguistic anthropology
  EDSL/*64*; FDLP/*anthropological linguistics*.
linguistic arbitrariness
  EDSL/*130*.
linguistic areas
  GLT.
linguistic association
  EDSL/*60*.
linguistic atlas
  FDLP/*dialect*; FDLP/*iso-*; GLT; ME/*398*.
linguistic category
  EDSL/*111*.
Linguistic Circle of Copenhagen
  FDLP/*glossematics*.
Linguistic Circle of Prague
  FDLP/*Prague School*.
linguistic competence
  FDLP/*communication*.
linguistic convention
  LGEP/*12*.
linguistic criteria
  FDLP/*criteria*.

linguistic determinism
FDLP/*relativity*.

linguistic distribution
GLT.

linguistic environment
FDLP/*environment*.

linguistic form
GLT.

linguistic forms
FDLP/*form*.

linguistic geography
FDLP/*dialect*; GLT.

linguistic interaction
FDLP/*address*; FDLP/*ethnolinguistics*.

linguistic island
GLT.

linguistic metalanguage
FDLP/*metalanguage*.

linguistic minority
GLT.

linguistic norm (doctrine of the)
GLT.

linguistic ontogeny
GLT.

linguistic philosophy
FDLP/*philosophical linguistics*.

linguistic relativity
FDLP/*relativity*.

linguistic replacement
GLT.

linguistics
DLTC; DLTS; EDSL/*294*; FDLP; FDLP/*accent*; GLT; HL; ME/*397*.

linguistics and poetics
PEPP.

linguistic science
FDLP/*linguistics*.

linguistic sciences
FDLP/*phonetics*; FDLP/*linguistics*.

linguistics, descriptive
EDSL/*137*.

linguistic segmentation
EDSL/*135*.

linguistic semantics
FDLP/*semantics*.

linguistic sign
FDLP/*sign*; GLT.

linguistic substrate
FDLP/*substrate*.

linguistic system
FDLP/*system*.

linguistic theory
EDSL/*40*.

linguistic thought
FDLP/*Cartesian linguistics*.

linguistic typology
GLT.

linguistic units
EDSL/*134*.

linguo
FDLP/*lingual*.

linguolabial
FDLP/*lingual*.

linkage
FDLP/*co-ordination*; GLT.

linked rhyme
DLTC; HL; PH/*rhyme*.

linked sentences
EDSL/*285*.

linked sonnet
DLTC.

linking
EDSL/*298*; EDSL/*268*; FDLP; GLT.

linking verb
ME/*398*.

link sonnet
HL.

link word
GLT.

lipogram
DLTC; DLTS.

lip position
GLT.

lips
FDLP/*articulation*.

liquid
FDLP; GLT.

lira
DLTC; PEPP.

list
GLT.

listening discrimination
GLT.

litany
DLTC; DLTS; HL.

literacy
GLT.

literacy coefficient
GLT.

literal
DLTC; DLTS; HL.

literal language
ME/*180*.

Literary and Philosophical Society of Newport
OCAL.

literary ballad
DLTS; HL; PH/*ballad*.

literary ballads
DLDC/*ballad*.

Literary Club, The
HL.

literary criticism
CR/*Index*.

literary epic
DLTS; HL.

literary history
EDSL/*144*.

literary language
GLT.

literary prizes and grants
ME/*180*.

literary rhetoric
CR/*Index*.

literary stylistics
FDLP/*stylistics*.

literati
DLTC.

literature
DLDC; DLTC; DLTS; DMCT; FDLP/*accent*.

literature of escape
DLTC.

literature of sensibility
DLDC/*sentimental*.

Lithuanian
FDLP/*length*; FDLP/*chroneme*.

Lithuanian poetry
PEPP.

litōtes
OCEL.

litotes
CODEL; DLDC/*figurative language*; DLTC; DLTS; EDSL/*278*; GLT; HL; LGEP/*166*; LGEP/*168*; LGEP/*170*; ME/*182*; PEPP.

littérateur
DLTS.

litterateur
HL.

littérateur
DLTC.

Little Giant
OCAL.

little magazine
DLTS; HL; OCAL.

little magazines
ME/*182*.

Littlepage Manuscripts
OCAL.

little theater
DLTS; OCAL.

little theater movement
HL.

liturgical coefficient
GLT.

liturgical drama
DLTC; DLTS; HL.

liturgical language
GLT.

165 □ logical inference

liturgy
DLTS.
Liverpool Poets
DLTC.
living newspaper
DLTC.
living theater
ME/*183*.
livre à clef
DLTC.
ljóðaháttr
PEPP.
ljoðaháttr
DLTC.
l.m.
PEPP.
loa
DLTC.
loan
FDLP; GLT.
loan blend
GLT.
loan blends
FDLP/*loan*.
loan-shift
GLT.
loan shifts
FDLP/*loan*.
loan translation
GLT.
loan translations
FDLP/*loan*; FDLP/*calque*.
loan word
DLTC; GLT; ME/*399*.
loan words
FDLP/*borrow*; FDLP/*loan*.
local
FDLP/*dialect*; FDLP.
local color
DLTS; ME/*183*; OCAL.
local color movement
DLDC/*realism*.
local color writing
HL.

local colour
DLTC.
locale
DLTS; HL.
localism
DLTS; FDLP; GLT; ME/*399*.
localist
FDLP/*case*; FDLP/*localism*.
localization
GLT.
locational
FDLP/*case*.
locative
FDLP; FDLP/*case*; ME/*399*.
loc. cit.
DLTS.
loci
CR/*Index*.
loco citato
DLTC.
locus
FDLP.
locus communis
CR/*Index*.
locution
DLTS; HL.
locutionary
FDLP/*locus*.
locutionary act
EDSL/*343*.
Loeb Classical Library
OCAL.
logaoedic
DLTC; HL; PEPP; PH.
logic
CR/*Index*.
logical aggregate
EDSL/*195*.
logical conjunction
GLT/*disjunction*.
logical hexagon
EDSL/*115*.
logical inference
EDSL/*286*.

logical order
DLTS.
logical positivism
HL.
logical stress
DLTC; PH.
logical structure
PH/*structure*.
logicistic
EDSL/*286*.
logocentrism
EDSL/*349*.
logogram
GLT.
logograph
GLT.
logographers
CR/*Index*.
logography
EDSL/*194*.
logogriph
DLTC.
logomachy
DLTC.
logopoeia
DLTC; PH.
logorrhoea
DLTC.
logos
GLT.
logos: **Christian**
CR/*Index*.
logos: **in Aristotle**
CR/*Index*.
logosyllabic
GLT; GLT.
logotactics
GLT.
log-rolling
DLTC.
Lollards
HL; ME/*185*.
London
FDLP/*area*; FDLP/*dialect*.
London-influenced dialects
FDLP/*area*.
long
FDLP/*length*; PEPP.
long measure
DLTC; DLTS; HL; PH/*common measure*.
long meter
PEPP.
long syllable
DLTC.
Loop
OCAL/*Chicago*.
loopback
FDLP/*locus*; FDLP/*backlooping*.
loose and periodic sentence
DLTC.
loose sentence
DLDC/*style*; DLTS; HL; ME/*185*.
loose vowel
GLT.
Los Angeles
OCAL.
loss of inflection
GLT.
loss of words
GLT.
lost generation
DLTS; HL; OCAL.
Lotos Club
OCAL.
loudness
FDLP; FDLP/*attitudinal*; GLT.
love casuistry
ME/*187*.
love poetry
DLTC.
low
EDSL/*155*; FDLP.
low burlesque
DLDC/*burlesque*.
low comedy
DLTC; HL.

167 □ **lysiody**

Lowell Institute
OCAL.
lower
FDLP.
lower verb
FDLP/*higher*.
Low Latin
GLT.
low style
DLDC/*style*.
low vowel
FDLP/*close*; GLT; ME/*399*.
Luganda
FDLP/*length*.
lullaby
DLTC; DLTS.
lungs
FDLP/*air-stream mechanism*.
lü-shih
DLTC.
Luska, Sydney
OCAL.

Lutherans
OCAL.
Lyceum
CR/*Index*.
lyceums
OCAL.
lying
FDLP/*co-operative principle*.
Lyon School
DLTC.
lyric
CODEL; DLDC; DLTC; DLTS; DMCT; EDSL/*153*; HL; ME/*187*; PEPP; PH.
lyrical caesura
PEPP.
lyrical drama
HL.
lyrisme romantique
DLTC; PEPP.
lysiody
DLTC.

M

Mabinogion
 HL.
Mabinogion, The
 CODEL; OCEL.
macabre
 DLTC; DLTS.
macaronic
 DLTC; DLTS; ME/*188*.
macaronic verse
 CODEL; DLDC; HL; OCEL;
 PEPP; PH.
Machiavel
 DLTC.
machinery
 DLDC/*epic*; DLTC; HL.
machine translation
 GLT.
macrocosm
 DLTS.
macrokinesic recording
 GLT.
macrolinguistics
 FDLP; GLT.
macrology
 DLTC; DLTS.
macron
 DLTC; DLTS; GLT; HL; PEPP;
 PH/*mora*.
macronym
 OO.

macrosegment
 GLT.
madness
 CR/*Index*.
madness, poetic
 PEPP.
madrigal
 DLTC; DLTS; HL; ME/*188*;
 PEPP; PH.
magazine
 DLTC; DLTS; HL.
magic
 CR/*Index*.
magnum opus
 DLTC; DLTS; HL.
magody
 DLTC.
Magyar poetry
 PEPP.
main
 FDLP.
main clause
 FDLP/*clause*; FDLP/*main*.
main clause sentence
 ME/*400*.
Maithili poetry
 PEPP.
major
 FDLP.

major class feature ☐ **170**

major class feature
  FDLP.
major form class
  GLT.
Major Jones
  OCAL.
major premise
  ME/*189*.
major sentence
  FDLP/*major*.
major term
  ME/*189*.
majuscule
  GLT.
makeshift language
  GLT.
málaháttr
  DLTC; PEPP.
malaprop
  DLDC.
malapropism
  DLDC/*malaprop*; DLTS; GLT; HL; ME/*189*.
malaproprism
  DLTC.
Malayalam poetry
  PEPP.
Malay poetry
  PEPP.
malediction
  DLTS; HL.
male rhymes
  CODEL.
male speech
  FDLP/*area*.
malformation
  GLT.
mal mariée
  DLTC; PEPP.
mammon
  DLTS.
Mandarin
  FDLP/*dialect*.

Manichaeism
  HL.
manifest
  FDLP.
manifestation
  EDSL/*22*; FDLP/*manifest*.
manifestation mode
  FDLP/*manifest*.
manifest destiny
  OCAL.
manifesto
  DLTC; DLTS.
manifest story-line
  ME/*189*.
manner
  FDLP/*manner of articulation*;
  FDLP/*co-operative principle*;
  FDLP/*adverb*.
manner adverbials
  FDLP/*manner of articulation*.
mannerism
  CR/*Index*; DLDC/*style*; DLTC; DLTS; DMCT; PEPP.
manner (mode) of articulation
  GLT.
manner of articulation
  FDLP.
manner of discourse
  FDLP/*manner of articulation*.
manners
  DMCT; HL.
manqué
  DLTS.
mantra
  DLTC.
Mantua
  CR/*Index*.
manuscript
  DLTC; DLTS.
manuscript, medieval
  HL.
mapped
  FDLP/*mapping*.
mapping
  FDLP.

171 □ Massachusetts Institute of Technology

maqāma
　DLTC.
Marathi poetry
　PEPP.
Märchen
　DLDC/*short story*; DLTC; DLTS;
　HL.
margin
　FDLP; GLT.
marginal
　GLT.
marginal archaism
　GLT.
marginal area
　GLT.
marginal auxiliaries
　FDLP/*auxiliary*.
marginalia
　DLTC; DLTS; HL.
marginally grammatical
　FDLP/*acceptability*.
marginal sounds
　GLT.
margin of security
　GLT.
Maria del Occidente
　OCAL.
Marinism
　DLTC; DLTS; HL; PEPP.
Mariolatry
　DLTS.
Marivaudage
　DLTC.
mark
　GLT.
marked
　EDSL/*112*; FDLP/*markedness*.
marked member
　GLT.
markedness
　FDLP/*markedness*; FDLP.
marker
　FDLP; GLT; ME/*400*.

marking
　FDLP/*markedness*.
Mark Littleton
　OCAL.
mark of correlation
　FDLP/*correlation*; GLT.
Marprelate Controversy
　HL.
Marxism
　HL.
Marxist
　DLTS.
Marxist criticism
　DLDC/*criticism*; PEPP.
masculine caesura
　DLTC.
masculine ending
　DLDC/*versification*; DLTS; HL;
　PEPP; PH/*feminine ending*.
masculine rhyme
　DLDC/*versification*; DLTC; HL;
　PEPP.
masculine rhymes
　CODEL.
mask
　DLDC/*drama*; DLDC/*persona*;
　DMCT.
masked comedy
　HL.
masks
　OCEL.
masque
　DLDC/*drama*; DLTC; DLTS;
　HL; ME/*189*; PEPP.
masques
　CODEL; OCEL/*masks*.
mass
　FDLP.
Massachusetts Bay Company
　OCAL.
Massachusetts Historical Society
　OCAL.
Massachusetts Institute of Technology
　FDLP/*MIT*.

mass literature
ME/*190*.
mass noun
GLT; ME/*400*.
mass word
GLT.
Mastersingers
PEPP.
material content
GLT.
materialism
DLTS.
material style
CR/*Index*.
mathematical linguistics
FDLP/*linguistics*; FDLP; PEPP.
mathematics
FDLP/*bracketing*.
matin
DLTS; HL.
matrix
DLTS; EDSL/*231*; FDLP.
matrix sentence
FDLP/*matrix*; ME/*400*.
matronym
OO.
matronymic
GLT.
matter
EDSL/*21*.
maxim
DLDC/*aphorism*; DLTC; DLTS; HL; ME/*190*.
maxims
CR/*Index*.
maximum scene technique
DLTC.
maximum silence
GLT.
Mayflower
OCAL.
MDP
FDLP; FDLP/*minimal-distance principle*.

meaning
DLTC; EDSL/*122*; FDLP; HL; LGEP/*39*.
meaning-changing
FDLP.
meaning, chief
EDSL/*257*.
meaning effect
EDSL/*122*.
meaningful
FDLP/*meaning*.
meaning, head
EDSL/*257*.
meaningless
FDLP/*empty*.
meaning of meaning
FDLP/*meaning*.
meaning-preserving
FDLP/*meaning-changing*.
meaning, problem of
PEPP.
mean length
FDLP/*length*.
mean length of utterance
FDLP.
measure
DLTC; DLTS; EDSL/*187*; HL; LGEP/*106*; PEPP; PH.
measures
LGEP/*63*.
mechanic form
DLTC.
mechanism
DLTC; EDSL/*31*.
mechanistic
FDLP/*behaviourism*.
mechanistic theory
GLT.
mechanistic theory of change
GLT.
medial
FDLP; GLT.
medial accent
GLT.

173 □ mentalism

medial alliteration
DLDC/*versification*.
medial articulation
FDLP/*acute*.
medial censura
PH/*cesura*.
medial consonant
GLT.
medial position
GLT.
median resonant
GLT.
mediation
EDSL/*70*.
medieval
DLTS.
medieval drama
HL.
medievalism
DLTC.
medieval poetics
PEPP.
medieval poetry
PEPP.
medieval romance
HL; ME/*190*; PEPP.
mediopalatal
GLT.
meditative
FDLP/*rate*.
meditative poetry
HL.
medium
FDLP.
medium vowel
GLT.
meiosis
CODEL; DLTC; DLTS; HL; OCEL; PEPP.
Meistergesang
DLTC.
Meistersinger
PEPP.

meiurus
DLTC; PEPP.
melete
CR/*Index*.
melic poetry
DLTC; HL; PEPP.
melioration
GLT.
meliorism
HL.
mellow
FDLP.
melodrama
CODEL; DLDC/*drama*; DLTC; DLTS; HL; ME/*190*; OCEL.
melody
FDLP/*intonation*; GLT.
Melopoeia
PH/*logopoeia*; DLTC.
mels
FDLP/*pitch*.
melting pot
OCAL.
memoir
DLDC/*biography*; DLTS.
memoirs
DLTC; HL.
memorabilia
DLTS.
memory
CR/*Index*.
Menippean
DLTS.
Menippean satire
DLDC/*satire*; DLTC; HL.
Mennonites
OCAL.
menology
DLTC.
mens sana
DLTS.
mentalism
EDSL/*31*; FDLP.

mentalistic linguistics ☐ **174**

mentalistic linguistics
  FDLP/*mentalism.*
mentalistic theory
  GLT.
merde, mystique de la
  DLTC.
merge
  FDLP/*merger.*
merged form
  GLT.
merged verb
  GLT.
merger
  FDLP.
merisms
  EDSL/*173.*
merismus
  DLTC.
Merry Mount
  OCAL.
mesode
  DLTC; PEPP.
mesostich
  DLTC; DLTS; HL; PEPP.
message
  FDLP/*communication.*
message information
  GLT.
messenger
  DLTC.
mester de clerecia
  DLTC.
mesur tri-thrawiad
  DLTC; PEPP.
meta-
  HL.
metacriticism
  HL; PEPP/*951.*
metafiction
  HL.
metahpor, animistic
  LGEP/*158.*
metalanguage
  EDSL/*23*; FDLP; GLT.

metalepsis
  DLTC.
metalinguistic
  EDSL/*341.*
metalinguistics
  FDLP/*metalanguage*; GLT; ME/*400.*
metamorphosis
  DLTS.
metanalysis
  FDLP/*error*; GLT.
metanoia
  DLTC.
metanym
  OO.
metaphone
  GLT.
metaphony
  GLT.
metaphor
  CODEL; CR/*Index*; DLDC/*figurative language*; DLTC; DLTS; DMCT; EDSL/*278*; GLT; HL; LGEP/*49*; LGEP/*153*; LGEP/*173*; LGEP/*156*; LGEP/*150*; ME/*191*; OCEL; PEPP; PH.
metaphor, animistic
  LGEP/*158.*
metaphor, compound
  LGEP/*159.*
metaphor, concretive
  LGEP/*158.*
metaphor, extended
  LGEP/*159.*
metaphor, humanizing ('anthropomorphic')
  LGEP/*158.*
metaphoric
  EDSL/*111.*
metaphor, mixed
  LGEP/*161.*
metaphor, synaesthetic
  LGEP/*158.*
metaphrase
  GLT.

metaphysical
DLTC; DMCT.
metaphysical conceit
DLDC/*metaphysical poets*; HL.
metaphysical poetry
DLTS; HL; PEPP; PH.
Metaphysical Poets
CODEL; ME/*192*; OCEL; DLDC.
metaphysical verse
OCAL.
metaplasm
GLT.
metastasis
DLTC.
metatheatre
DLTC.
metathesis
CODEL; DLTC; DLTS; FDLP; GLT; HL; ME/*400*; OCEL.
metempsychosis
DLTS.
meter
DLDC/*versification*; DLTC; DLTS; EDSL/*186*; HL; ME/*192*; PEPP.
Methodism
OCAL.
metonomy
CODEL.
metonym
ME/*195*; OO.
metonymic
EDSL/*111*.
metonymy
DLDC/*figurative language*; DLTC; DLTS; EDSL/*278*; GLT; HL; LGEP/*152*; ME/*195*; PEPP; PH.
metre
CODEL; DMCT; FDLP/*accent*; LGEP/*103*; OCEL; PH.
metre, English
LGEP/*111*.

metrical
FDLP/*rhythm*.
metrical accent
HL.
metrical pause
PH; PH/*compensation*.
metrical romance
DLTC; DLTS; HL; ME/*196*; PEPP.
metrical stress
PH/*metre*.
metrical variation
LGEP/*121*.
metrical variations
DLTC; PEPP.
metric pause
EDSL/*187*.
metric prose
EDSL/*188*.
metrics
DLTS; FDLP; HL; ME/*196*.
metric, simplicity
FDLP/*simplicity*.
Metricus
PEPP.
metron
DLTC; PEPP.
metronym
OO.
Metropolitan Museum of Art
OCAL.
Metropolitan Opera Company
OCAL.
Mexican poetry
PEPP.
Mexican War
OCAL.
mezzo-zeugma
DLTC.
M-H-Q
FDLP/*modification*.
microcosm
DLTS.

microkinesic recording
GLT.

microlinguistics
FDLP; GLT.

microsegment
GLT.

mid
FDLP.

middle
EDSL/*155*.

Middle Border
OCAL.

Middle Colonies
OCAL.

middle comedy
DLTC.

middle consonant
GLT.

Middle English
CODEL; DLTS; HL; ME/*401*; OCEL.

Middle English period
HL.

middle rhyme
DLTC; HL.

middle style
CR/*Index*; DLDC/*style*; LGEP/*17*.

middle term
ME/*196*.

middle voice
FDLP/*voice*; GLT.

middle vowel
GLT.

Middle West
OCAL.

Midland dialect
ME/*401*.

mid verb
ME/*402*.

mid vowel
FDLP/*close*.

mid-vowel
GLT.

Mieza
CR/*Index*.

migration theory
GLT.

Milan
CR/*Index*.

miles gloriosus
DLDC/*braggart soldier*; DLTC; DLTS; HL; ME/*196*.

milieu
DLTS; HL; ME/*196*.

Millenial Church
OCAL/*Shakers*.

Millerites
OCAL.

millisecond
FDLP/*duration*.

Miltonic
DLTS.

Miltonic sonnet
DLTC; HL; PH/*sonnet*.

mime
DLTC; DLTS; HL; PEPP.

mimes
ME/*197*.

mimesis
CR/*Index*; DLDC/*imitation*.

mimesis
DLTC; DLTS; DMCT; HL; ME/*197*; PEPP.

mimetic
DLTS.

mimetic theories
EDSL/*81*.

mimetic theory of art
HL.

mimetic word
GLT.

minimal-distance principle
FDLP.

minimal free form
FDLP.

minimal language
GLT.

177 □ modal auxiliary

minimal pair
FDLP; GLT; ME/*403*.
minnesinger
DLTC; DLTS; HL.
Minnesingers
PEPP.
minnesingers
PH/*troubadour*.
minor
FDLP.
minor plot
HL.
minor premise
ME/*198*.
minor sentence
FDLP/*minor*; ME/*198*.
minstrel
DLTC; DLTS; HL; PEPP.
minstrel show
HL; OCAL.
minuscule
GLT.
minus juncture
GLT.
mirabile dictu
DLTS.
miracle play
DLDC/*drama*; DLTC; DLTS; HL.
miracle plays
CODEL; ME/*199*; OCEL; PEPP.
miscellany
DLTC; DLTS; HL; ME/*199*.
misderivation
FDLP.
mise en scène
DLDC/*drama*; DLTS; HL.
missal
DLTS.
missionary sermon
CR/*Index*.
Mississippi River
OCAL.

MIT
FDLP.
Mitteleuropa
DLTS.
mixed figures
HL.
mixed language
GLT.
mixed metaphor
DLDC/*figurative language*; DLTC; DLTS; ME/*200*; PH/*metaphor*.
mixed-relational element
GLT.
mixed vowel
GLT.
mixing of levels
FDLP/*level*.
mixture
GLT.
MLU
FDLP/*mean length of utterance*; FDLP.
mnemonics
DLTS; ME/*200*.
mock drama
HL.
mock epic
DLTS; HL; ME/*200*.
mock-epic
DLDC/*burlesque*; DLTC; DMCT.
mock epic, mock heroic
PEPP.
mock-form
GLT.
mock heroic
DLTS; HL/*mock epic*; LGEP/*176*.
mock-heroic
CODEL; DLTC.
modal
FDLP.
modal auxiliaries
FDLP/*auxiliary*.
modal auxiliary
ME/*403*.

modal content
GLT.
modalities
EDSL/*282*.
modality
EDSL/*313*; FDLP/*modal*; FDLP/*mood*.
modalizing
EDSL/*325*.
modal logic
FDLP/*alethic*.
modal predicate
GLT.
mode
FDLP; FDLP/*mood*; HL; ME/*200*.
model
FDLP; GLT.
mode of action
EDSL/*311*; FDLP/*adverb*.
mode of articulation
GLT.
mode of discourse
FDLP/*mode*.
mode of signifying
EDSL/*47*.
modern
HL.
Modern English
ME/*403*.
modernism
DLTC; DMCT.
modernismo
DLTC; PEPP.
Modernist Period in English Literature, The
HL.
modern poetics
PEPP.
modes of representation
EDSL/*261*.
modification
FDLP; GLT; ME/*403*.
modified language
GLT.

modifier
GLT.
modifiers
FDLP/*modification*; ME/*403*.
modists
EDSL/*47*.
modulation
DLTS; FDLP; GLT; HL; PEPP.
modus
EDSL/*313*.
molecule
GLT.
molossus
DLTC; ME/*201*; PEPP.
momentary aspect
GLT.
moneme
EDSL/*201*; GLT.
moneme, grammatical
EDSL/*202*.
moneme, lexical
EDSL/*202*.
Mongolian poetry
PEPP.
mongrel word
GLT.
Monk's Tale stanza
DLTC; PEPP; PH/*stanza*.
mono-
FDLP.
monodrama
DLTC; HL.
monody
CR/*Index*; DLDC/*elegy*; DLTC; DLTS; DMCT; HL; PEPP.
monogatari
DLTC.
monogenesis theory
GLT.
monoglot
GLT.
monograph
DLTC; DLTS.

monolabial
FDLP/*bilabial*.
monolingual
FDLP/*multilingual*; GLT.
monologue
CODEL; DLTC; DLTS; EDSL/*303*; HL; ME/*201*; PEPP.
monologues
DLDC/*soliloquy*.
monometer
DLDC/*versification*; DLTC; DLTS; HL; PEPP; PH/*metre*.
monomorphemic
FDLP/*mono-*; FDLP/*morpheme*.
mononym
OO.
monophone
GLT.
monophthong
FDLP; FDLP/*diphthong*; GLT; ME/*404*.
monophthongisation
FDLP/*monophthong*.
monophthongization
GLT.
monopody
DLTS.
monopolylogue
DLTC.
monorhyme
DLTC; HL; PEPP.
monosemy
FDLP/*mono-*.
monostich
DLTC; HL; PEPP.
monosyllabic
FDLP/*mono-*; GLT.
monosyllabic language
GLT.
monosyllable
DLTS; FDLP/*syllable*; GLT.
monosystemic
FDLP/*polysystemic*; FDLP/*mono-*.
monotony test
GLT.

monotransitive
FDLP/*di-transitive*.
montage
DLTS; HL.
Montague grammar
FDLP.
Monte Cassino
CR/*Index*.
mood
DLTS; FDLP; HL; ME/*404*.
mora
DLTC; DLTS; EDSL/*181*; GLT; HL; PEPP; PH.
morae
HL.
moral
DLTC.
moral criticism
HL; PEPP.
moral interlude
DLTC.
moralist
DLTS.
moralities
CODEL; OCEL.
morality
DLTS; HL.
morality play
DLDC/*drama*; DLTC; DLTS; HL; ME/*201*.
morality plays
PEPP.
Moravian Church
OCAL.
Morgan Library
OCAL.
Mormon
OCAL.
morology
DLTC.
morph
FDLP/*morpheme*; GLT.

morpheme
DLTC; DLTS; EDSL/*200*;
EDSL/*200*; FDLP; GLT; ME/*404*.
morpheme alternant
EDSL/*201*.
morphemes
EDSL/*23*.
morpheme structure conditions
FDLP/*morpheme structure rules*.
morpheme structure rules
FDLP.
morpheme types
GLT.
morpheme word
GLT.
morphemically conditioned alternation
GLT.
morphemic alternant
GLT.
morphemic alternants
FDLP/*allo-*.
morphemic analysis
FDLP/*morphology*; FDLP/*morpheme*.
morphemics
FDLP/*morphology*; FDLP/*morpheme*; GLT.
morphemic segment
EDSL/*201*.
morphemic variants
FDLP/*morpheme*.
morphemic writing system
GLT.
morphemography
EDSL/*194*.
morpho-
GLT.
morphographemic
ME/*404*.
morphological
EDSL/*53*; FDLP/*morphology*.
morphological analysis
FDLP/*morphology*.

morphological assimilation
GLT.
morphological conditioning
ME/*404*.
morphological construction
GLT.
morphological doublets
GLT.
morphological extension
GLT.
morphological processes
GLT.
morphological relic
GLT.
morphological school
EDSL/*82*.
morphological word
GLT.
morphology
EDSL/*51*; FDLP; GLT; ME/*405*.
morphomatic
GLT.
morphome
GLT.
morphonology
EDSL/*54*; FDLP/*morphophonemics*.
morphophoneme
FDLP; GLT.
morphophonemic
GLT; ME/*405*.
morphophonemic allomorph
GLT.
morphophonemic alternation
GLT.
morphophonemic economy
GLT.
morphophonemic rules
FDLP/*morphophonemics*.
morphophonemics
FDLP; GLT.
morphophonemic stress
GLT.

181 □ multilateral opposition

morphophonological
EDSL/*54.*
morphophonology
FDLP/*morphophonemics.*
morphosyntactic
FDLP.
morphotactics
FDLP/*tactics*; FDLP/*morpheme*;
GLT.
mosaic
HL.
mosaic rhyme
DLTC; PEPP.
mosaic verse
DLTC.
mot
DLTC.
mote
DLTC; PEPP.
motet
DLTC.
Mother Lode
OCAL.
mother node
FDLP/*node.*
mother tongue
FDLP/*native-speaker.*
mother-tongue
FDLP/*acquisition.*
mother-tongue education
FDLP/*applied linguistics.*
motif
DLDC; DLTC; DLTS; DMCT;
EDSL/*217*; HL; ME/*201.*
motion pictures
OCAL.
motivation
DLDC/*plot*; DLTS; EDSL/*130*;
EDSL/*263*; HL.
motive
HL/*motif.*
mot juste
DLTS.
Motor Boys, The
OCAL.

motor phonetics
GLT.
motor theory
FDLP/*syllable*; FDLP.
motto
DLTS.
mouth
FDLP/*articulation.*
movable speech organs
GLT.
movement
DLTC; DLTS; FDLP/*allo-*;
FDLP; HL.
Movement, the
DLTC.
movement transformation
FDLP/*movement.*
Mozarabic lyric
DLTC.
mozarabic lyrics
PEPP.
M. Quad
OCAL.
msec
FDLP/*duration.*
mucker pose
GLT.
muckrakers
HL.
muckraking
DLTS.
Muckraking movement
OCAL.
mudanza
DLTC.
muddy transition (juncture)
GLT.
multidimensional scaling
FDLP.
multilateral
FDLP/*opposition*; FDLP.
multilateral opposition
GLT.

multilingual ☐ **182**

multilingual
   FDLP; GLT.
multilingualism
   EDSL/*60*; FDLP/*multilingual*; GLT.
multipartite
   GLT.
multipartite system
   GLT.
multiple-complex transformation
   ME/*405*.
multiple meaning
   LGEP/*39*.
multiple meanings
   HL.
multiple or polysyllabic rhyme
   DLTC; PEPP.
multiple substitution frame
   GLT.
multiplicative numeral
   GLT.
multiply ambiguous
   FDLP/*ambiguity*.
multisyllabic
   FDLP/*polysyllable*.
multivalence
   EDSL/*302*.
multiverbal endocentric structure
   GLT.
multum in parvo
   DLTS.
mumbo jumbo
   DLTS.
mummery
   DLTS; HL.
mumming play
   DLTC.
mummings
   HL.
Münchener Dichterkreis
   DLTC; PEPP.
Murmelvokal
   GLT.
murmur
   FDLP/*breathy*.
murmur (murmured) vowel
   GLT.
muscular movement
   FDLP/*articulatory phonetics*.
Muse
   PH; DLTC; DLTS; ME/*201*; PEPP.
muses
   HL.
Museum of Modern Art
   OCAL.
music
   CR/*Index*; LGEP/*93*.
musical accent
   GLT.
musical comedy
   DLTC; DLTS; HL.
music and poetry
   PEPP.
music of the spheres
   DLTS.
mutation
   FDLP; GLT; ME/*405*.
mutation vocalique
   GLT.
mutatis mutandis
   DLTS.
mute
   GLT.
mutual influence
   FDLP/*contact*; FDLP/*assimilation*.
muwashshah
   DLTC; PEPP.
mycterism
   DLTC.
myodynamic
   FDLP/*dynamic*.
myoelastic theory
   FDLP/*vocal cords*.
mysteries
   CODEL; OCEL.

mystery and miracle plays
  PEPP.
mystery play
  DLTC; DLTS; HL; ME/*201*.
mystery plays
  DLDC/*drama*.
mystery story
  DLTS; HL; OCAL.
mysticism
  DLTS; HL.
myth
  DLDC; DLTC; DLTS; DMCT; HL; ME/*201*; PEPP.
myth criticism
  PEPP/*955*.
mythic criticism
  HL.
mythography
  EDSL/*193*.
mythology
  DLDC/*myth*.
mythopoeia
  PEPP.
mythopoeic
  DLDC/*myth*.
mythopoesis
  DLTS; PH.
mythopoet
  PH/*mythopoesis*.
mythopoetics
  HL; ME/*203*.
mythos
  DMCT.

N

nadsat
  DLTC.
nagauta
  PEPP.
naive hero
  HL/*naive narrator.*
naive narrator
  HL.
naive-sentimental
  PEPP.
naiv und sentimentalisch
  DLTC.
name
  FDLP/*noun.*
name word
  GLT.
naming word
  GLT.
Naples
  CR/*Index.*
narcissism
  DLTS.
narodne pesme
  DLTC.
narration
  CR/*Index*; DLTS; HL; ME/*205.*
narrative
  DLDC; DMCT; EDSL/*297*; EDSL/*319*; HL.

narrative essay
  HL.
narrative hook
  DLTS; HL; ME/*206.*
narrative poem
  HL.
narrative poetry
  PEPP.
narrative textual analysis
  EDSL/*295.*
narrative verse
  DLTC.
narrator
  DLTC; DLTS; EDSL/*329*; HL.
narratorial distances
  EDSL/*331.*
narratorial knowledge
  EDSL/*332.*
narratorial presence
  EDSL/*331.*
narreme
  GLT.
narrow
  FDLP/*diphthong.*
narrowed meaning
  GLT.
narrowing
  FDLP/*fricative.*
narrow transcription
  FDLP/*transcription*; GLT.

narrow transcription symbols
  GLT.
narrow vowel
  GLT.
nasal
  FDLP.
nasal cavity
  FDLP/*cavity*.
nasal consonant
  ME/*406*.
nasal consonants
  GLT.
nasalisation
  FDLP/*nasal*.
nasalised
  FDLP/*nasal*.
nasalised consonant
  FDLP/*nasal*.
nasality
  FDLP/*nasal*.
nasalization
  GLT.
nasalized
  GLT.
nasal plosion
  FDLP/*nasal*.
nasal (sound)
  GLT.
nasal twang
  FDLP/*nasal*; GLT.
nasal vowel
  FDLP/*nasal*.
nasal vowels
  GLT.
National Academy of Design
  OCAL.
National Book Awards
  DLTS; OCAL.
National Gallery of Art
  OCAL.
National Institute of Arts and Letters
  OCAL/*American Academy*.

nationalism
  DLTS.
nationalistic (nationalistic) coefficient
  GLT.
national language
  GLT.
national language policy
  FDLP/*applied linguistics*.
National Medal for Literature
  OCAL.
native-like
  FDLP/*native-speaker*.
native-speaker
  FDLP.
native tradition
  DLTC.
native word
  GLT.
nativistic theory
  GLT.
natural class
  FDLP/*naturalness*.
natural conversation
  FDLP/*assimilation*.
natural gender
  FDLP/*grammar*; FDLP/*gender*; GLT.
Naturalism
  OCAL; DLDC; DLTC; DLTS; DMCT; HL; ME/*206*; PEPP.
Naturalistic and Symbolistic Period in American Literature
  HL.
naturalistic drama
  DLTC.
naturalization, language of
  GLT.
naturalized word
  GLT.
natural languages
  FDLP/*language*.
naturalness
  FDLP.
natural school, the
  DLTC.

187 □ neoplatonism

natural symbol
DLDC/*symbolism.*
nature
CR/*Index*; HL; ME/*207*; PEPP.
nature, training, practice
CR/*Index.*
natya
DLTC.
Navaho poetry
PEPP.
near rhyme
PEPP; PH/*rhyme.*
near-rhyme
DLDC/*versification*; DLTC; DLTS; HL; ME/*207.*
neatness of pattern
GLT.
necrophilia
DLTS.
negation
DLTC; EDSL/*314*; FDLP.
negative
FDLP/*negation.*
negative capability
DLDC; DLTC; DLTS; HL; ME/*207*; PEPP/*958.*
negative particle
FDLP/*adjunction.*
negative to affirmative
ME/*207.*
negative transfer
FDLP/*transfer.*
negative transformation
ME/*406.*
Négritude
DLTC.
Negroes in America
OCAL.
Negro literature
ME/*208.*
Negro minstrels
OCAL/*Minstrel show.*
Negro poetry
PEPP.

nemesis
DLTC; DLTS; HL.
neo-Aristotelianism
DMCT.
neo-classical
PH/*classical.*
neoclassical poetics
PEPP.
Neo-Classicism
ME/*208.*
Neoclassicism
CR/*Index*; DLTC; PEPP.
neo-classicism
DMCT.
neoclassicism
DLTS; HL.
neoclassicists
DLDC/*classic.*
Neoclassic Period
HL.
neo-Firthian
FDLP/*Firthian*; FDLP/*Hallidayan.*
Neogongorism
PEPP.
neogrammarian
FDLP.
neogrammarian hypothesis
FDLP/*neogrammarian.*
Neogrammarians
GLT; EDSL/*13.*
Neo-humanism
PEPP.
Neolinguists
GLT.
neologism
DLTC; DLTS; GLT; HL; LGEP/*42*; LGEP/*61*; PH.
Neoplatonism
CODEL; CR/*Index*; DLTS; HL; OCEL; PEPP.
neo-Platonism
DMCT.
neoplatonism
DLDC/*platonism.*

neoteric
  DLTC.
neoterici
  PEPP.
Neo-thomism and poetry
  PEPP.
nervous system
  GLT.
nested
  FDLP/*nesting*.
nesting
  FDLP; GLT.
neural program
  FDLP/*neurolinguistics*.
neurochronaxiac theory
  FDLP/*vocal cords*.
neurolinguistics
  FDLP/*linguistics*; FDLP.
neurological linguistics
  FDLP/*neurolinguistics*.
neurological responses
  FDLP/*auditory phonetics*.
neuronym
  OO.
neurophysiological models
  FDLP/*biolinguistics*.
neutral
  EDSL/*114*; FDLP; FDLP/*accent*.
Neutral Ground
  OCAL.
neutralisable
  FDLP/*opposition*; FDLP/*neutralisation*.
neutralisation
  FDLP.
neutralise
  FDLP/*syncretism*.
neutralised
  FDLP/*neutralisation*.
neutralization
  EDSL/*112*; GLT.
neutralization of vowels
  ME/*406*.

neutral omniscience
  DLDC/*point of view*.
neutral vowel
  GLT.
neutral vowels
  FDLP/*centre*.
new
  FDLP/*given*; FDLP.
New Comedy
  DLDC/*comedy*; HL; DLTC.
New Criticism
  DLTC; DLTS; HL; OCAL; DLDC/*criticism*; DMCT; EDSL/*83*; PEPP.
New Critics
  ME/*208*.
New England
  OCAL.
New England Company
  OCAL/*Massachusetts Bay Company*.
New England Renaissance
  OCAL.
Newgate
  HL.
New Harmony
  OCAL.
New Humanism
  DLTC; HL; ME/*209*; PEPP.
New Norse
  PEPP.
New Norwegian
  GLT.
new novel
  HL.
New Orleans
  OCAL.
Newsbooks
  OCEL; CODEL; DLTC.
Newsletters
  OCEL; CODEL; DLTC.
newspeak
  DLTC.
New Testament
  CR/*Index*.

189 □ nominative

New York
   FDLP/*dialect*.
New York, City of
   OCAL.
New York Poets
   PEPP/*958*.
New York Public Library
   OCAL.
New Zealand
   CR/*Index*.
New Zealand poetry
   PEPP.
nexus
   EDSL/*240*; GLT.
Nibelungen stanza
   PEPP.
Nibelungenstrophe
   DLTC.
Nicaraguan poetry
   PEPP.
Nick Carter
   OCAL.
nihilism
   DLTS.
nihil obstat
   DLTS; HL.
Nil Volentibus Arduum
   PEPP; DLTC.
Nine Worthies
   DLTC.
nine worthies, the
   HL.
nirvana
   DLTS.
niveaux
   EDSL/*238*.
Nō
   DLTC; PEPP.
noa word
   GLT.
Nobel prize
   DLTS; HL; ME/*209*.
Nobel Prizes
   OCAL; OCEL.
noble savage
   DLDC/*primitivism*; DLTC; HL; ME/*210*.
nocturne
   DLTS; HL.
node
   FDLP; ME/*406*.
noeme
   GLT.
Noh
   DLTC/*Nō*.
Noh (Nō) Plays
   HL.
noh
   DLTS.
Noh Plays
   CODEL; OCEL.
noise
   EDSL/*26*; FDLP/*communication*; GLT.
NOM
   FDLP/*arc*.
nom de guerre
   DLTS/*nom de plume*.
nom de plume
   DLTC; DLTS.
nom de plume (pen name)
   HL.
nomenclature
   EDSL/*20*.
nomic spelling
   GLT.
nominal
   EDSL/*281*; FDLP; GLT; ME/*406*.
nominal group
   FDLP/*noun*.
nominal groups
   FDLP/*class*.
nominalisation
   FDLP/*nominal*.
nominalism
   DLTS; HL.
nominative
   FDLP/*case*; FDLP.

nominative case
ME/*407*.

nomos
CR/*Index*.

non-agentive passive
FDLP/*passive*.

non-anterior
FDLP/*anterior*.

non-areal
FDLP/*area*.

non-artistic proof
CR/*Index*.

non-automatic alternation
GLT.

non-back sounds
FDLP/*back*.

non-breathy
FDLP/*breathy*.

non-causative
FDLP/*causative*.

nonce
FDLP.

nonce-form
GLT.

nonce-formation
LGEP/*42*.

nonce word
CODEL; DLTS; GLT; HL; ME/*407*; ME/*210*.

nonce-word
DLTC; OCEL.

non-consonantal
FDLP/*consonant*.

non-contiguous assimilation
FDLP/*assimilation*; GLT.

non-continuant
FDLP/*continuant*.

non-continuous
FDLP/*continuous*.

non-contrastive distribution
GLT.

non co-referential
FDLP/*co-referential*.

non-co-referential
FDLP/*referential indices*.

non-coronal
FDLP/*coronal*.

non-covered
FDLP/*covered*.

non-definite types
FDLP/*article*.

non-discrete
FDLP/*discrete*.

nondiscrete grammar
FDLP.

non-distributed
FDLP/*distributed*.

non-equivalent
FDLP/*equivalence*.

non-factive
FDLP/*factive*.

non-favourite
FDLP/*favourite*.

nonfiction
DLTS.

non-finite
FDLP/*finite*.

non-functional feature
GLT.

non-glottalised sounds
FDLP/*checked*.

non-high
FDLP/*high*.

nonhuman nouns
ME/*407*.

non-immediate situation
GLT.

non-lateral
FDLP/*lateral*.

non-linear
GLT.

non-linguistic
FDLP/*feature*; FDLP/*arbitrariness*.

non-linguistic criteria
FDLP/*criteria*.

191 □ **notational device**

non-low
  FDLP/*low*.
non-nasal
  GLT.
non-perfective
  FDLP/*perfect*.
non-phonemic
  GLT.
non-predicative
  FDLP/*predicate*.
non-primitive
  FDLP/*primitive*.
non-productive
  FDLP/*productivity*; GLT.
non-progressive
  FDLP/*continuous*; FDLP/*progressive*.
non-restrictive
  FDLP/*restrictive*.
nonrestrictive modifier
  ME/*407*.
non-rounded
  FDLP/*rounding*.
nonsense
  DLTC; FDLP.
Nonsense verse
  PH/*light verse*; DLDC/*light verse*; DLTS; HL; PEPP.
non-sibilant
  FDLP/*sibilant*.
non-silent pause
  FDLP/*filled pause*.
non-sonorant
  FDLP/*sonorant*.
non-standard
  FDLP/*bidialect*; FDLP/*standard*.
non-strident
  FDLP/*strident*.
non-syllabic
  GLT.
non-tense
  FDLP/*tension*.
non-terminal
  FDLP/*terminal*.

non-velarised
  FDLP/*velar*.
non-vocalic
  FDLP/*vocalic*.
Nō Plays
  OCEL/*Noh Plays*; CODEL/*Noh Plays*.
norm
  EDSL/*124*; EDSL/*126*; EDSL/*125*; FDLP; GLT.
normal grade
  GLT.
Norman Conquest
  HL.
normative
  EDSL/*343*; FDLP/*norm*; GLT.
normative grammar
  ME/*407*.
Norse prosody
  PEPP.
Norske Selskab, Det
  PEPP.
North American Phalanx
  OCAL.
Northwest
  OCAL.
Northwest Territory
  OCAL.
North Woods
  OCAL.
Norwegian
  FDLP/*dialect*.
Norwegian poetry
  PEPP.
nostalgia
  DLTS.
Nostratic
  GLT.
notaries
  CR/*Index*.
notation
  FDLP.
notational device
  FDLP/*notation*.

notebook
    DLTC.
notion
    FDLP/*notional*.
notional
    FDLP/*form*; FDLP.
notional word
    GLT.
noumenon
    DLTS.
noun
    FDLP; ME/*407*.
noun adjunct
    ME/*408*.
noun-banging
    ME/*210*.
noun clause
    ME/*408*.
noun cluster
    GLT.
noun complement position
    ME/*408*.
noun, grammatical proper
    EDSL/*251*.
noun-headed construction
    ME/*408*.
nouniness
    FDLP/*nondiscrete grammar*.
noun, logical proper
    EDSL/*251*.
noun of quantity
    ME/*408*.
Noun Phrase
    FDLP/*assign*; FDLP/*noun*; FDLP/*adjective*; ME/*409*.
noun, proper
    EDSL/*250*.
noun replacives
    ME/*409*.
nouveau roman
    DLTC.
nouvelle
    DLTC; HL.

nouvelle vague
    DLTC.
Novanglus
    OCAL.
novas rimadas
    DLTC; PEPP.
novel
    CODEL; DLDC; DLTC; DLTS; DMCT; HL; ME/*211*.
novelette
    DLTC; DLTS; HL; ME/*212*.
novelization
    HL.
novella
    DLTC; DLTS; HL; ME/*212*.
novellat
    DLTC.
novel of character
    HL.
novel of incident
    HL.
novel of manners
    HL.
novel of sensibility
    DLTC; HL.
novel of the soil
    DLTC; HL.
novel, picaresque
    CODEL.
NP
    FDLP; FDLP/*analysable*.
nuclear
    FDLP/*nucleus*.
nuclear stress
    FDLP/*nucleus*.
Nuclear Stress Rule
    FDLP/*cycle*; FDLP/*nucleus*.
nuclear syllable
    FDLP/*nucleus*.
nuclear tone
    FDLP/*tone group*; FDLP/*nucleus*.
nucleus
    EDSL/*213*; FDLP/*syllable*; FDLP; GLT.

Nudelverse
   DLTC.
null element
   FDLP/*zero*.
number
   DLTC; FDLP; ME/*409*.
numbers
   PEPP; PH.
numeral classifier
   GLT.
numerals
   FDLP/*cardinal*.
numerative classifier
   GLT.

numerical code
   FDLP/*cardinal vowels*.
numerical metanalysis
   GLT.
numerology
   DLTS.
nuntius
   DLDC/*tragedy*.
nursery rhyme
   DLTC; DLTS; HL; PH.
nursery rhymes
   PEPP.
Nynorsk
   GLT.

O

obiter dicta
DLTS; HL.
obiter dicta
DLTC; ME/*214*.
obituary
DLTS.
object
EDSL/*118*; FDLP; ME/*410*.
object complement
FDLP/*complement*; ME/*410*.
objective
DLDC/*subjective*; FDLP/*object*.
objective and objectivity
DLTC.
objective aspects
EDSL/*311*.
objective case
ME/*410*.
objective correlative
DLDC; DLTC; DLTS; DMCT; HL; ME/*214*; PEPP; PH.
objective point of view
DLDC/*point of view*.
objective theories
EDSL/*81*.
objective theory of art
HL.
Objectivism
OCAL; PEPP.

objectivity
DLTS; HL; PEPP.
object language
FDLP/*metalanguage*; GLT.
object-raising
FDLP/*raising*.
obligatory
FDLP.
obligatory categories
GLT.
obligatory scene
DLTC; DLTS; HL.
obligatory transformation
FDLP/*obligatory*; ME/*410*.
oblique
DLTS; FDLP.
oblique case
GLT; ME/*410*.
oblique context
EDSL/*249*.
oblique rhyme
DLTC; HL; ME/*214*; PEPP.
obscenity
ME/*214*.
obscurantism
DLTS.
obscuration
GLT.
obscurity
CR/*Index*; DLTC; DMCT; PEPP.

observational adequacy
EDSL/39; FDLP/adequacy.
obsolescence
GLT.
obsolescent
GLT.
obsolete
GLT.
obsolete diction
DLTS.
obstructive
GLT.
obstruent
FDLP; GLT/obstructive; ME/410.
obtrusion
GLT.
obviative
FDLP.
Occam's razor
FDLP/economy.
occasion
CR/Index.
occasional poem
DLDC.
occasional poetry
PH.
occasional verse
DLTC; DLTS; HL; ME/216; PEPP.
occlusion
FDLP; GLT.
occlusive
FDLP/occlusion; GLT.
occupational dialect
FDLP/dialect.
occurrence, privilege of
GLT.
oclus pastoralis
CR/Index.
octameter
DLDC/versification; DLTC; DLTS; HL; ME/216; PEPP.
octastich
DLTC; DLTS; HL.

octateuch
DLTC.
octave
DLDC/versification; DLTC; DLTS; HL; PEPP; PH.
Octave Thanet
OCAL.
octavo
DLDC/folio; DLTC; DLTS; HL.
octet
DLTS; HL.
octonarius
DLTC; PEPP.
octosílabo
PEPP.
octosyllabic
CODEL; OCEL.
octosyllabic couplet
DLDC/versification.
octosyllabic verse
DLTC; HL; PEPP; PH.
ode
CODEL; DLDC; DLTC; DLTS; DMCT; HL; ME/216; OCEL; PEPP; PH.
odl
PEPP.
Oedipus complex
DLTS; HL.
oesophageal
FDLP.
oesophageal cavity
FDLP/cavity.
oesophageal voice
FDLP/air-stream mechanism.
oesophagus
FDLP/cavity; FDLP/air-stream mechanism.
off-Broadway
DLTC.
off-glide
FDLP/glide; FDLP/off-/on- glide; GLT.
officialese
DLTC; ME/216.

197 □ onomatopoeic expressions

official language
GLT.
officia oratoris
CR/*Index*.
off-rhyme
DLDC/*versification*; DLTS; ME/*216*.
O. Henry
OCAL.
O. Henry Awards
OCAL.
Okies
OCAL.
old
GLT.
Old Comedy
DLDC/*comedy*; DLTC; HL.
Old Corner Bookstore
OCAL.
Old English
DLTS; FDLP/*analogy*; ME/*410*.
Old English language
HL.
Old English Period
HL.
Old English versification
HL.
Old French
DLTC.
Old Germanic prosody
PEPP.
Old Norse poetry
PEPP.
Old Southwest
OCAL.
Oldstyle, Jonathan
OCAL.
Oldstyle, Oliver
OCAL.
Old Testament
CR/*Index*.
old wives' tale
DLTS.

Olympia
CR/*Index*.
Omar Khayyám quatrain
DLTC; PEPP.
omission of sounds
FDLP/*elision*.
omnibus
HL.
omnibus edition
DLTC.
omnipotent vowel
GLT.
omniscience
DLTS.
omniscient point of view
DLDC/*point of view*; HL.
one-acter
DLTS.
one-act play
DLTC; HL.
Oneida Community
OCAL.
one-word sentences
FDLP/*holophrase*.
ongkos
CR/*Index*.
on-glide
FDLP/*off-/on- glide*; FDLP/*glide*; GLT.
onomasiology
FDLP; GLT.
onomasticon
DLTC.
onomastics
DLTS; FDLP; GLT.
onomatology
GLT.
onomatopoeia
CODEL; DLDC/*versification*; DLTC; DLTS; DMCT; FDLP/*sound-symbolism*; HL; LGEP/*96*; ME/*216*; OCEL; PEPP; PH.
onomatopoeic expressions
FDLP/*arbitrariness*.

onomatopoeic words
FDLP/*correspond*.

onomatopo(i)eia
GLT.

onomatopo(i)etic theory
GLT.

onset
FDLP/*syllable*; FDLP; GLT.

ontogenetic
FDLP/*ontogeny*.

ontogeny
FDLP; GLT/*linguistic*.

ontology
DLTC; DLTS.

-onym
OO.

opaque context
EDSL/*249*.

op. cit.
DLTS.

open
FDLP/*close*; FDLP.

open book
ME/*217*.

open class
FDLP/*open*.

open-class words
GLT.

open construction
GLT.

open couplet
DLTC; HL; PH.

opening sound
GLT.

open juncture
FDLP/*juncture*; GLT.

open list
GLT.

open repertory
GLT.

open stress
GLT.

open syllabification
GLT.

open syllable
FDLP/*syllable*; GLT; ME/*410*.

open transition
FDLP/*transition*; GLT.

open vowel
GLT.

opera
CODEL; DLTC; DLTS; HL; OCEL.

opéra bouffe
HL.

opera bouffe
OCEL.

opéra bouffe
DLTS.

opera bouffe
CODEL.

operator
GLT.

opere citato
DLTC.

operetta
DLTC; DLTS; HL.

oppositeness
FDLP/*antonym*.

oppositeness of meaning
FDLP/*converse*.

opposition
EDSL/*19*; FDLP; GLT.

oppositional signification
EDSL/*237*.

opposition of meaning
EDSL/*27*.

optative mood
ME/*410*.

Optic, Oliver
OCAL.

optional
FDLP; GLT.

optional element
FDLP/*adjunct*; ME/*410*.

optional external sandhi
GLT.

optional transformation
ME/*410*.
optional variants
GLT.
oracy
FDLP/*oral*.
oral
FDLP.
oral cavity
FDLP/*cavity*.
oral composition
DMCT.
orality
CR/*Index*.
oral poetry
PEPP.
oral sound
GLT; ME/*411*.
oral tradition
DLTC.
oral transmission
DLDC/*ballad*; DLTS; HL.
orama
GLT.
oration
DLTS; HL.
orator, duties of
CR/*Index*.
orator, ideal
CR/*Index*.
oratory, kinds of
CR/*Index*.
order
DLTS; FDLP; GLT.
order class
GLT.
ordering
FDLP/*order*.
ordering, conjunctive
FDLP/*disjunction*.
ordering, disjunctive
FDLP/*disjunction*.
order, logical
EDSL/*296*.

order of mention
FDLP/*order*.
order, spatial
EDSL/*296*.
order, temporal
EDSL/*296*.
ordinal
FDLP.
ordinary language
EDSL/*95*.
Oregon Trail
OCAL.
organic
DMCT.
organic form
DLTC; HL; PH/*form*.
organic metaphor
DLTC; PH/*metaphor*.
organic shifting
GLT.
organic unity
DLDC/*unity*.
organism
PEPP.
organization
DLTS.
organonym
OO.
organs of speech
GLT.
Oriental theater
DLTS.
orientation
FDLP/*canonical*.
oriented
EDSL/*116*.
origin
FDLP/*case*.
originality
DLTC; DLTS; DMCT; HL; PEPP.
orismology
DLTC.

Oriya poetry ☐ **200**

Oriya poetry
  PEPP.
ormonym
  OO.
ornament
  PEPP/*958*.
ornamentation
  CR/*Index*.
Orpheus C. Kerr
  OCAL.
orta oyunu
  DLTC.
orthodoxy
  DLTS.
orthoepy
  DLTS.
orthography
  DLTS; GLT; ME/*411*.
orthotone
  DLTC.
Oscan Fable
  DLTC.
oscillogram
  GLT.
oscillograph
  GLT.
oscilloscope
  GLT.
Ossianic Controversy
  HL.
Ossianism
  DLTC.
otiose
  HL.
Otis, James
  OCAL.
ottava rima
  DLTC; HL.
ottava rima
  CODEL; DLDC/*versification*;
  DLTS; ME/*217*; OCEL; PEPP;
  PH/*stanza*.
outer closure
  GLT.

outline
  DLTS; GLT; ME/*217*.
output
  GLT.
output conditions
  FDLP/*constraint*.
outride
  HL.
outrides
  DLTC.
over-all frame
  GLT.
over-all pattern
  GLT.
over-correction
  GLT.
over-differentiation
  GLT.
overextension
  FDLP.
overgeneralisation
  FDLP/*general*; FDLP.
Overland Trail
  OCAL.
overlap
  FDLP/*overlapping*; GLT.
overlapping
  FDLP.
overlearn
  GLT.
overphrasing
  ME/*219*.
overpredication
  ME/*219*.
overstatement
  DLDC/*figurative language*.
overt
  FDLP.
overt meaning
  LGEP/*172*.
overtone
  DLTS.

Oxford Movement
CODEL; DLTC; DLTS; HL; ME/*219*; OCEL.

Oxford Reformers
HL.

Oxford school
EDSL/*95*.

Oxford University
CR/*Index*.

oxymoron
CR/*Index*.

oxymoron
CODEL; DLDC/*figurative language*; DLTC; DLTS; EDSL/*278*; HL; LGEP/*140*; LGEP/*132*; ME/*219*; OCEL; PEPP; PH.

oxytone
DLTC; GLT.

P

pace
  DLTS.
pace-egging play
  DLTC.
Pacing Mustang
  OCAL.
paean
  CODEL; DLTC; DLTS; HL; ME/*221*; OCEL; PEPP.
paedonym
  OO.
paeon
  CODEL; CR/*Index*; DLTC; DLTS; HL; ME/*221*; OCEL; PEPP; PH.
paeonic metre
  LGEP/*117*.
paganism
  DLTS.
pageant
  DLTC; DLTS; HL.
Paget-Gorman Sign System
  FDLP/*sign*.
painting
  CR/*Index*.
painting and poetry
  PEPP.
pair-networks
  FDLP/*arc*.

palaeography
  DLTC.
palatal
  FDLP/*palatalisation*; GLT.
palatalisation
  FDLP; FDLP/*articulation*.
palatalised
  FDLP/*palatalisation*.
palatalization
  GLT; ME/*412*.
palatalized consonant
  GLT.
palatal law
  GLT.
palatal sound
  ME/*412*.
palatal vowel
  GLT.
palate
  FDLP; FDLP/*alveolar*.
palato-alveolar
  FDLP.
palatograms
  FDLP/*palate*.
palatograph
  FDLP/*articulatory phonetics*.
palatography
  FDLP/*palate*.
paleface and redskin
  ME/*221*.

paleography
DLTS; GLT.

palillogy
PEPP.

palilogy
DLTC; DLTS; HL.

palimbacchius
DLTC; PEPP.

palimpsest
CODEL; DLTC; DLTS; HL; OCEL.

palindrome
CODEL; DLDC; DLTC; DLTS; HL; ME/*221*; OCEL; PEPP.

palinode
CODEL; DLDC; DLTC; DLTS; HL; OCEL; PEPP.

palinodic
DLTC; PEPP.

palliata
DLTC.

pamphlet
CODEL; DLTC; DLTS; HL; OCEL.

panchronic grammar
GLT.

panchronic laws
GLT.

pandialectal
FDLP.

P and Q Celtic
GLT.

panegyric
CR/*Index*; DLTC; DLTS; HL; PEPP.

panegyrical sermon
CR/*Index*.

pangram
DLTS.

Panhellenism
CR/*Index*.

Panjabi poetry
PEPP.

panlectal
FDLP.

panorama
DLTS.

panoramic method
DLTC; HL.

Pantaloon
DLTC; OCEL; CODEL.

pantheism
DLTS; HL.

pantomime
CODEL; DLDC/*drama*; DLTC; DLTS; HL; OCEL.

pantoum
DLTS; HL; PEPP; PH.

pantun
DLTC.

parabasis
DLTC; DLTS; HL; PEPP.

parable
CR/*Index*; DLDC/*allegory*; DLTC; DLTS; HL; ME/*221*.

paradiastole
DLTC.

paradigm
DLTC; DLTS; EDSL/*111*; EDSL/*108*; FDLP/*paradigmatic*; GLT; ME/*412*.

paradigmatic
FDLP.

paradigmatic economy
GLT.

paradigmatic pattern
GLT.

paradigmatic sound change
GLT.

paradox
DLDC; DLTC; DLTS; DMCT; HL; LGEP/*142*; LGEP/*132*; ME/*221*; PEPP.

paragoge
DLTS; GLT; HL.

paragogue
FDLP/*intrusion*.

paragram
DLTC; EDSL/*359*.

paragraph
  DLTC; DLTS; EDSL/*294*; ME/*222*.
paralanguage
  FDLP.
paraleipsis
  DLTS; PEPP.
paralinguistic
  FDLP/*paralanguage*.
paralinguistics
  GLT.
paralipomena
  DLTC.
paralipsis
  EDSL/*278*.
parallelism
  DLTC; DLTS; EDSL/*185*; HL; LGEP/*67*; LGEP/*89*; LGEP/*62*; ME/*224*; PEPP; PH.
parallelism, rhythmic
  LGEP/*111*.
parallelism, verbal
  LGEP/*79*.
parallel structure
  DLDC/*form*.
parameter
  FDLP/*parametric phonetics*.
parametric phonetics
  FDLP/*dynamic*; FDLP.
paraphasias
  EDSL/*163*.
paraphrase
  DLDC/*form*; DLTC; DLTS; DMCT; EDSL/*287*; FDLP; GLT; HL; ME/*225*.
paraphrase, heresy of
  PEPP.
paraplasm
  GLT.
para-rhyme
  DLTC.
pararhyme
  PEPP.
parasitic vowel
  GLT.

parasynthetic derivation
  GLT.
paratactic
  FDLP.
parataxis
  DLTC; DLTS; FDLP/*paratactic*; GLT; HL.
parent
  FDLP/*family*.
parenthesis
  DLTC; DLTS; HL.
parenthesis notation
  FDLP/*bracketing*.
pariosis
  CR/*Index*.
parison
  CR/*Index*.
Paris, University of
  CR/*Index*.
parisyllabic
  GLT.
parlance
  DLTS.
Parnassian poetry
  PH.
Parnassians
  DLTC; HL; PEPP.
Parnassian School
  CODEL; OCEL.
Parnassus
  DLTS; HL; PEPP; PH.
parodos
  PEPP.
parody
  CODEL; DLDC/*burlesque*; DLTC; DLTS; DMCT; EDSL/*256*; HL; ME/*226*; PEPP.
paroemiac
  PEPP.
parole
  DLTC/*langue* and *parole*.
parole
  EDSL/*118*; FDLP; GLT; ME/*413*.

paromoeosis
　CR/*Index*.
paronomasia
　CODEL; DLDC/*figurative language*; DLTC; DLTS; EDSL/*278*; HL; ME/*227*; OCEL; PEPP.
paronym
　DLTC; GLT; OO.
paronymy
　EDSL/*256*.
paroxytone
　DLTC; GLT.
parrhesia
　DLTS.
parsing
　FDLP; ME/*413*.
partial closure
　FDLP/*closure*.
partial complementation
　GLT.
partial overlap
　FDLP/*overlapping*.
participating character
　ME/*227*.
participation
　EDSL/*114*.
participial
　FDLP/*particple*.
participial phrase
　ME/*413*.
participle
　FDLP; ME/*413*.
Participles Anonymous
　ME/*227*.
particle
　FDLP; GLT; ME/*413*.
particula pendens
　PEPP.
particular
　DLDC/*concrete*.
particular statement
　ME/*227*.
particular to universal
　ME/*227*.

partimen
　DLTC; PEPP.
partition
　CR/*Index*.
part of speech
　FDLP; ME/*413*.
parts of oration
　CR/*Index*.
parts of speech
　EDSL/*203*; GLT.
part-song
　DLTC.
pasigraphy
　GLT.
pasimology
　GLT.
paso
　DLTC.
pasquinade
　DLTC; HL.
Pasquin, Anthony
　OCAL.
passim
　DLTS.
passion play
　DLTC; DLTS; HL; PEPP.
passive
　FDLP.
passive articulators
　FDLP/*articulation*.
passive transformation
　ME/*413*.
passive voice
　ME/*414*.
passivisation
　FDLP/*cross-over*; FDLP/*govern*; FDLP/*passive*.
passivise
　FDLP/*passive*.
passus
　DLTC.
past
　FDLP/*affix*.

pastiche
　HL.
pastiche
　CODEL; DLTC; DLTS; DMCT; ME/*227*; OCEL.
pastoral
　DLDC; DLTC; DLTS; DMCT; HL; ME/*228*; PEPP; PH.
pastoral drama
　HL.
pastoral elegy
　HL.
pastoral poetry
　CODEL; OCEL.
pastoral romance
　HL.
pastourelle
　DLTC; DLTS; HL; PEPP.
past participle
　ME/*414*.
past perfect tense
　ME/*414*.
past tense
　ME/*414*.
past use
　FDLP/*attested*.
pataphysics
　DLTC.
patavinity
　CODEL; DLTC; OCEL.
patent theaters
　HL.
paternoster
　DLTS.
path
　FDLP.
pathetic fallacy
　CODEL; DLDC/*figurative language*; DLTC; DLTS; DMCT; HL; ME/*228*; PEPP; PH.
pathological forms
　FDLP/*biolinguistics*.
pathopoeia
　DLTC.

pathos
　CR/*Index*.
pathos
　DLDC; DLTC; DLTS; HL; PEPP.
patient
　FDLP/*goal*; FDLP.
patois
　DLTC; DLTS; EDSL/*58*; GLT.
Patrick, John
　OCAL.
patron
　CR/*Index*; DLTS.
patronage
　DLTC.
patronym
　DLTS; OO.
patronymic
　GLT.
pattern
　DLTC; DLTS; FDLP; GLT.
pattern congruity
　FDLP/*pattern*; GLT.
pattern drill
　FDLP/*pattern*.
pattern drills
　FDLP/*substitution*.
patterned congruence
　GLT.
pattern poetry
　DLTC; PEPP.
pattern pressure
　GLT.
patterns of development
　FDLP/*developmental linguistics*.
patter song
　DLTC; DLTS.
paucal number
　GLT.
pausal phenomena
　FDLP/*pause*.
pause
　DLTC; FDLP; LGEP/*107*.

pause of silence ☐ **208**

pause of silence
GLT.
pause pitch
GLT.
Pavia
CR/*Index*.
Paxton, Philip
OCAL.
payada
DLTC; PEPP.
peak nucleus
GLT.
peak (of sonority)
GLT.
peak satellite
GLT.
Pecos Bill
OCAL.
pedagese
DLTS.
pedagogical grammar
FDLP/*grammar*.
pedagogical novel
ME/*228*.
pedantry
DLTS; HL.
pedigree theory
GLT.
Pegasus
DLTS; HL; PEPP.
pejoration
GLT.
pejorative
DLTS; GLT.
Pekingese
FDLP/*dialect*.
Peking Mandarin Chinese
FDLP/*tone*.
Pelagianism
HL.
pendant
GLT.

pen name
DLTS; HL/*nom de plume*; ME/*pseudonym*, 239.
Pennsylvania Dutch
OCAL.
penny dreadful
DLTC; DLTS; HL.
pensée
DLTC.
pentad
ME/*228*.
pentameter
CODEL; DLDC/*versification*; DLTC; DLTS; HL; ME/*228*; OCEL; PEPP; PH/*metre*; PH.
pentapody
DLTC; PEPP.
pentarsic
DLTC; PEPP.
pentastich
DLTC; DLTS; HL; PEPP.
Pentateuch
DLTC.
penthemimer
PEPP.
penthimimer
DLTC.
penult
GLT/*penultimate*.
penultimate
DLTS.
perception
FDLP.
perceptual
FDLP/*perception*.
perceptual response
FDLP/*auditory phonetics*.
Percy, Florence
OCAL.
Perennialism
ME/*228*.
perfect
FDLP.
Perfectionism
OCAL.

perfective
FDLP/*aspect*; FDLP/*perfect*; GLT.
perfective aspect
EDSL/*307*.
perfect rhyme
DLTC; DLTS; PH.
perfect rhymes
DLDC/*versification*.
perfect tense
FDLP/*perfect*; ME/*414*.
perfect, true, or full rhyme
PEPP.
performance
EDSL/*120*; FDLP; LGEP/*104*; ME/*414*.
performance disorders
EDSL/*165*.
performance grammar
FDLP/*performance*; FDLP/*grammar*.
performance utterance
FDLP/*performative*.
performative
EDSL/*342*; FDLP.
performative verb
FDLP/*performative*.
period
DLTC.
periodical
DLTC; DLTS; HL.
periodical essay
HL.
periodic sentence
DLDC/*style*; DLTS; HL; ME/*229*.
periodic style
CR/*Index*.
Period of Criticism and Conformity in American Literature, 1930-1960
HL.
Period of the Confessional Self in American Literature, 1960
HL.
periods
EDSL/*151*.
periods of English and American literary history
HL.
peripatetics
CODEL.
peripatetic school
CR/*Index*.
peripeteia
DLDC/*tragedy*; DLDC/*plot*.
peripeteia
DLTC.
peripety
DLDC/*tragedy*; DLDC/*plot*; DLTS; HL; ME/*230*.
peripheral language
GLT.
peripheral theory
GLT.
periphrasis
CODEL; DLDC; DLTC; DLTS; FDLP; HL; LGEP/*132*; LGEP/*138*; ME/*230*; OCEL; PEPP.
periphrastic
FDLP/*periphrasis*.
periphrastic construction
ME/*415*.
perlocutionary
FDLP.
perlocutionary act
EDSL/*343*.
permutability
FDLP/*ascriptive*.
permutation
FDLP.
peroration
CR/*Index*; DLTC; DLTS; HL.
perseveration
FDLP.
Persian poetry
PEPP.
persiflage
DLTS; HL.

persistence of vision
HL.

person
FDLP; ME/*415*.

persona
DLDC; DLTC; DLTS; DMCT; HL; ME/*230*; PEPP/*959*.

personal
EDSL/*254*; FDLP/*person*.

personal essay
DLTS; HL.

personal heresy, the
DLTC.

personal pronouns
FDLP/*pronoun*.

personification
DLDC/*figurative language*; DLTC; DLTS; HL; ME/*231*; PEPP; PH/*metaphor*.

perspective
DLTS.

persuasion
CR/*Index*; DLTS; HL.

Peruvian poetry
PEPP.

Peter Parley
OCAL.

Peter Porcupine
OCAL.

petitio
CR/*Index*.

Petrarchan
DLTS.

Petrarchan Conceit
HL.

Petrarchan conceits
DLDC/*metaphysical poets*.

Petrarchan Sonnet
HL; CODEL; DLDC/*versification*; DLTC; ME/*231*.

Petrarchism
DLTC; PEPP.

petrification
GLT.

petroglyph
GLT.

pevăci
DLTC.

Pfaff's Cellar
OCAL.

phalaecean
PEPP.

phanopoeia
DLTC; PH/*logopoeia*.

phantasy
DMCT; PH/*fancy*.

phantom word
DLTC; GLT.

pharyngeal
FDLP.

pharyng(e)al
GLT.

pharyngeal cavity
FDLP/*cavity*.

pharyngealisation
FDLP/*pharyngeal*; FDLP/*articulation*.

pharyngealised
FDLP/*pharyngeal*.

pharyngealization
GLT.

pharynx
FDLP/*pharyngeal*.

phatic
EDSL/*342*.

phatic communion
FDLP.

phatic function
FDLP/*phatic communion*.

phatic language
DLTC; FDLP/*phatic communion*.

phememe
GLT.

phenomenology
HL; PEPP/*961*.

pheno-text
EDSL/*360*.

Pherecratean
  PEPP.
Pherecretean
  DLTC.
Phi Beta Kappa
  OCAL.
phi effect
  HL/*phi phenomenon*.
Philadelphia
  OCAL.
Philemon Perch
  OCAL.
Philenia
  OCAL.
philippic
  DLTC; DLTS; HL.
Philippine poetry
  PEPP.
Philistine
  DLTC.
Philistinism
  HL; ME/*231*.
philological conditions
  GLT.
Philological Society
  OCAL.
philologist
  FDLP/*philology*.
philology
  DLTC; DLTS; FDLP; GLT; HL; ME/*415*; ME/*231*.
philosophical grammar
  GLT.
philosophical linguistics
  FDLP.
philosophical semantics
  FDLP/*semantics*.
philosophy and poetry
  PEPP.
philosophy of language
  EDSL/*92*; FDLP/*philosophical linguistics*; FDLP/*semantics*.
philter
  DLTS/*philtre*.

phi phenomenon
  HL.
Phoenix, John
  OCAL.
phonaestheme
  FDLP/*phonaesthetics*.
phonaesthesia
  FDLP/*phonaesthetics*.
phonaesthetics
  FDLP.
phonation
  FDLP; GLT.
phonation type
  FDLP/*phonation*.
phone
  FDLP; GLT; ME/*415*.
phonema
  GLT.
phonematic
  EDSL/*176*; GLT.
phonematics
  GLT.
phonematic unit
  FDLP.
phoneme
  DLTC; DLTS; EDSL/*171*; FDLP; GLT; ME/*416*; PEPP; PH.
phoneme-grapheme correspondence
  FDLP/*phoneme*.
phonemes
  LGEP/*63*.
phonemic
  GLT.
phonemically conditioned alternation
  GLT.
phonemic analysis
  FDLP/*phoneme*; GLT.
phonemic change
  GLT.
phonemic clause
  FDLP/*phoneme*.
phonemic inventory
  FDLP/*inventory*.

phonemicists
FDLP/*phoneme*.

phonemic loan
GLT.

phonemic merger
FDLP/*merger*.

phonemic overlapping
FDLP/*overlapping*.

phonemic phonology
FDLP/*phoneme*.

phonemic phrase
GLT.

phonemics
EDSL/*171*; FDLP/*phoneme*; GLT; PH.

phonemic shape
GLT.

phonemic stress
GLT.

phonemic structure
FDLP/*phoneme*.

phonemic substitution
GLT.

phonemic system
FDLP/*phoneme*.

phonemic transcription
FDLP/*transcription*; FDLP/*phoneme*; GLT; ME/*416*.

phonemization
GLT.

phonestheme
GLT.

phone substitution
GLT.

phonetic
GLT.

phonetic/phonemic transcription
ME/*416*.

phonetic alphabet
FDLP/*transcription*; GLT.

phonetic alternation
GLT.

phonetic assimilation
ME/*416*.

phonetic change
GLT.

phonetic complement
GLT.

phonetic equivalence
PEPP.

phonetician
FDLP/*phonetics*.

phonetic indicator
GLT.

phonetic law
EDSL/*8*; GLT.

phonetic modification
GLT.

phonetics
DLTS; EDSL/*119*; EDSL/*170*; EDSL/*171*; FDLP; GLT; ME/*416*.

phonetic segment
FDLP/*phonology*.

phonetic shape
FDLP/*allo-*.

phonetic spelling
GLT.

phonetic symbolism
EDSL/*255*.

phonetic symbols
GLT.

phonetic transcription
FDLP/*transcription*; GLT.

phonetic variant
FDLP/*allo-*.

phonetic variants
GLT.

phonetic writing
GLT.

phoneti(ci)zation
GLT.

phoniatry
GLT.

phonic continuum
FDLP/*phone*.

phonics
DLTS; GLT.

phonic substance
FDLP.
phonocentric
EDSL/*349*.
phonogenetic phonetics
GLT.
phonogram
GLT.
phonography
EDSL/*195*.
phonological analyses
FDLP/*cost*.
phonological component
EDSL/*54*; FDLP/*component*; FDLP/*phonology*.
phonological components
GLT.
phonological conditioning
FDLP/*morpheme*; ME/*416*.
phonologically conditioned alternants
FDLP/*alternation*.
phonological unit
FDLP/*phonology*.
phonological universals
EDSL/*174*.
Phonologie
GLT.
phonologist
FDLP/*phonology*.
phonology
EDSL/*119*; EDSL/*170*; FDLP; GLT; LGEP/*39*; LGEP/*37*; ME/*416*.
phonology, diachronic
EDSL/*141*.
phonology, generative
EDSL/*174*.
phon(o), phon(e)
GLT.
phonostylistics
FDLP/*stylistics*.
phonosymbolism
GLT.
phonotactics
FDLP/*tactics*; FDLP; GLT.

phrasal
FDLP/*phrase*.
phrasal verb
FDLP/*verb*; FDLP.
phrasal verbs
FDLP/*complement*.
phrase
FDLP; ME/*417*.
phrase marker
ME/*417*.
phrase-marker
FDLP.
phraseology
DLTS.
phrase-structure
FDLP.
phrase-structure component
FDLP/*phrase-structure*.
phrase structure grammar
ME/*417*.
phrase structure
EDSL/*PS, 227*.
phrase structure rules
ME/*417*.
phylogenetic
FDLP/*phylogeny*.
phylogeny
FDLP; GLT/*linguistic*.
physical correspondence
FDLP/*arbitrariness*.
physical phonetics
GLT.
physical solutions
FDLP/*acoustic phonetics*.
physical units
FDLP/*exponent*.
physiological movements
FDLP/*articulation*.
physiological phonetics
FDLP/*articulatory phonetics*; GLT.
physiophonetics
GLT.
physis
CR/*Index*.

picaresque □ 214

picaresque
CODEL; DLTS; DMCT; OCEL.
picaresque novel
DLDC/*novel*; DLTC; HL; ME/*232*.
picaroon
DLTC.
Pickwickian sense
CODEL; OCEL.
pictogram
GLT; ME/*417*.
pictographic writing
GLT.
picturesque
HL.
pidgin
DLTS; EDSL/*59*; FDLP/*relexification*; FDLP; GLT; ME/*417*.
pidginised
FDLP/*pidgin*.
pièce à thèse
DLTC.
pièce bien faite
DLDC; DLTC; HL.
pièce de résistance
DLTS.
pie quebrado
DLTC; PEPP.
Pierpont Morgan Library, The
OCAL/*Morgan Library*.
Pike
OCAL.
Pilgrims
OCAL.
Pindaric
DLTS.
Pindaric ode
DLDC/*ode*; DLTC; HL; ME/*232*; PEPP; PH/*ode*.
pirated edition
DLTS; HL; ME/*232*.
Pisa
CR/*Index*.
pistis
CR/*Index*.

pitch
DLTS; EDSL/*177*; FDLP; GLT; PEPP.
pitch accent
GLT.
pitch functions
GLT.
pitch level
FDLP/*level*; GLT.
pitch levels
FDLP/*cline*; ME/*418*.
pitch meter
FDLP/*pitch*.
pitch patterns
FDLP/*intonation*.
pitch range
GLT.
pitch registers
GLT.
Pittsburgh
OCAL.
pivot
FDLP.
pivot word
DLTC.
piyyut
DLTC.
place
FDLP/*adverb*.
placebo
DLTS.
place-holder
FDLP/*dummy*.
place of articulation
FDLP.
plagiarism
DLTC; DLTS; DMCT; HL; ME/*232*.
plain
FDLP.
plainsong
DLTS; HL.
Plains region
OCAL.

plain style
CR/*Index*; DLDC/*style*; HL; LGEP/*17*.
plaint
DLTC; DLTS; HL; PEPP/*964*.
planh
DLTC; PEPP.
plateresco
DLTC.
platitude
DLTC; DLTS; ME/*233*.
platonic
DLTS.
Platonic criticism
HL.
Platonic love
DLDC/*platonism*.
Platonism
DLDC; DLTC; DLTS; DMCT; HL.
Platonism and poetry
PEPP.
Platonists, The Cambridge
CODEL; OCEL.
plausibility
DLTS.
play
DLTC; DLTS; HL; ME/*233*.
Players, The
OCAL.
play on antonyms
LGEP/*210*.
play-within-a-play
DLTS.
Playwrights' Company
OCAL.
Playwrights Theatre
OCAL/*Provincetown Players*.
pleasure
DMCT.
Pléiade
HL; PEPP.
Pléiade
DLTC.

Pléiade, La
OCEL.
Pléiade, La
CODEL.
pleonasm
DLTC; DLTS; HL; LGEP/*137*; LGEP/*132*; ME/*233*.
plereme
FDLP; GLT.
pleremes
EDSL/*23*.
pliego suelto
DLTC.
ploce
LGEP/*77*; PEPP.
plosion
FDLP/*plosive*; FDLP/*affricate*.
plosive
FDLP; GLT.
plot
DLDC; DLTC; DLTS; DMCT; EDSL/*298*; HL; ME/*233*; PEPP.
plot, action
EDSL/*298*.
plot, admiration
EDSL/*299*.
plot, affective
EDSL/*299*.
plot, cynical
EDSL/*298*.
plot, disillusionment
EDSL/*299*.
plot, education
EDSL/*299*.
plot, maturing
EDSL/*299*.
plot, pathetic
EDSL/*298*.
plot, punitive
EDSL/*298*.
plot, reform
EDSL/*299*.
plot, revelation
EDSL/*299*.

plot, sentimental
EDSL/*299.*

plots of character
EDSL/*299.*

plots of fortune
EDSL/*298.*

plots of thought
EDSL/*299.*

plot, testing
EDSL/*299.*

plot, tragic
EDSL/*298.*

Plough Monday play, the
DLTC.

pluperfect
FDLP/*perfect.*

pluperfect tense
ME/*418.*

plural formation
FDLP/*analogy.*

plural inflection
ME/*418.*

pluralism
DMCT.

plurality
FDLP/*allo-.*

plural of approximation
GLT.

plurative
GLT.

plurilingualism
FDLP/*multilingual.*

plurisegmental
FDLP/*plosive.*

plurisignation
DLTC; DLTS; HL; PEPP.

plus juncture
FDLP/*juncture*; GLT.

Plymouth Colony
OCAL.

Plymouth Company
OCAL/*Virginia Company.*

PM
FDLP/*plosive*; FDLP/*phrase-marker.*

pnigos
DLTC.

poecilonym
OO.

poem
DLTC; DLTS; HL; ME/*233*; PH.

poëme
DLTC; PEPP.

poesie
DLTC; PEPP.

poesy
DLTS; PH.

poet
HL; PH.

poetaster
DLTC; DLTS; HL.

poète maudit
DLTC; DLTS; PEPP.

poetic
EDSL/*341*; LGEP/*26*; PH.

poetical miscellanies
HL.

poetic closure
PEPP/*964.*

poetic contests
DLTC; PEPP.

poetic contractions
DLTC; PEPP.

poetic diction
CODEL; DLDC/*diction*; DLTC; DLTS; DMCT; HL; LGEP/*15*; PEPP; PH.

poetic drama
HL; PEPP.

poetic function
FDLP/*poetics.*

poeticism
ME/*234.*

poetic justice
DLDC; DLTC; DLTS; HL; ME/*234.*

217 □ Polish poetry

poetic licence
DLTC; DMCT; LGEP/36.
poetic license
DLDC; DLTS; HL; ME/234; PEPP; PH.
poetic madness
PEPP.
poetic prose
DLTC; DLTS; LGEP/26.
poetics
CR/Index; DLTS; EDSL/79; FDLP/plosive; HL; PH.
poetics and rhetoric
PEPP.
poetics, conceptions of
PEPP.
Poetischer Realismus
PEPP.
poet laureate
CODEL; DLTC; DLTS; HL; ME/234; OCEL; PEPP.
poetry
CR/Index; DLDC/literature; DLTC; DLTS; DMCT; EDSL/153; FDLP/poetics; FDLP/accent; HL; ME/233; PH.
poetry and fine arts
PEPP.
poetry and history
PEPP.
poetry and knowledge
PEPP.
poetry and music
PEPP.
poetry and philosophy
PEPP.
poetry and religion
PEPP.
poetry and rhetoric
CR/Index.
poetry and science
PEPP.
poetry and semantics
PEPP.

poetry and society
PEPP.
poetry and the other arts
PEPP/965.
poetry and truth
PEPP.
poetry, oral
CR/Index.
poetry reading
PEPP/967.
poetry, theories of
PEPP.
poetry therapy
PEPP/970.
poikilonym
OO.
pointer
GLT/word.
point of articulation
FDLP/place of articulation; GLT.
point of attack
DLTC; HL.
point of rest
DLTC.
point of turning
DLTC.
point of view
DLDC; DLTS; DMCT; EDSL/328; HL; ME/234.
point of view shot
HL.
polarity
FDLP.
polemic
DLTC; HL.
polemic: Christian
CR/Index.
polemics
DLTS.
Polish
FDLP/alveolo-palatal.
Polish poetry
PEPP.

Polish prosody
PEPP.
political novel
HL.
politics
CR/*Index.*
politics and poetry
PEPP/*970.*
polygenesis
GLT.
polyglot
GLT.
polylectal
FDLP.
polymorphemic
FDLP/*morpheme.*
Polynesian
FDLP/*canonical.*
Polynesian poetry
PEPP.
polyonomy
GLT.
polyonym
OO.
polyphonic prose
DLTC; DLTS; HL; ME/*234*; OCAL; PEPP; PH.
polyphony
GLT.
polyptoton
HL.
polyrhythmic
DLTC; PEPP.
polyschematic
DLTC.
polyschematist
PEPP.
polysemia
FDLP/*polysemy.*
polysemic
FDLP/*polysemy.*
polysemous
FDLP/*polysemy.*

polysemy
DMCT; EDSL/*236*; FDLP; GLT; LGEP/*39*; LGEP/*206.*
polysemy, grammatical
LGEP/*207.*
polysemy, lexical
LGEP/*206.*
polysyllabic
FDLP/*polysyllable.*
polysyllabication
DLTS.
polysyllabic rhyme
DLTC; PEPP.
polysyllable
FDLP/*syllable*; FDLP.
polysyndeton
DLTC; HL; ME/*235*; PEPP.
polysynthesis
FDLP/*polysynthetic.*
polysynthetic
FDLP/*incorporating*; FDLP.
polysynthetic language
GLT.
polysystemic
FDLP.
polysystemicism
FDLP/*polysystemic.*
polytonic language
GLT.
pooh-pooh theory
GLT.
pop literature
ME/*235.*
popular ballad
DLTS; HL.
popular etymology
GLT.
popular word (form)
GLT.
Populist party
OCAL.
pornography
DLTC; DLTS; DMCT; HL; ME/*235.*

Porson's law
  PEPP.
portemanteau morph
  EDSL/*201*.
portmanteau
  FDLP.
portmanteau morph
  FDLP/*morpheme*.
portmanteau morpheme
  GLT.
portmanteau word
  DLDC/*figurative language*; DLTC; DLTS; GLT; ME/*418*.
portmanteau words
  HL; ME/*235*.
portrayal
  DLTS.
Port Royal
  FDLP.
Port-Royalists
  CR/*Index*.
Portuguese
  FDLP/*relexification*; FDLP/*diminutive*; FDLP/*diphthong*; FDLP/*nasal*.
Portuguese poetry
  PEPP.
position
  FDLP; GLT; ME/*418*.
positional mobility
  FDLP.
positional variant
  FDLP/*position*; GLT.
position class
  ME/*418*.
position of articulation
  GLT.
positions
  FDLP/*canonical*.
positive
  FDLP.
positive degree
  ME/*419*.
positive transfer
  FDLP/*transfer*.
positivism
  DLTS; HL.
possession
  FDLP/*case*.
possessive inflection
  ME/*419*.
possessive pronoun
  FDLP/*pronoun*.
possessive relationship
  FDLP/*alienable*.
post-
  FDLP.
post-alveolar
  FDLP/*alveolar*.
post-article
  FDLP/*post-*.
post-dental
  GLT.
post-determiner
  FDLP/*post-*.
postdeterminer
  ME/*419*.
post-dorsal
  GLT.
post-modern
  HL.
Post-Modernist Period in English Literature, The, 1965-
  HL.
postmodification
  FDLP/*modification*; FDLP/*post-*.
post-modifying genitive
  FDLP/*genitive*.
Post-Nicene Fathers
  OCEL/*Ante-Nicene Fathers*.
postnominal modification
  ME/*420*.
post-palatal
  GLT.
postposition
  FDLP/*post-*; GLT.
post-tonic
  GLT.

post-tonic syllable ▢ **220**

post-tonic syllable
GLT.
postulational method
FDLP/*postulates*.
posture
FDLP/*parametric phonetics*.
post-velar
GLT.
post-verbal
FDLP/*adjective*; FDLP/*post-*.
posy
HL.
potboiler
DLTC; DLTS; HL.
potentialities, semantic
GLT.
potential pause
FDLP/*pause*; FDLP.
potpourri
DLTS.
poulter's measure
CODEL; DLTC; DLTS; HL; OCEL; PEPP; PH.
power
FDLP.
powerful
FDLP/*power*.
power, literature of
DLTC.
practical critic
DLDC/*criticism*.
practical criticism
DMCT; HL; PEPP.
practical knowledge
CR/*Index*.
praeexercitamina
CR/*Index*.
praemunitio
CR/*Index*.
pragmatics
EDSL/*338*; FDLP.
pragmatic theories
EDSL/*81*.

pragmatic theory of art
HL.
Pragmatism
OCAL.
pragmatism
DLTS; HL.
Prague School
FDLP.
Prairie region
OCAL.
praise and blame
CR/*Index*.
Prākrits poetry
PEPP.
praxis
DLTC.
pre-
FDLP.
preaching
CR/*Index*.
pre-adjective
GLT.
pre-adjunct order
GLT.
preamble
DLTS; HL; ME/*235*.
pre-article
FDLP/*pre-*.
precept
DLTS; ME/*236*.
préciosité
PEPP.
préciosité, la
DLTC.
preciosity
DLTS; HL.
précis
DLTC; DLTS; HL; ME/*236*.
pre-dental
GLT.
predestination
DLTS; HL.
pre-determiner
FDLP/*pre-*.

predeterminer
ME/*420*.
predicables
CR/*Index*.
predicate
EDSL/*270*; EDSL/*213*; EDSL/*210*; EDSL/*217*; EDSL/*212*; FDLP; ME/*420*.
predicate adjective
ME/*420*.
predicate attribute
GLT.
predicate calculus
FDLP/*predicate*.
predicated
FDLP/*predicate*.
predicate logic
FDLP.
predicate, logical
EDSL/*269*.
predicate noun
ME/*420*.
predicate objective
ME/*420*.
predicate, psychological
EDSL/*271*.
predication
FDLP/*predicate*; ME/*420*.
predicative
FDLP/*predicate*.
predicative construction
GLT.
predicative syntagm
GLT.
predicator
FDLP/*predicate*.
predispositions
FDLP/*cultural transmission*.
pre-dorsal
GLT.
preface
DLTC; DLTS; HL; ME/*236*.
prefix
DLTS; EDSL/*200*; FDLP; GLT; ME/*420*.

prefixal morpheme
GLT.
prefixation
FDLP/*affix*; FDLP/*prefix*.
pregnant construction
GLT.
pre-grammar
GLT.
pregunta
DLTC; PEPP.
pre-head
FDLP/*tone group*.
pre-lexical structures
FDLP.
prelinguistics
FDLP; GLT.
prelude
DLTS; HL; ME/*236*.
premise
DLTS; ME/*236*.
premises
CR/*Index*.
premodification
FDLP.
premodify
FDLP/*premodification*.
premodifying
FDLP/*modification*.
pre-palatal
GLT.
preparatory conditions
FDLP/*felicity conditions*.
pre-pausal juncture
GLT.
preposition
FDLP; ME/*420*.
preposition adverb
ME/*421*.
prepositional
FDLP/*preposition*.
prepositional phrase
ME/*421*.
Pre-Raphaelite
DLTS.

Pre-Raphaelite Brotherhood
CODEL; OCEL; PEPP.

Pre-Raphaelites
DLTC; ME/*237*.

Pre-Raphaelitism
HL.

prerequisites
FDLP.

preromanticism
PEPP.

Presbyterianism
OCAL.

prescriptive
FDLP; GLT.

prescriptive grammar
GLT; ME/*421*.

prescriptivism
FDLP/*prescriptive*.

prescriptivist
FDLP/*prescriptive*.

presence vs. absence
FDLP/*markedness*.

present
FDLP/*affix*.

presentational affix
GLT.

presentative
GLT.

presentiment
DLTS.

presentive word
GLT.

present participle
ME/*421*.

present perfect tense
ME/*421*.

present tense
ME/*421*.

present use
FDLP/*attested*.

Presslaute
GLT.

Presstimme
GLT.

pressure
FDLP.

pressures, paradigmatic and syntagmatic
GLT.

pressure stop
FDLP/*stop*; GLT.

prestige center
GLT.

prestige dialect
ME/*422*.

prestige language
FDLP/*basilect*; GLT/*dialect*.

presuppose
FDLP/*presupposition*.

presupposed
EDSL/*272*.

presupposes
EDSL/*109*.

presupposition
FDLP.

preterit-present verbs
ME/*422*.

preterit tense
ME/*422*.

preternatural
DLTS.

pretonic
GLT.

pretonic syllable
GLT.

prevarication
FDLP.

preverb
GLT.

pre-verbal
FDLP/*pre-*.

Priamel
PEPP; DLTC.

priapean
DLTC; PEPP.

primacy
EDSL/*351*.

primary accent and secondary accent
  DLTC.
primary analogy
  GLT.
primary articulation
  FDLP/*secondary articulation.*
primary co-articulation
  FDLP/*articulation.*
primary compound
  GLT.
primary epic
  DLDC/*epic.*
primary language
  GLT.
primary linguistic data
  FDLP/*data.*
primary medium
  FDLP/*medium.*
primary phoneme
  GLT.
primary responses
  FDLP/*secondary response.*
primary source
  DLTS.
primary stress
  GLT; ME/*422.*
primary vowels
  GLT.
primary vowel types
  FDLP/*cardinal vowels.*
primary
  GLT/*prime.*
prime
  FDLP/*primitive.*
primer
  DLTC; DLTS.
primeval
  DLTS.
primitive
  FDLP; GLT.
primitive name
  EDSL/*130.*
Primitive Romance
  GLT.

primitivism
  DLDC; DLTC; DLTS; HL; PEPP.
principal parts
  ME/*422.*
printing
  CR/*Index*; DLTS; HL.
printing, introduction into American Colonies
  HL.
printing, introduction into England
  HL.
private press
  DLTC.
private symbol
  DLDC/*symbolism.*
private theaters
  HL.
privative
  EDSL/*112*; FDLP; FDLP/*opposition*; GLT.
privative opposition
  GLT.
privilege of occurrence
  FDLP; GLT.
pro-adjective
  GLT.
probability
  CR/*Index.*
problem novel
  DLTS; HL.
problem play
  DLDC/*drama*; DLTC; DLTS; HL; ME/*237.*
procedural semantics
  FDLP/*semantics.*
procedure
  FDLP.
proceleusmatic
  DLTC; PEPP.
process
  FDLP; GLT.
processing abilities
  FDLP/*acceptability.*

process verb
  GLT.
prochronism
  DLTC; DLTS.
proclitic
  GLT.
proclitics
  FDLP/*clitic.*
Procrustean
  DLTS.
production
  FDLP.
productions
  EDSL/*226.*
productive
  FDLP/*productivity*; FDLP/*production*; GLT.
productive knowledge
  CR/*Index.*
productive prefix
  GLT/*suffix.*
productivity
  EDSL/*357*; FDLP; GLT.
proem
  DLTC; DLTS; HL; ME/*237.*
proemium
  CR/*Index.*
proest
  PEPP.
profanity
  DLTS.
profile
  DLTS; HL.
pro-form
  FDLP; ME/*422.*
progress
  HL; ME/*237.*
progressive
  FDLP.
progressive assimilation
  FDLP/*assimilation*; FDLP/*progressive*; GLT.
progressive dissimilation
  GLT.

progressive tense
  ME/*424.*
progymnasmata
  CR/*Index.*
prohemio
  DLTC.
project
  FDLP.
projection-rules
  FDLP/*project.*
projective poetry
  DLDC.
projective verse
  HL; ME/*237*; PEPP/*972*; PH.
prolegomena
  CR/*Index.*
prolegomena
  ME/*238.*
prolegomenon
  DLTC; DLTS; HL.
prolepsis
  DLTC; DLTS; HL; ME/*238.*
proletarian
  DLTS.
proletarian literature
  OCAL.
proletarian novel
  DLTC.
proletarskaya kul'tura
  DLTC.
prolixity
  ME/*238.*
pro-locative
  FDLP/*pro-form.*
prologue
  DLDC; DLTC; DLTS; HL; ME/*238.*
prominence
  FDLP.
prominent
  FDLP/*prominence.*
promythium
  DLTC.

pro-nominal
FDLP/*pro-form*.
pronoun
FDLP; ME/*424*.
pronunciation
FDLP/*accent*.
pronunciation borrowing
GLT.
pronuntiatio
CR/*Index*.
pro-ode
DLTC; PEPP.
proof
CR/*Index*.
prop
DLTS; FDLP.
propaganda
DLTC; DLTS.
propaganda devices
ME/*238*.
propaganda novel
DLTC; HL.
propaganda play
DLTC.
proparalepsis
HL.
proparoxytone
GLT.
propemptic
CR/*Index*.
proper
FDLP.
proper compound
GLT.
proper name
FDLP/*proper*; GLT.
proper noun
ME/*425*.
proper nouns
FDLP/*proper*.
properties
DLDC/*drama*.
prophecy
CR/*Index*.

pro-phrase
GLT.
proportion
DLTS.
proportional
FDLP; FDLP/*opposition*.
proportional analogy (extension)
GLT.
proportional opposition
GLT.
propos
DLTC.
proposition
CR/*Index*; DLTC; DLTS; FDLP.
propositional calculus
FDLP/*proposition*.
propositional meaning
FDLP/*proposition*.
propositions
FDLP/*alethic*; FDLP/*axiomatic*.
pro-predicate complement
GLT.
pro-presentative
GLT.
propriety
CR/*Index*; DLTC; HL.
prop word
GLT.
prop words
FDLP/*prop*.
prosaic
LGEP/*26*.
prosaic poetry
LGEP/*26*.
prosaic strength
LGEP/*26*.
proscenium
DLTS; HL.
proscriptive
FDLP.
prose
CR/*Index*; DLDC; DLTC; DLTS; DMCT; EDSL/*185*; HL; ME/*239*.

prose/poetry
  LGEP/26.
prose and verse
  PEPP.
prose, baroque
  CR/Index.
prose hymns
  CR/Index.
prose poem
  DLTC; PEPP; PH.
prose poetry
  HL.
prose rhythm
  DLTC; HL; LGEP/103; PEPP.
prosiopesis
  FDLP/elision; GLT.
prosodeme
  GLT.
prosodemes
  EDSL/23; FDLP/prosody.
prosodic
  EDSL/176; FDLP/prosody.
prosodic features
  GLT.
prosodic notation
  PEPP.
prosodic phonology
  FDLP/prosody.
prosodic sign
  GLT.
prosodic symbols
  PH.
prosodion
  DLTC; PEPP.
prosody
  DLDC/versification; DLTC; DLTS; EDSL/183; FDLP; GLT; HL; LGEP/103; ME/239; PEPP; PH.
prosopopeia
  PH/metaphor.
prosopopoeia
  CR/Index.

prosopopoeia
  DLDC/figurative language; DLTC; DLTS; HL; PEPP.
prospectus
  DLTS.
prosphonetic
  CR/Index.
prosthesis
  DLTS.
prosthesis, prosthetic
  GLT.
protagonist
  DLDC/plot; DLTC; DLTS; DMCT; EDSL/223; HL; ME/239.
protasis
  DLTC; DLTS; HL.
protatic character
  DLTC.
protected consonant
  GLT.
Protestant Episcopal Church
  OCAL.
prothalamion
  DLTC; HL; PH/epithalamion.
prothesis
  FDLP/intrusion; GLT; HL.
prothetic
  FDLP.
prothetic vowel
  GLT.
proto-
  FDLP; GLT; ME/425.
proto-conversion
  FDLP/proto-.
Proto-Indo-European
  FDLP/proto-; ME/425.
proto language
  FDLP/comparative.
protonym
  OO.
Proto-Romance
  FDLP/proto-.
proto-sentence
  FDLP/proto-.

227 □ psycholinguistics

prototype
DLTS; HL.
protozeugma
DLTC.
protreptic
DLTC.
Provençal poetry
PEPP.
provenance
ME/*provenience, 239.*
provenience
ME/*239.*
pro-verb
FDLP/*pro-form*; GLT.
proverb
DLDC/*aphorism*; DLTC; DLTS; HL; ME/*239*; PEPP.
proverbe dramatique
DLTC.
Providence Plantations
OCAL.
Provincetown Players, The
OCAL.
provincialism
DLTS; HL.
proxemics
FDLP.
pruning poem
DLTC; HL.
pryddest
PEPP.
PS
FDLP/*phrase-structure*; FDLP.
psalm
DLTC; DLTS; HL; PEPP/*973.*
psalms
CR/*Index.*
psalter
DLTC.
pseudepigrapha
DLTC; DLTS.
pseudo-cleft sentence
FDLP.

pseudo-intransitive
FDLP/*transitivity.*
pseudonym
DLTC; DLTS; HL; ME/*239*; OO.
pseudonymous literature
DLTC.
pseudo-procedure
FDLP.
pseudo-semantic development
GLT.
pseudo-Shakespearean plays
HL.
pseudo-statement
DLTC; PEPP.
pseudo-subjunctive
GLT.
PSG
FDLP/*phrase-structure*; FDLP/*PS.*
psittacism
DLTC.
psyche
DLTS.
psychedelic
DLTS; ME/*239.*
psychical distance
DLDC.
psychic distance
DLTC; HL; ME/*240*; PEPP/*973.*
psychoanalysis
ME/*240.*
psychoanalysis and poetry
PEPP.
psychoanalytical criticism
HL.
psychogogia
DMCT.
psychograph
DLTS.
psychography
DLTC.
psycholinguistics
EDSL/*71*; FDLP/*linguistics*; FDLP/*applied linguistics*; FDLP; GLT; ME/*425.*

psychological criticism
PEPP.

psychological linguistics
FDLP/*psycholinguistics*.

psychologically connected items
FDLP/*association*.

psychological novel
DLDC/*novel*; DLTC; DLTS; HL.

psychological phonetics
GLT.

psychological processes
FDLP/*correspond*.

psychological responses
FDLP/*auditory phonetics*.

psychological solutions
FDLP/*acoustic phonetics*.

psychological subject
FDLP/*topicalisation*.

psychology
DMCT.

psychology and poetry
PEPP/*973*.

psychomechanics
EDSL/*122*.

psychophonetics
GLT.

public theaters
HL.

Publius
OCAL.

Puerto Rican poetry
PEPP/*977*.

puffery
DLTC.

puissance
DLTS.

Pulitzer prize
DLTS.

Pulitzer Prizes
HL; OCEL.

Pulitzer Prizes in Journalism and Letters
OCAL.

pulmonic
FDLP.

pulmonic cavity
FDLP/*cavity*.

pulp magazine
DLTS.

pulp magazines
HL.

pulps, the
ME/*241*.

pulp writer
DLTS.

pulse
FDLP/*chest pulse*.

pulse theory
FDLP/*syllable*.

pun
DLDC/*figurative language*; DLTC; DLTS; HL; LGEP/*209*; ME/*241*; PEPP.

pun, asyntactic
LGEP/*211*.

punctuation
ME/*425*.

pun, etymological
LGEP/*211*.

pun, homonymic
LGEP/*209*.

punning repetition
LGEP/*210*.

pun, polysemantic
LGEP/*209*.

puns
FDLP/*homonym*.

puppetry
DLTS.

pure linguistics
FDLP/*applied linguistics*.

pure marker
GLT.

pure poetry
DLDC/*didactic literature*; DLTC; HL; PEPP; PH.

pure-relational element
GLT.

pure vowel
FDLP/*vowel*; FDLP.
purgation
DLTS.
purism
DLTC; FDLP.
purist
DLTS; FDLP/*purism*; HL.
Puritan Interregnum
DLDC/*puritanism*.
Puritanism
DLTS; HL; OCAL; DLDC.
Puritansim
ME/*242*.
purple passage
DLDC; ME/*242*.
purple patch
DLTC; HL; PEPP.
purple prose
DLTS.
purpose
DLTS.

purpose in communicating
ME/*243*.
Puseyism
HL.
putative author
HL.
puzzlement
FDLP/*intonation*.
pyramidal structure
DLDC/*plot*.
pyrrhic
CODEL; DLDC/*versification*; DLTC; DLTS; HL; ME/*243*; OCEL; PEPP; PH.
pythiambic
PEPP.
pythiambic verse
DLTC.
pythian meter
DLTC; PEPP.

Q

qasida
  PEPP.
qasida
  DLTC.
Q Celtic
  GLT.
quadrilabial
  FDLP/*bilabial*.
quadrivium
  CR/*Index*; DLTC; DLTS; HL; OCEL.
quadruplets
  GLT.
Quakers
  OCAL.
qualification
  FDLP.
qualifier
  FDLP/*qualification*; GLT; ME/*426*.
qualify
  FDLP/*qualification*.
qualitative
  FDLP/*quality*.
qualitative accent
  GLT.
qualitative gradation
  GLT.

quality
  FDLP/*co-operative principle*; FDLP; GLT.
quality, stasis of
  CR/*Index*.
quantifiable noun
  GLT.
quantification
  FDLP/*quantifier*.
quantifier
  FDLP; GLT.
quantifier-floating
  FDLP/*quantifier*.
quantitative accent
  GLT.
quantitative gradation
  GLT.
quantitative linguistics
  FDLP.
quantitative verse
  DLDC/*versification*; DLTS; HL; PH/*metre*.
quantity
  DLTC; EDSL/*186*; FDLP; FDLP/*co-operative principle*; GLT; HL; PEPP; PH.
quantity mark
  GLT.
quart d'heure
  DLTC.

Quarterly Review
  OCEL.
Quarterly Review
  CODEL.
Quarterly Review, The
  HL.
quartet
  DLTC.
quarto
  CODEL; DLDC/*folio*; DLTC; DLTS; HL; OCEL.
quasi-auxiliary
  GLT.
quaternarius
  DLTC; PEPP.
quaternion
  HL.
quatorzain
  PEPP.
quatorzain
  DLTC; DLTS; HL.
quatrain
  CODEL; DLDC/*versification*; DLTC; DLTS; EDSL/*192*; HL; ME/*244*; PEPP; PH.
Quechua
  FDLP/*ejective*; FDLP/*glottal*.
Queen's English
  FDLP/*accent*.
quem quaeritis
  DLTS.
quem quaeritis **trope**
  DLTC.
question
  FDLP; ME/*426*.
questione della lingua
  DLTC.

questione della lingua
  GLT.
question, epic
  DLTC; PEPP.
question transformation
  ME/*426*.
question word
  FDLP/*question*.
quibble
  DLTS; HL.
quidproquo
  DLTC.
quinary
  DLTC.
quintain
  DLTC; DLTS; HL.
quintessence
  DLTS.
quintet
  DLTC; HL/*quintain*; PEPP.
quintilla
  DLTC; PEPP.
quinzain
  DLTC.
quip
  DLTS; HL; ME/*244*.
Quod, John
  OCAL.
quod semper quod ubique
  DLTC.
quotation
  EDSL/*327*.
quotations, introducing
  ME/*246*.
quotation titles
  DLTC.

R

Rabelaisian
  DLTC; DLTS.
radiation of synonyms
  GLT.
radical
  FDLP/*root*; GLT.
Radical Club, The
  OCAL.
radical flection
  GLT.
radicalism
  DLTS.
radical language
  GLT.
radicaux
  EDSL/*200*.
Ragusan poetry
  PEPP.
Rahmenerzählung
  DLTC.
raising
  FDLP.
raison d'ètre
  DLTS.
raisonneur
  DLDC/*chorus*; DLTC.
raisonneur
  HL.
random variations
  GLT.

range
  GLT.
rank
  EDSL/*240*; FDLP; GLT.
ranks
  FDLP/*incompatibility*.
rank scale
  FDLP/*rank*.
rankshift
  FDLP/*rank*.
Rappists
  OCAL.
rasa
  PEPP.
rasa
  DLTC.
rate
  FDLP.
ratiocinatio
  CR/*Index*.
ratiocination
  DLTS; HL; ME/*247*.
rationalism
  DLTC; DLTS; HL; ME/*247*.
rationalize
  HL.
Räuberroman
  DLTC.
Ravenna
  CR/*Index*.

r-coloured □ **234**

r-coloured
    FDLP/*retroflex*.
reaction
    EDSL/*290*.
reader
    EDSL/*329*; EDSL/*81*.
reader identification
    DLTS.
reading
    CR/*Index*; EDSL/*80*.
readjustment rule
    FDLP/*diacritic*.
ready-made utterances
    FDLP/*idiom*.
realisation
    FDLP.
realisational analysis
    FDLP/*realisation*.
realise
    FDLP/*realisation*.
Realism
    OCAL; CODEL; DLDC; DLTC; DLTS; DMCT; EDSL/*260*; HL; ME/*247*; OCEL; PEPP.
realistic comedy
    HL.
realistic novel
    HL.
Realistic Period in American Literature, 1865-1900
    HL.
Realistic Period in English Literature, 1870-1914
    HL.
realist theory
    HL.
realization
    GLT; LGEP/*37*.
re-analysis
    FDLP/*error*.
reason
    DMCT.
Reason, Age of
    DLTS.

rebus
    DLTS; EDSL/*196*.
rebuttal
    DLTS; HL.
recantation
    DLTS; HL; PEPP/*979*.
Received Pronunciation
    DLTS; FDLP; GLT.
received standard pronunciation
    ME/*428*.
receiver
    EDSL/*341*; FDLP/*object*; FDLP/*communication*.
recension
    DLTC; HL.
receptor
    DLTC.
recessive accent
    DLTC; GLT; HL; PEPP; PH.
recherche
    DLTS.
recipient
    FDLP/*goal*; FDLP/*passive*.
reciprocal
    FDLP.
reciprocal assimilation
    FDLP/*coalescence*; FDLP/*assimilation*; GLT.
reciprocal social roles
    FDLP/*converse*.
reciprocus versus
    PEPP.
récit
    EDSL/*297*.
recitation
    CR/*Index*.
recognition
    DLDC/*tragedy*; DLDC/*plot*; DLTC; EDSL/*332*; PEPP.
recognition plot
    HL.
recognition scene
    HL.
recoil
    DLTC.

recomposition
GLT.
Reconstruction
OCAL; EDSL/*10*; FDLP; GLT; ME/*428*.
recorded speech
FDLP/*corpus*.
recorded usage
FDLP/*attested*.
recto
DLTS.
recto and verso
DLTC.
recuesta
DLTC.
recursive
EDSL/*231*; FDLP/*recursiveness*.
recursive-complex transformation
ME/*428*.
recursiveness
FDLP; ME/*428*.
recutting
GLT.
redaction
DLTC; DLTS; HL.
rederijkers
DLTC; PEPP.
red herring
ME/*247*.
redondilla
DLTC; PEPP.
reduced
FDLP.
reduced grade
GLT.
reduced sentence
GLT.
reduced vowel
GLT.
reductio ad absurdum
DLTS; HL; ME/*248*.
reduction
GLT.

redundancy
DLTS; FDLP; GLT; ME/*429*; ME/*248*.
redundancy rules
FDLP/*redundancy*.
redundant
EDSL/*26*; HL.
redundant verse
DLTC.
reduplicated
FDLP/*reduplication*.
reduplication
FDLP; GLT; ME/*430*; ME/*248*.
reduplicative compound
FDLP/*reduplication*.
reduplicative morpheme
GLT.
reference
FDLP/*referent*; GLT.
reference grammars
FDLP/*grammar*.
reference of pronouns
ME/*430*.
reference, point of
DLTC.
referend
GLT.
referent
EDSL/*101*; FDLP; GLT; ME/*248*.
referential
EDSL/*341*.
referential function
EDSL/*247*.
referential indices
FDLP.
referentiality
FDLP/*co-referential*.
referential language
DLTC.
referential meaning
FDLP/*referent*; GLT.
referred speech
GLT.

reflection
  EDSL/*322*.
reflectiveness
  FDLP/*reflexive*.
reflex
  GLT.
reflexive
  FDLP.
reflexive middle
  GLT.
reflexiveness
  FDLP/*reflexive*.
reflexivisation
  FDLP/*reflexive*.
reflexivity
  FDLP/*reflexive*.
reformation
  DLTS.
Reform Bill
  CODEL; OCEL.
Reform Bill of 1832
  HL.
Reformed Church in America
  OCAL.
Reformed Church in the United States
  OCAL.
refrain
  DLDC/*versification*; DLDC/*ballad*; DLTC; DLTS; DMCT; EDSL/*192*; HL; ME/*248*; PEPP; PH/*stanza*.
refrán
  DLTC; PEPP.
refrein
  DLTC; PEPP.
refutation
  CR/*Index*.
regional
  FDLP/*accent*.
regional accents
  FDLP/*accent*.
regional dialects
  FDLP/*dialect*; FDLP/*geographical linguistics*.

Regionalism
  OCAL; DLTS; HL.
regional language
  GLT.
regionally distinctive
  FDLP/*dialect*.
regional novel
  DLTC.
Regions
  OCAL.
register
  DLTC; FDLP; LGEP/*9*.
register study
  LGEP/*41*.
regressive
  FDLP.
regressive assimilation
  FDLP/*anticipatory*; FDLP/*assimilation*.
regular
  EDSL/*229*; FDLP.
regular alternation
  GLT.
regularisation
  FDLP/*analogy*.
regularist
  GLT.
regularity
  FDLP/*regular*.
regular ode
  PH.
regular sound change
  GLT.
reification
  HL; ME/*249*.
reiteration
  FDLP.
Reizianum
  PEPP.
rejet
  PEPP.
rejet
  DLTC.

relation
FDLP; FDLP/*co-operative principle.*
relation(al)
GLT.
relational
FDLP/*relation.*
relational complement
EDSL/*211.*
relational grammar
FDLP.
relational network
FDLP/*arc.*
relational word
GLT.
relative
FDLP.
relative adverb
ME/*430.*
relative arbitrariness
EDSL/*131.*
relative clause
FDLP/*relative*; ME/*430.*
relative pitch
GLT.
relative pronoun
EDSL/*282*; FDLP/*relative*; FDLP/*pronoun.*
relative pronouns
ME/*431.*
relativisation
FDLP/*relative.*
relativism
DLTC.
relativism in criticism
PEPP.
relativist critic
DLDC/*criticism.*
relativity
FDLP.
release
FDLP; GLT.
release, delayed
FDLP/*delayed.*

relevant
FDLP/*distinctive*; GLT.
relexification
FDLP.
relic area
GLT; ME/*431.*
relic areas
FDLP/*area.*
relic form
GLT.
relief scene
HL.
religion and poetry
PEPP.
religious contexts
FDLP/*common.*
religious drama
HL.
religious factor
GLT.
religious situations
FDLP/*appropriate.*
relique
DLTS; HL.
remate
DLTC; PEPP.
Renaissance
CODEL; DLDC; DLTC; DLTS; HL; ME/*249*; OCEL.
renaissance grammars
FDLP/*grammar.*
Renaissance poetics
PEPP.
Renaissance poetry
PEPP.
rendering
HL; ME/*251.*
renewal of connection
FDLP/*connection.*
renga
PEPP.
re-ordering
FDLP.

repartee □ 238

repartee
  DLTC; DLTS; HL; ME/*252*.
repeated elements
  FDLP/*cycle*.
repeated structure
  DLDC/*form*.
repertoire
  DLTS; FDLP.
repertory
  FDLP/*repertoire*; GLT.
repetend
  DLTC; DLTS; HL; ME/*252*; PEPP.
repetitio
  CR/*Index*.
repetition
  DLTC; EDSL/*278*; HL; ME/*252*; PEPP.
repetition, free
  LGEP/*77*.
repetition, immediate
  LGEP/*77*.
repetition, intermittent
  LGEP/*77*.
repetitive compound
  GLT.
replacement
  GLT.
replacive
  FDLP; GLT.
replacive allomorph
  ME/*431*.
replevin
  DLTC.
replica
  GLT.
report
  DLTS.
reportage
  DLTS.
reported discourse
  EDSL/*302*.
reported speech
  FDLP/*indirect*.

representation
  DMCT; EDSL/*101*; FDLP.
representational
  GLT.
representationality
  EDSL/*302*.
representative
  EDSL/*281*; FDLP.
representative function
  EDSL/*341*.
requiem
  DLTS; HL.
research paper
  ME/*252*.
reshaping
  GLT.
residual phoneme (residue)
  GLT.
residue forms
  GLT; ME/*431*.
residuum
  DLTS.
resolution
  DLDC/*plot*; DLTC; DLTS; HL; PEPP.
resolution of medial groups
  GLT.
resolved stress
  HL.
resonance
  FDLP; GLT.
resonance chambers
  FDLP/*resonance*.
resonant
  FDLP; GLT.
response
  DMCT.
rest
  DLTC; PEPP; PH.
Restoration
  CODEL; DLDC/*comedy*; DLDC; ME/*253*; DLTS.
Restoration Age
  HL.

Restoration comedy
DLTC.
Restoration Period
DLTC.
Restoration, The
OCEL.
restraint
HL.
restricted
FDLP.
restricted code
FDLP/*elaborated*; FDLP/*restricted*.
restricted language
FDLP/*restricted*.
restricted rules
FDLP/*context*.
restricted stress
GLT.
restrictions
FDLP/*collocation*.
restrictive
FDLP.
restrictive modifier
ME/*432*.
résumé
DLTS.
retracted
FDLP; GLT.
retroencha
DLTC; PEPP.
retroflex
FDLP; GLT.
retroflexed
FDLP/*retroflex*.
retroflexion
FDLP/*retroflex*; GLT.
retroflex *r*
ME/*432*.
re(tro)gressive assimilation
GLT.
re(tro)gressive dissimilation
GLT.

re(tro)gressive formation
GLT.
retrospect
DLDC/*plot*.
revenge play
DLDC/*tragedy*.
revenge tragedy
DLTC; DLTS; HL.
reverdie
DLTC; PEPP.
Reverie, Reginald
OCAL.
reversal
DLDC/*tragedy*; DLDC/*plot*; DLTC; FDLP; HL; PEPP.
reversed consonance
PH/*rhyme*.
reversed foot
PH.
reverse spelling
GLT.
Revesby play
DLTC.
review
DLTC; DLTS; HL; ME/*254*.
Revised Extended Standard Theory
FDLP.
revising
ME/*254*.
Revolutionary Age in American Literature, 1765-1790
HL.
Revolutionary and Early National Period in American Literature, 1765-1830
HL.
Revolutionary Romances
OCAL.
Revolutionary War
OCAL.
revue
DLTC; DLTS; HL.
rewrite rule
ME/*432*.

rewrite-rule
FDLP.

rewriting rule
FDLP/*rewrite-rule*.

rewriting rules
EDSL/*227*.

rhapsodist
PEPP.

rhapsody
CODEL; DLTC; HL; OCEL; PEPP.

Rheins
CR/*Index*.

rhematic
FDLP/*rheme*.

rhematic aspects
FDLP/*communication*.

rheme
FDLP.

rhetor
CR/*Index*.

Rhetores Latini Minores
CR/*Index*.

rhetoric
CR/*Index*; DLDC; DLTC; DLTS; DMCT; EDSL/*294*; EDSL/*73*; FDLP/*elision*; HL; ME/*255*.

rhetorical accent
HL; PEPP.

rhetorical criticism
HL.

rhetorical exercises
CR/*Index*.

rhetorical figure
DLTC.

rhetorical figures of speech
HL.

rhetorical irony
DLTC.

rhetorical question
DLTC; DLTS; HL; LGEP/*184*; ME/*256*; PEPP.

rhetorical schools
CR/*Index*.

rhetorical stress
PH/*metre*.

rhetorical textual analysis
EDSL/*295*.

rhetoric and philosophy
CR/*Index*.

rhetoric and poetics
PEPP.

rhetoric, deduced
CR/*Index*.

rhetoric, induced
CR/*Index*.

rhetoric, internal
CR/*Index*.

rhetoric, literary
CR/*Index*.

rhetoric, philosophical
CR/*Index*.

rhetoric, prescriptive
CR/*Index*.

rhetoric, primary
CR/*Index*.

rhetoric, secondary
CR/*Index*.

rhetoric, sophistic
CR/*Index*.

rhetoric, technical
CR/*Index*.

rhetoric, traditional
CR/*Index*.

rhétoriqueurs
DLTC; PEPP.

Rhodes
CR/*Index*.

Rhodes Scholarships
OCAL.

rhopalic verse
CODEL; DLTC; HL; OCEL; PEPP.

rhotacised
FDLP/*retroflex*.

rhotacism
GLT; ME/*432*.

rhotacization
  GLT.
rhupynt
  PEPP.
rhyme
  DLDC/*versification*; DLTC;
  DLTS; DMCT; EDSL/*190*; GLT;
  HL; ME/*256*; PEPP; PH.
rhyme, alternating
  EDSL/*191*.
rhyme, antigrammatical
  EDSL/*191*.
rhyme, antisemantic
  EDSL/*191*.
rhyme counterpoint
  DLTC.
rhyme-counterpoint
  PEPP.
rhyme, end
  EDSL/*190*.
rhyme, enveloping
  EDSL/*191*.
rhyme, equivocal
  EDSL/*191*.
rhyme, eye
  EDSL/*190*.
rhyme, feminine
  EDSL/*191*.
rhyme, grammatical
  EDSL/*191*.
rhyme, hyperdactylic
  EDSL/*191*.
rhyme: male or masculine
  CODEL; OCEL.
rhyme, masculine
  EDSL/*191*.
rhyme, near
  EDSL/*191*.
rhyme, oxytonic
  EDSL/*191*.
rhyme, paroxytonic
  EDSL/*191*.
rhyme, proparoxytonic
  EDSL/*191*.

rhyme, rich
  EDSL/*190*.
rhyme royal
  DLDC/*versification*; DLTC;
  DLTS; HL; ME/*256*; OCEL;
  PEPP; PH/*stanza*.
rhyme-royal
  CODEL.
rhyme scheme
  DLTC; DLTS; HL; PEPP.
rhyme, semantic
  EDSL/*191*.
rhyme, true
  EDSL/*190*.
rhyme word
  GLT.
rhyming slang
  DLTC.
rhythm
  DLDC/*versification*; DLTC;
  DLTS; DMCT; EDSL/*187*;
  FDLP/*duration*; FDLP; GLT;
  HL; ME/*257*; PEPP; PH.
rhythmical pause
  DLTC; PEPP; PH.
rhythmici
  PEPP.
rhythmic measure
  LGEP/*91*.
rhythm, prose
  CR/*Index*.
Richmond
  OCAL/*Virginia*.
riddle
  DLTC; DLTS; HL; PEPP.
riddles
  FDLP/*homonym*.
ridicule
  DLTS.
riding rhyme
  DLTC; DLTS.
right
  FDLP/*correct*.
right-branching
  FDLP/*depth hypothesis*; FDLP.

right recursive
   FDLP/*right-branching*.
Riksmål
   GLT.
rill spirant
   GLT.
rim
   FDLP.
rime
   DLTC; ME/*rhyme, 256*; PEPP; PH/*rhyme*.
rime couée
   DLTC; HL.
rime couée
   PH/*stanza*.
rime riche
   HL.
rime riche
   DLTS; PEPP; PH/*rhyme*.
rimes riches
   DLTC.
rimes suffisantes
   DLTC.
rímur
   PEPP.
rise
   FDLP/*rising*.
rising
   FDLP.
rising action
   DLDC/*plot*; DLTC; DLTS; HL; PEPP.
rising diphthong
   GLT.
rising-falling
   FDLP/*nucleus*.
rising juncture
   FDLP/*juncture*.
rising meter
   DLDC/*versification*.
rising rhythm
   DLTC; HL; LGEP/*113*; PEPP.
rispetto
   DLTC; PEPP.

ritornello
   DLTC; PEPP.
ritornello
   DLTS.
ritual
   DLDC; DMCT.
rímur
   DLTC.
Roanoke Island
   OCAL.
Robin Hood theme
   DLTS.
rocking rhythm
   DLTC; HL; PEPP; PH.
rock lyric
   PEPP/*979*.
rock verse
   ME/*257*.
rococo
   DLTC; DLTS; HL; ME/*257*; PEPP.
rodomontade
   DLTC; DLTS; HL.
rogue
   DLTS.
rogue comedies
   DLDC/*comedy*.
role
   EDSL/*224*; LGEP/*9*.
roll
   DLTC; FDLP.
rolled
   FDLP/*roll*.
rolled consonant
   GLT.
Rollo books
   OCAL.
roman
   DLDC/*classic*.
roman à clef
   DLDC/*novel*; DLTC; HL; ME/*258*.
roman à clef
   DLTS.

243 □ Romany

roman à deux sous
DLTC.
roman à thèse
DLTS.
roman à tiroirs
DLTC.
Roman Catholic Church
OCAL.
romance
DLTC.
romance
DLDC/*novel*; DLTC; DLTS; DMCT; HL; ME/*259*; OCAL; PEPP; PH.
Romance languages
DLTC; GLT.
romance, medieval
PEPP.
romance prosody
PEPP.
romancero
DLTC.
romance-six
DLTC.
romance-six
PEPP.
Romanesque
DLTS; HL.
roman-feuilleton
DLTC.
roman-fleuve
DLTC.
roman-fleuve
DLTS.
Roman grammarians
FDLP/*grammar*.
Romanization
GLT.
roman noir
DLTC.
roman policier
DLTC.
roman policier
DLTS.

romans Bretons
DLTC.
romans courtois
DLTC.
romans d'antiquité
DLTC.
romans d'aventure
DLTC.
Romansh poetry
PEPP.
romantic
CODEL; DLDC/*classic*; OCEL; PH.
romantic comedies
DLDC/*comedy*.
romantic comedy
DLTC; HL.
romantic criticism
HL.
romantic epic
HL.
Romantic irony
DLDC/*irony*; DLTC; PH/*irony*.
Romanticism
DMCT; OCAL; PH/*romantic*; DLTC; DLTS; HL; ME/*259*; PEPP.
Romantic Movement
DLDC/*classic*; CODEL; OCEL.
romantic novel
HL.
romantic period
DLTC.
Romantic Period in American Literature, 1830-1865
HL.
Romantic Period in English Literature, 1798-1870
HL.
romantic revival
DLTC.
romantic tradegy
HL.
Romany
DLTS; HL; OCEL.

Romany poetry
PEPP.
romería
DLTC.
rondeau
CODEL; DLTC; DLTS; EDSL/
192; HL; ME/*260*; OCEL; PEPP;
PH.
rondeau redoublé
DLTC; PEPP.
rondeau redoublé
PH.
rondel
PEPP.
rondel
CODEL; DLTC; DLTS; HL;
ME/*261*; OCEL; PH/*rondeau*.
rondelet
DLTC.
roof of the mouth
FDLP/*articulation*.
root
DLTS/*stem*; EDSL/*200*; FDLP/
base; FDLP/*node*; FDLP; FDLP/
affix; GLT; ME/*432*.
root base
GLT.
root-inflected
FDLP/*root*.
root inflection
GLT.
root-isolating
FDLP/*root*.
root, nominal
EDSL/*207*.
root, pronominal
EDSL/*207*.
roots
EDSL/*10*.
root transformation
FDLP/*root*.
round
DLTS; HL.
round character
DLTC; DLTS; EDSL/*223*; HL.

round characters
DLDC/*plot*.
rounded
FDLP/*rounding*.
rounded vowel
GLT.
rounded vowels
ME/*433*.
roundel
DLTC; DLTS; HL; ME/*261*;
PEPP; PH/*rondeau*.
roundelay
DLTC; DLTS; HL; ME/*262*.
Roundheads
CODEL; HL; OCEL.
rounding
FDLP; GLT.
roundlet
DLTC.
Round Table
DLTS.
routine licence
LGEP/*17*; LGEP/*36*.
Rover Boys
OCAL.
Royal Society of London
CR/*Index*.
RP
FDLP/*received pronunciation*.
rubāʿī
PEPP.
Rubaiyat
DLTS.
rubáʿiyát
DLTC.
rubáiyát
HL.
rubaiyat
PH.
Rubáiyát stanza
HL.
rubric
DLTS; HL.

Rückbildung
GLT.
Rück-umlaut
GLT.
rule
FDLP.
rule features
FDLP.
rule of grammar
ME/*433*.
rules
DLTC; PEPP.
rule schema
FDLP/*rule*.
Rumanian poetry
PEPP.
rune
CODEL; DLTC; DLTS; HL; OCEL; PEPP.
runes
PH.
runic
OCEL.
runic writing
ME/*434*.
running rhythm
DLTC; PEPP; PH.

running style
CR/*Index*.
run-on line
DLDC/*versification*; DLTC; DLTS; LGEP/*123*; PEPP.
run-on lines
HL.
rural novel
DMCT.
Russell, Lillian
OCAL.
Russell's Bookstore Group
OCAL.
Russian
FDLP/*frequentative*; FDLP/*article*; FDLP/*hard consonant*; FDLP/*soft consonant*; FDLP/*aspect*; FDLP/*palatalisation*; FDLP/*equative*.
Russian Formalism
PEPP; EDSL/*82*.
Russian poetics
PEPP.
Russian poetry
PEPP.
Russian prosody
PEPP.

S

S
  FDLP.
SAAD
  FDLP.
saber
  DLTC.
sabir
  GLT.
Sacco-Vanzetti Case
  OCAL.
sacra rappresentazione
  DLTC.
sacred books
  DLTC.
saga
  CODEL; DLDC; DLTC; DLTS; HL; ME/*263*; OCEL.
saga novel
  DLTC.
Saint John, Hector
  OCAL.
Saint-Simonism
  OCAL.
saints' lives
  CR/*Index*; HL.
saint's play
  HL.
salamander
  DLTS.

Salem witchcraft trials
  OCAL.
salon
  DLTC; DLTS.
salutatio
  CR/*Index*.
samizdat
  DLTC.
sample
  FDLP/*adequacy*.
sandhi
  FDLP; GLT.
sandhi alternants
  GLT.
sandhi form
  GLT; ME/*435*.
San Francisco
  OCAL.
San Francisco Renaissance
  PEPP/*980*.
Sanskrit
  FDLP/*fusional*.
Sanskrit poetics
  CR/*Index*.
Sanskrit poetry
  PEPP.
Santa Fe Trail
  OCAL.
Sapir-Whorf hypothesis
  FDLP/*sandhi*.

Sapphic
DLTS; HL; PEPP.
Sapphic ode
DLTC.
sapphics
PH.
Sapphic stanza
CODEL; OCEL.
sarcasm
DLDC/*irony*; DLTS; FDLP/*attitudinal*; FDLP/*intonation*; FDLP/*co-operative principle*; HL; LGEP/*172*; ME/*263*.
sarcasm of tone
LGEP/*176*.
Sassenach
DLTS.
satanic
DLTS.
Satanic School
CODEL; DLTC; HL; OCEL; PEPP; DLTS/*satanic*.
Satanism
HL.
satellite
GLT.
satellite language
GLT.
satem languages
GLT; ME/*435*.
satire
CODEL; DLDC; DLTC; DLTS; DMCT; HL; ME/*263*; OCEL; PEPP; PH.
satire bernesque
DLTC.
satirical comedy
DLTC.
satiric comedies
DLDC/*comedy*.
satiric poetry
HL.
satura
DLTC.

satura
PEPP.
Saturday Club
HL.
Saturday Club, The
OCAL.
Saturnian
PEPP.
Saturnian metre
CODEL; DLTC; OCEL.
satyriasis
DLTS.
satyric drama
CODEL; OCEL.
satyr play
DLTC; DLTS; HL.
Saunders, Richard
OCAL.
Saussurean
FDLP.
Saussurianism
EDSL/*14*.
Savoyard
DLTC.
Saybrook Platform
OCAL.
saying
DLTS.
SC
FDLP/*structural change*.
scald
HL/*skald*; HL/*skald*; PEPP; PH.
scale-and-category grammar
FDLP.
scales
FDLP/*incompatibility*.
Scandinavian languages
FDLP/*area*.
scansion
DLDC/*versification*; DLTC; DLTS; EDSL/*186*; HL; ME/*265*; PEPP; PH.
Scapigliatura
DLTC.

scatology
DLTC; DLTS.
scazon
CODEL; DLTC; OCEL; PEPP.
scenario
CODEL; DLTC; DLTS; HL; ME/*265*; OCEL.
scene
DLDC/*plot*; DLDC; DLTS; EDSL/*332*; ME/*265*.
scène à faire
DLTC; HL.
scene and summary
ME/*265*.
scenes (of a drama)
HL.
scenic method
HL.
schema
CR/*Index*.
schema
EDSL/*125*.
scheme
DMCT; HL; LGEP/*73*.
schemes
LGEP/*74*.
Schlüsselroman
DLTC; HL.
scholasticism
CR/*Index*; DLTC; DLTS; HL; OCEL.
scholiast
DLTS; HL.
school
DLTC.
school drama
DLTC.
schoolgirl style
DLTS.
school grammar
ME/*435*.
school grammars
FDLP/*grammar*.
schoolmen
HL.

School of Night
PEPP; HL.
School of Spenser
DLTC; HL; PEPP.
school plays
HL.
Schüttelreim
DLTC; PEPP.
schwa
FDLP; GLT; ME/*435*.
Schwank
DLTC.
Schwellvers
DLTC.
science and poetry
PEPP.
science fiction
CODEL; DLDC; DLTC; DLTS; HL; OCAL; OCEL.
science of language
GLT.
scientific language
FDLP/*language*.
scolion
DLTC; PEPP.
scop
DLDC/*bard*; DLTC; DLTS; HL; PEPP.
Scopes Trial
OCAL/*Fundamentalism*.
Scotticism
DLTS.
Scottish Chaucerians
CODEL; DLTC; HL; PEPP.
Scottish Gaelic poetry
PEPP.
Scottish literature
HL.
Scottish poetry
PEPP.
Scottish Text Society
CODEL; OCEL.
Scottsboro Case
OCAL.

screen play
DLTS.

Scriblerus Club
CODEL; DLTC; HL; OCEL.

script
FDLP/*transcription*.

scriptorium
DLTC.

scriptural drama
HL.

sculpture
CR/*Index*.

scurrility
DLTS.

SD
FDLP/*structural description*.

sea shanties
PEPP.

sea shanty
DLTC.

secentismo
DLTC.

seci
DLTC.

second articulation
GLT.

secondary apertures
FDLP.

secondary articulation
FDLP; GLT.

secondary co-articulation
FDLP/*articulation*.

secondary compound
GLT.

secondary derivative
GLT.

secondary element
FDLP/*adjunct*.

secondary epic
DLDC/*epic*.

secondary features
GLT.

secondary language
GLT.

secondary meaning
FDLP/*medium*.

secondary phoneme
GLT.

secondary response
FDLP.

secondary source
DLTS.

secondary stress
GLT; HL.

secondary vowel
GLT.

secondary vowel types
FDLP/*cardinal vowels*.

secondary word
GLT.

second language
FDLP/*acquisition*; FDLP/*bilingual*; FDLP/*language*.

secondness
EDSL/*104*.

second person
FDLP/*person*.

second rhetoric
CR/*Index*.

second signaling system
EDSL/*68*.

Second Sophistic
CR/*Index*.

secretion
GLT.

seer
DLTC.

segment
FDLP.

segmental
GLT.

segmental elements
EDSL/*176*.

segmental phoneme
ME/*435*.

segmental phonemes
GLT.

251 □ semantic rejuvenation

segmental phonemics
GLT.
segmental phonology
FDLP/*segment*; FDLP/*phonology*.
segmentation
EDSL/*17*; FDLP/*segment*; GLT.
segmentator
FDLP/*segment*.
segment (of speech)
GLT.
segrel
DLTC.
segue
DLTS.
seguidilla
DLTC; PEPP.
selectional
FDLP.
selectional restriction
EDSL/*266*.
selective listening
FDLP.
selective omniscience
DLDC/*point of view*.
selective representation
ME/*265*.
self-consistency
FDLP/*exhaustiveness*.
self-effacing author
HL.
self-embedding
FDLP.
self-expression
ME/*expression, 119*.
semanalysis
EDSL/*362*.
semanteme
GLT.
sémantèmes
EDSL/*200*.
semantic amalgam
GLT.
semantic anomalies
EDSL/*128*.

semantic aspect
EDSL/*295*.
semantic change
GLT.
semantic combinatorial
EDSL/*264*.
semantic complement
GLT.
semantic component
EDSL/*54*; FDLP/*component*; FDLP/*semantics*.
semantic contagion
GLT.
semantic coordination
EDSL/*285*.
semantic determiner
EDSL/*196*.
semantic differential
FDLP/*semantics*.
semantic equivalence
FDLP/*equivalence*.
semantic extension
GLT.
semantic feature
EDSL/*265*.
semantic feature hypothesis
FDLP/*semantics*.
semantic features
FDLP/*component*; FDLP/*semantics*.
semantic fields
EDSL/*135*; FDLP/*field*.
semantic field theory
FDLP/*semantics*.
semantic indicator
GLT.
semanticity
FDLP/*semantics*.
semantic meaning
GLT.
semantic potentialities
GLT.
semantic rejuvenation
GLT.

semantic relations
FDLP/*semantics*.

semantic representation
FDLP/*semantics*.

semantics
DLTC; DLTS; EDSL/*338*; FDLP; GLT; LGEP/*39*; LGEP/*37*; ME/*435*; ME/*266*.

semantics and poetry
PEPP.

semantic shift
GLT.

semantic source
EDSL/*281*.

semantic triangle
FDLP/*semantics*; GLT.

semantic universals
FDLP/*universal*.

semasiography
GLT.

semasiology
FDLP/*semiotics*; GLT.

sematology
GLT.

semblance
DLTS.

seme
FDLP; GLT.

semeiology
DLTC; FDLP/*semiotics*; GLT.

sememe
EDSL/*266*; FDLP; GLT; ME/*435*.

sememics
FDLP/*sememe*.

semes
EDSL/*265*.

semi-auxiliaries
FDLP/*auxiliary*.

semic analysis
EDSL/*265*.

semi-consonant
GLT.

semi-consonants
FDLP/*consonant*.

semi-contoid
GLT.

semi-learned
GLT.

seminal
DLTS.

semiology
DMCT; FDLP/*glossematics*; GLT.

semiotic function
EDSL/*69*.

semiotics
DLTS; DMCT; EDSL/*84*; FDLP; GLT; HL; PEPP/*980*.

semi-plosive
GLT.

semi-productive
FDLP/*productivity*.

semi-sentence
FDLP.

semi-syntactic compound
GLT.

semi-vocoid
GLT.

semi-vowel
FDLP; GLT.

semivowel
ME/*435*.

semi-vowels
FDLP/*consonant*.

semology
FDLP/*semiotics*; FDLP.

semotactics
FDLP/*tactics*; FDLP/*sememe*.

senarius
DLTC; PEPP.

sender
EDSL/*341*.

Senecan
DLTS.

Senecan sentence
DLDC/*style*.

Senecan style
HL.

Senecan tragedy
  CODEL; DLDC/*tragedy*; DLTC; HL; ME/*267*.
senhal
  DLTC; PEPP.
senryū
  PEPP.
sense
  DLTC; FDLP.
sense associations
  FDLP/*association*.
sense relations
  FDLP/*relation*; FDLP/*sense*.
sense stress
  PH/*metre*.
sensibility
  DLDC; DLTC; DLTS; DMCT; HL; ME/*268*; PEPP; PH.
sensibility, dissociation
  PEPP.
sensory words
  DLTS.
sensual
  HL.
sensuous
  HL.
sentence
  DLTS; FDLP/*analytic*; FDLP; GLT; HL; ME/*436*.
sentence accent
  FDLP/*accent*.
sentence connectors
  FDLP/*adverb*.
sentence, kernel
  EDSL/*244*.
sentence length
  FDLP/*length*.
sentence modifiers
  FDLP/*adverb*.
sentence pattern
  GLT; ME/*436*.
sentence-patterns
  FDLP/*acceptability*.
sentence phonetics
  GLT.

sentence rhythm
  GLT.
sentence stress
  FDLP/*stress*; GLT.
sentence word
  GLT.
sententia
  DLTC; HL.
sententia
  DLDC/*aphorism*; DLTS.
sententiae
  CR/*Index*.
sentimental
  DLDC.
sentimental comedy
  CODEL; DLDC/*sentimental*; DLTC; HL; OCEL.
sentimental drama
  DLDC/*sentimental*.
sentimentalism
  DLTS; HL; ME/*271*.
sentimentality
  DLTC; HL; PEPP.
sentimental novel
  DLDC/*sentimental*; DLTC; HL; ME/*269*.
separable prefix
  GLT.
separable suffix
  GLT.
Separatists
  OCAL.
septenarius
  DLTC; PEPP.
septenary
  DLDC/*versification*; HL; PEPP; PH/*metre*.
septet
  DLTC; DLTS; HL; PEPP.
Septuagint
  CR/*Index*; DLTS; HL.
sequel
  DLTS; HL; ME/*272*.
sequence
  DLTC; EDSL/*297*; FDLP.

sequence of tenses ☐ **254**

sequence of tenses
   FDLP/*sequence*.
sequence sentence (utterance)
   GLT.
sequencing
   FDLP/*sequence*.
sequential
   FDLP/*constraint*.
sequential constraints
   FDLP/*phonotactics*.
sequential expansion
   GLT.
Serapionovy Bratya
   DLTC.
Serbo-Croatian poetry
   PEPP.
serenade
   DLTC; DLTS; HL.
serendipity
   DLTS.
serial ordering
   FDLP/*cycle*.
series
   FDLP; GLT.
sermo
   CR/*Index*.
sermo cotidianus
   GLT/*sermo familiaris*.
sermo familiaris
   GLT.
sermon
   DLTC; DLTS.
sermons
   CR/*Index*.
sermo plebeius
   GLT/*sermo familiaris*.
sermo rusticus
   GLT/*sermo familiaris*.
serpentine verse
   CODEL; DLTC; HL; OCEL.
serranilla
   DLTC; PEPP.
sesquipedalian
   DLTC; DLTS; HL.

sesquipedalianism
   ME/*272*.
sestet
   DLDC/*versification*; DLTC;
   DLTS; HL; PEPP; PH.
sestina
   CODEL; DLTC; DLTS; HL;
   ME/*272*; OCEL; PEPP; PH.
set, structural
   GLT.
setting
   DLDC/*atmosphere*; DLTC; DLTS;
   HL; ME/*274*.
sevdalinke
   DLTC.
seven arts, the
   DLTC; ME/*274*.
seven cardinal virtues
   HL.
seven deadly sins
   CODEL; DLTS; HL; ME/*274*;
   OCEL.
seven liberal arts
   DLTS; HL.
seven virtues
   DLTS.
Seven Wonders of the World
   DLTS.
sexain
   DLTC; PEPP.
sextilla
   PEPP.
sextilla
   DLTC.
SFH
   FDLP; FDLP/*semantics*.
shadow show
   DLTC.
shaggy dog story
   DLTC.
Shakespearean sonnet
   DLDC/*versification*; DLTC;
   DLTS; HL; PH/*sonnet*.
Shakespeare, early editions of
   HL.

shanty
  HL; HL/*chantey*; PEPP.
shape change
  GLT.
shaped poetry
  DLDC.
shaped verse
  HL; PEPP/*982*.
shape, phonemic
  GLT.
sharacans
  DLTC.
sharp
  FDLP.
sharp transition
  GLT.
Shays's Rebellion
  OCAL.
shelta
  DLTC.
shibboleth
  DLTS; GLT.
shifter
  GLT.
shifters
  EDSL/*252*.
shifting definition
  ME/*274*.
shifting stress
  GLT.
shift of accent
  GLT.
shift signs
  GLT.
shih
  DLTC; PEPP.
shoptalk
  DLTS.
short
  FDLP/*length*; PEPP.
Short, Bob
  OCAL.
short couplet
  DLTC; HL; PH.

shortening
  GLT.
short fiction
  DMCT.
shorthand
  CR/*Index*.
short measure
  DLTC; DLTS; HL; PH/*common measure*.
short meter
  DLTC; HL; PEPP.
short novel
  DLTC; HL.
short particular measure
  PH/*common measure*.
short short story
  DLTS.
short-short story
  HL; ME/*274*.
short story
  DLDC; DLTC; DLTS; HL; ME/*274*.
short term memory
  FDLP/*depth hypothesis*.
Short-Title Catalogue
  DLTC.
showboats
  OCAL.
shwa
  FDLP/*schwa*; GLT.
Siamese poetry
  PEPP.
sibilance
  FDLP/*sibilant*.
sibilant
  FDLP; GLT; ME/*437*.
sibilants
  DLTS.
sic
  DLTC; DLTS.
Sicilian octave
  DLTC; PEPP.
Sicilian school
  DLTC; PEPP.

sick verse □ **256**

sick verse
  DLTC.
sideronym
  OO.
Sidney, Edward William
  OCAL.
Sidney, Margaret
  OCAL.
sigmatic
  GLT.
sigmatism
  DLTC; DLTS; HL.
sign
  DLDC/*symbolism*; EDSL/*100*;
  FDLP; GLT; PEPP.
signal
  EDSL/*103*; GLT.
signalling system
  FDLP/*code*.
signals
  FDLP/*sign*; FDLP/*communication*.
signal syndrome
  GLT.
signature
  DLTC; DLTS; HL.
signifiant
  FDLP/*sign*.
significance
  LGEP/*40*.
significans
  FDLP/*sign*; GLT.
significant
  FDLP/*sign*; GLT.
significatio
  PEPP.
significatio
  EDSL/*248*.
signification
  EDSL/*100*; FDLP/*sign*.
significatum
  FDLP/*sign*; GLT.
significs
  FDLP/*sign*; FDLP/*semiotics*;
  GLT.

signifié
  FDLP/*sign*.
signified
  EDSL/*100*; GLT.
signifier
  EDSL/*100*; GLT.
signifying capacity
  EDSL/*105*.
signifying chain
  EDSL/*353*.
sign language
  FDLP/*sign*.
sign, linguistic
  GLT.
sign, prosodic
  GLT.
signs
  CR/*Index*.
sign system
  EDSL/*104*; FDLP/*sign*.
sign-token
  GLT.
sign-type
  GLT.
sijo
  DLTC; PEPP.
silence
  FDLP/*juncture*; FDLP/*continuant*.
silent pause
  FDLP/*pause*.
silent stress
  FDLP/*stress*; LGEP/*114*.
Silesian school
  PEPP.
sillographer
  DLTC; PEPP.
silva
  DLTC; PEPP.
Silver-Fork School
  HL.

257 □ **skald**

simile
   CODEL; CR/*Index*; DLDC/*figurative language*; DLTC; DLTS; DMCT; EDSL/*278*; LGEP/*156*; ME/*276*; OCEL; PEPP; PH/*metaphor*.
similitude
   DLTC; DLTS.
simpatico
   DLTS.
simple
   FDLP/*progressive*; FDLP.
simple forms
   EDSL/*155*.
simple sentence
   ME/*437*.
simple transformation
   EDSL/*290*; ME/*437*.
simplex word
   GLT.
simplicity
   FDLP.
simplification
   GLT.
simultaneity
   EDSL/*322*.
simultaneous
   FDLP/*constraint*.
sincerity
   DLTC; DMCT; HL; PEPP.
Sindhi
   FDLP/*implosive*.
single-bar
   FDLP/*juncture*.
single-base
   FDLP/*double-base*; FDLP.
single-moulded line
   DLTC.
single rhyme
   DLTC.
sing-song theory
   GLT.
Singspiel
   DLTC.

singular
   DLDC/*concrete*.
singular form
   ME/*437*.
singulary
   FDLP.
singulative
   GLT.
Sinhalese poetry
   PEPP.
Sinn
   EDSL/*249*.
sinnverleihend
   EDSL/*340*.
sirvente
   CODEL; OCEL; PH/*troubadour*.
sirventes
   DLTC; PEPP.
sistant
   GLT.
sister-adjunction
   FDLP/*adjunction*.
sister node
   FDLP/*node*.
situation
   DLTS; FDLP; HL.
situational comedy
   DLDC/*comedy*.
situational context
   FDLP/*context*.
situational dialect
   GLT.
situational distinctive feature
   EDSL/*337*.
situational meaning
   FDLP/*situation*.
situation utterance
   GLT.
Sitz im Leben
   CR/*Index*.
sixain
   DLTS.
skald
   PEPP.

Skald
  CODEL; DLTC; DLTS; HL; OCEL.
skaz
  DLTC.
Skeltoniads
  HL/*Skeltonic verse*.
Skeltonics
  DLTC; DLTS; HL/*Skeltonic verse*.
Skeltonic verse
  DLTC; HL; ME/*276*; PEPP; PH.
skepticism
  DLTS.
sketch
  DLTC; DLTS; HL.
skit
  DLTC; HL.
slack
  DLTC.
slack syllable
  HL.
slander
  DLTS.
slang
  DLTC; DLTS; EDSL/*59*; GLT; HL; ME/*438*.
slanting
  ME/*277*.
slant rhyme
  DLTC; DLTS; HL; ME/*277*; PEPP.
slant-rhyme
  DLDC/*versification*.
slapstick
  DLDC/*comedy*; DLTC; DLTS; HL; ME/*277*.
slashes
  FDLP/*bracketing*.
slave narratives
  HL.
Slavic
  FDLP/*palatalisation*.
Slavic poetics
  PEPP.

Slavic prosody
  PEPP.
Slavonic languages
  FDLP/*aspect*.
slender consonant
  GLT.
slender vowel
  GLT.
slice of life
  DLDC/*naturalism*; DLTC; DLTS; HL.
slick magazine
  DLTS; HL.
slicks, the
  ME/*277*.
slip of the brain
  FDLP/*tongue-slip*.
slip of the tongue
  FDLP/*tongue-slip*.
Slipslop
  DLTC.
slips of the brain
  FDLP/*error*.
slips of the tongue
  FDLP/*error*.
slit
  FDLP.
slit fricative
  GLT.
slit spirant
  GLT.
slogan
  DLTC; DLTS.
śloka
  DLTC.
śloka
  PEPP.
slot
  FDLP; GLT.
slot-and-filler
  FDLP/*slot*.
Slovak poetry
  PEPP.

259 □ soft consonant

slur
  GLT.
smear
  GLT.
Smithy Poets
  DLTC; PEPP.
smooth-edged
  FDLP/*mellow*.
snyopsis
  DLTS.
sobriquet
  DLTS.
social/cultural situation
  FDLP/*conditioned*.
social accents
  FDLP/*accent*.
social background
  FDLP/*developmental linguistics*.
social determinants
  FDLP/*communicative competence*.
social dialect
  ME/*438*.
social dialects
  FDLP/*dialect*; FDLP/*class*.
social function
  FDLP/*function*.
socialist realism
  DLTC.
social proximity
  FDLP/*contact*.
social relation
  LGEP/*9*.
social relations
  FDLP/*interpersonal*.
social settings
  FDLP/*bidialect*; FDLP/*correct*.
social situation
  FDLP/*appropriate*.
social situations
  FDLP/*domain*.
social status
  FDLP/*bilingual*.
social stratification
  GLT.

social systems
  FDLP/*code*.
sociative morpheme
  GLT.
society
  DLTS; DMCT.
society and poetry
  PEPP.
Society for the Propagation of the Gospel in Foreign Parts
  OCAL.
society verse
  DLTC; HL; PEPP.
sociocultural norms
  FDLP/*domain*.
sociolect
  FDLP.
sociolinguistics
  EDSL/*62*; FDLP/*linguistics*;
  FDLP.
sociological criticism
  PEPP.
sociological linguistics
  FDLP/*sociolinguistics*.
sociological novel
  DLTC; HL.
sociological novel, play
  DLTS.
sociology of language
  FDLP/*sociolinguistics*.
sociometry
  DLTC.
sock
  DLTS; HL.
Socratic
  DLTS; HL.
Socratic irony
  DLDC/*irony*; DLTC.
Socratic paradox
  CR/*Index*.
Socratic question
  CR/*Index*.
soft consonant
  FDLP; GLT.

soldiers' englyn □ 260

soldiers' englyn
PH/*Welsh forms.*
solecism
CODEL; DLTC; DLTS; HL; ME/*278*; OCEL.
solf palate
FDLP/*palate.*
solidarity
EDSL/*109*; GLT.
solid compound
GLT.
soliloquy
CODEL; DLDC; DLTC; DLTS; DMCT; HL; LGEP/*186*; ME/*278*; PEPP.
solipsism
DLTS.
Solomon Islands
CR/*Index.*
solution
DLTS; HL.
sonagram
FDLP/*sonagraph.*
sonagraph
FDLP.
sonant
GLT.
song
DLTC; DLTS; FDLP/*allo-*; HL; PEPP.
songbook
DLTC.
sonnet
CODEL; DLDC/*versification*; DLTC; DLTS; DMCT; EDSL/*192*; HL; ME/*278*; OCEL; PEPP; PH.
sonnet cycle
DLTC; ME/*280*; PEPP; PH/*sonnet.*
sonnet sequence
DLDC/*versification*; DLTS; HL; ME/*280*; PH/*sonnet.*
sonorant
FDLP; GLT.

sonority
FDLP; GLT.
sonorization
GLT.
sonorous
FDLP/*sonority.*
sonorousness
GLT.
Sons of Ben
HL.
sophism
CODEL; OCEL.
sophistication
DLTS.
sophistry
DLTS.
sophists and sophistry
CR/*Index.*
sophists and sophistry, Byzantine
CR/*Index.*
sophists and sophistry, Christian
CR/*Index.*
sophists and sophistry, Latin
CR/*Index.*
Sophoclean
DLTS.
Sophoclean irony
DLDC/*irony.*
sophrosyne
DLTS.
soprano
FDLP/*phonation.*
soraismus
DLTC.
sorites
DLTS; ME/*280*; PEPP.
sortilege
DLTS.
sotadean
DLTC; PEPP.
sotadic
CODEL; OCEL.
sotie
DLTC.

261 □ spatial linguistics

sotto voce
GLT.
sound
DLTS; DMCT; FDLP/*abrupt*.
sound and meaning
FDLP/*arbitrariness*.
sound change
FDLP; GLT; ME/*438*.
sound echoes
LGEP/*93*.
sound in poetry
PEPP.
sound law
FDLP/*sound change*; GLT.
sound-over
HL.
sound production
FDLP/*articulation*.
sounds
FDLP/*approximant*.
sound segment
FDLP/*assimilation*.
sound sensation
FDLP/*attribute*.
sound shift
FDLP/*sound change*; GLT.
sound spectrograph
FDLP/*spectrograph*; GLT.
sound symbolism
GLT.
sound-symbolism
FDLP.
sound system
FDLP.
sound type
GLT.
sound-units
FDLP/*articulation*.
source
DLTS; FDLP/*communication*; HL.
source-book
DLTC.
source feature
FDLP.

source language
GLT.
source sentence
ME/*438*.
South African poetry
PEPP.
South-East Asia
FDLP/*analytic*.
South-East Asian languages
FDLP/*isolating*.
southern gothic
ME/*280*.
South, The
OCAL.
Southwest
OCAL.
Souza, E.
OCAL.
space-direction sequence
GLT.
space order
DLTS.
Spain
CR/*Index*.
Spanish
FDLP/*nasal*; FDLP/*fricative*; FDLP/*clitic*.
Spanish American poetry
PEPP.
Spanish-American War
OCAL.
Spanish poetics
PEPP.
Spanish poetry
PEPP.
Spanish prosody
PEPP.
Spasmodic school
PEPP; DLTC; HL.
spatial form
HL.
spatial linguistics
GLT.

spatial relationships □ **262**

spatial relationships
FDLP/*converse.*
speaker
EDSL/*341*; EDSL/*324*; ME/*281.*
speaker's errors
FDLP/*error.*
speaker, speech, audience
CR/*Index.*
speaking in tongues
FDLP/*glossolalia.*
speaking voice
ME/*281.*
specialisation
FDLP.
specialization of meaning
GLT.
specialized meaning
GLT.
specification
EDSL/*290.*
specific grammatical category
GLT.
specifies
EDSL/*109.*
spectacle
DLTS; HL.
spectogram
GLT.
spectograph
GLT.
spectral
DLTS.
spectrogram
FDLP/*spectrograph.*
spectrograph
FDLP.
speech
EDSL/*126*; EDSL/*118*; FDLP/*accent*; FDLP; GLT.
speech act
EDSL/*343.*
speech-act
FDLP; FDLP/*speech.*

speech community
FDLP/*speech.*
speech deafness
EDSL/*163.*
speech disorder
EDSL/*161.*
speech, divisions of
DLTC.
speech event
FDLP/*speech.*
speech form
GLT.
speech island
GLT.
speech lapse
GLT.
speech organs
GLT.
speech perception
FDLP/*speech.*
speech processing
FDLP/*speech.*
speech production
FDLP/*production*; FDLP/*speech.*
speech reception
FDLP/*speech.*
speech recognition
FDLP/*speech.*
speech segment
GLT.
speech situation
EDSL/*333.*
speech stretcher
FDLP/*speech*; GLT.
speech synthesiser
FDLP/*speech.*
speech system
FDLP/*acceptability.*
speech-writer
CR/*Index.*
spell
PEPP.
spelling
GLT.

spelling pronunciation
GLT; ME/*438.*

Spenserian sonnet
DLTC; HL; PH/*sonnet.*

Spenserian stanza
CODEL; DLDC/*versification*;
DLTC; DLTS; HL; ME/*283*;
OCEL; PEPP; PH/*stanza.*

sphere of influence
GLT.

spirant
FDLP/*fricative*; GLT; ME/*439.*

spiritual
OCAL.

spirituals
PEPP.

split
GLT.

split infinitive
ME/*439.*

splitting
FDLP/*realisation*; GLT.

spoken chain
GLT.

spoken language
FDLP/*speech.*

spoken medium
FDLP/*speech.*

spondaic
DLDC/*versification*; FDLP/*foot*;
PH/*metre.*

spondaic verse
PEPP.

spondee
CODEL; DLDC/*versification*;
DLTC; DLTS; EDSL/*187*; HL;
ME/*284*; OCEL; PEPP.

spontaneity
DLTC; PEPP.

spontaneous phonology
GLT.

spontaneous sound change
GLT.

spoof
DLTC.

spoonerism
CODEL; DLTC; DLTS; GLT;
HL; ME/*284*; OCEL.

spoonerisms
FDLP/*metathesis.*

sporadic alternation
GLT.

sporadic change
GLT.

sporadic sound change
GLT.

Sprachgefühl
FDLP/*intuition.*

spreading
FDLP.

spread vowel
GLT.

Sprechakt
EDSL/*340.*

Sprechhandlung
EDSL/*340.*

Sprechspruch
DLTC.

Spruch
DLTC; PEPP.

sprung rhythm
DLDC/*versification*; DLTC;
DLTS; HL; ME/*284*; PEPP; PH.

spy story
DLTC.

Squibob
OCAL.

squinter
ME/*284.*

squish
FDLP.

stable
FDLP/*case.*

stage directions
DLTC; DLTS.

stages of acquisition
FDLP/*acquisition.*

stage whisper
DLTS.

Stagira
CR/*Index*.
Stammbaumtheorie
GLT.
stances
PEPP/*982*.
stand
PH/*ode*.
standard
FDLP.
Standard English
ME/*439*; CODEL; DLTC; LGEP/*9*.
standardisation
FDLP/*standard*.
standardization
GLT.
standard language
GLT.
standard role
EDSL/*224*.
standard theory
FDLP.
Standish, Burt L.
OCAL.
stanza
CODEL; DLDC/*versification*; DLTC; DLTS; EDSL/*192*; HL; ME/*285*; PEPP; PH.
starred form
FDLP/*asterisk*; FDLP; GLT.
stasima
DLTS.
stasimon
DLTC; PEPP.
stasis
CR/*Index*; DLTS; DMCT.
state
FDLP.
statement
DLTC; FDLP; ME/*285*.
statement of fact
ME/*285*.
statement of opinion
ME/*285*.

state of a language
FDLP/*état de langue*.
states of languages
FDLP/*state*.
static character
DLTS; HL.
static consonant
GLT.
static linguistics
GLT.
statics
GLT.
statistical induction
ME/*285*.
statistical linguistics
FDLP.
statistical universals
FDLP/*universal*.
statistics
GLT.
stative
FDLP.
stativity
FDLP/*stative*.
status
CR/*Index*.
status
FDLP/*connotation*.
status verb
GLT.
stave
DLTC; DLTS; HL; PEPP; PH/*stanza*.
stem
DLTS/*root*; FDLP; FDLP/*affix*; GLT; ME/*439*.
stem base
GLT.
stem compound
GLT.
stem formative morpheme
GLT.
stemma
EDSL/*212*.

265 □ stream-of-consciousness

stereotype
HL; ME/285.
stereotyped sentences
FDLP/formulaic language.
-stich
HL.
stich
PEPP.
stichomythia
CODEL; DLDC/dialogue; DLTC; DLTS; HL; ME/stichomythy, 285; OCEL; PEPP; PH.
stichomythy
ME/285.
stichos
DLTC.
Stilforschung
PEPP.
stilnovismo
PEPP.
stimulus-plus-response
FDLP/adjacency pair.
Stirling, Arthur
OCAL.
St. Louis
OCAL.
stock
DLTC; GLT; PEPP.
stock character
DLTC; DLTS; ME/286.
stock characters
DLDC/convention; HL.
stock epithet
DLDC/epithet; ME/286.
stock epithets
DLDC/epic.
stock response
DLDC; DLTC; DLTS; HL; PEPP; PH.
stock situation
DLDC/convention; DLTC; DLTS; HL.
stod
GLT.

Stoicism
HL; DLTS.
Stoics
CR/Index.
stop
FDLP; GLT; ME/439.
storm and stress
DLTC; HL.
storm of association
DLTC.
stornello
DLTC; PEPP.
story
DLDC/plot; DLTS; DMCT; HL.
story-line
ME/286.
story within a story
DLTC.
story-within-a-story
DLTS.
stracittà
DLTC.
straight man
HL.
strambotto
DLTC; PEPP.
strapaese
DLTC.
stratal system
FDLP/stratificational.
strategy
DLTC; PEPP; PH.
stratificational
FDLP.
stratification of language
GLT.
stratum
FDLP/stratificational.
stream of consciousness
CODEL; DLTC; DLTS; DMCT; HL; ME/286.
stream-of-consciousness
OCAL.

stream of consciousness novel
  DLDC/*novel*.
stream-of-consciousness novel
  HL.
street ballad
  DLDC/*ballad*.
street songs
  DLTC.
strength
  FDLP/*fortis*; FDLP/*stress*.
stress
  DLDC/*versification*; DLTC;
  DLTS; DMCT; EDSL/*181*;
  FDLP; GLT; HL; LGEP/*105*;
  LGEP/*107*; ME/*440*; PEPP.
stress accent
  GLT.
stress contour
  FDLP/*contour*.
stressed
  FDLP/*stress*.
stress functions
  GLT.
stress group
  FDLP/*stress*; GLT.
stressonym
  OO.
stress phonemes
  GLT.
stress prosody
  PH/*metre*.
stress-timed
  FDLP; LGEP/*105*.
stretch of speech
  FDLP/*utterance*.
strict meter poetry
  DLTC.
strict-metre poetry
  PEPP.
strict roles
  LGEP/*12*.
strict subcategorisation
  FDLP.
stricture
  FDLP.
strident
  FDLP.
string
  FDLP; ME/*440*.
string (structured)
  GLT.
stroneme
  GLT.
strong
  FDLP/*lenis*; FDLP/*fortis*; GLT.
strong curtain
  HL.
strong form
  FDLP; GLT.
strong generative capacity
  FDLP/*capacity*.
strongly adequate
  FDLP/*adequacy*.
strongly equivalent
  FDLP/*equivalence*.
strong stress metre
  LGEP/*118*.
strong verb
  ME/*440*.
strophe
  CODEL; DLDC/*ode*; DLTC;
  DLTS; HL; ME/*286*; OCEL;
  PEPP; PH/*stanza*; PH/*ode*.
structural
  FDLP; GLT.
structural allophonic change
  GLT.
structural ambiguity
  FDLP/*ambiguity*; FDLP.
structural analysis
  EDSL/*83*; FDLP/*structural description*.
structural change
  FDLP.
structural description
  FDLP.
structural dialectology
  FDLP/*dialect*.
structural gap
  GLT.

structural grammar
ME/*440*.

structuralism
DMCT; FDLP/*structural*; GLT; HL; PEPP/*983*.

structuralist grammar
FDLP/*structural*.

structuralist linguistics
FDLP/*structural*.

structural linguistics
FDLP/*linguistics*; GLT.

structurally ambiguous
FDLP/*construction*.

structural marker
GLT.

structural meaning
GLT.

structural metaphor
DLTC; PH.

structural semantics
FDLP/*semantics*; FDLP/*structural*.

structural set
GLT.

structural similarity
GLT.

structural word
GLT.

structure
DLDC/*form*; DLTC; DLTS; DMCT; EDSL/*16*; FDLP; GLT; HL; PEPP; PH.

structure drill
FDLP/*pattern*.

structured string
GLT.

structure group word
ME/*441*.

structure index
FDLP/*structural description*; FDLP/*structure*.

structure preserving
FDLP/*cycle*.

structure word
GLT.

Stuart Period
DLTC.

studia humanitas
CR/*Index*.

stump word
GLT.

Sturm und Drang
CODEL; DLTC; HL; OCEL; PEPP.

Sturm und Drang
DLTS; ME/*286*.

stuttering
EDSL/*161*; FDLP/*neurolinguistics*.

style
CR/*Index*; DLDC; DLTC; DLTS; DMCT; EDSL/*300*; FDLP/*stylistics*; HL; ME/*287*; PEPP.

style, direct
EDSL/*303*.

style, emotive
EDSL/*303*.

style, evaluative
EDSL/*303*.

style, free indirect
EDSL/*303*.

style, indirect
EDSL/*303*.

style, modalizing
EDSL/*303*.

stylistics
DLTC; EDSL/*294*; EDSL/*75*; FDLP; GLT; PEPP.

stylistic variation
EDSL/*27*.

stylization
EDSL/*256*.

stylostatistics
FDLP/*stylistics*.

suasoriae
CR/*Index*.

suavity
DLTS.

subcategorisation, strict
FDLP/*category*.

sub-components ☐ 268

sub-components
FDLP/*component*.
subconscious
DLTS.
subdued metaphor
DLTC; PH/*metaphor*.
subject
EDSL/*210*; EDSL/*213*; FDLP; ME/*441*.
subject/predicate distinction
FDLP/*topicalisation*.
subject bibliography
HL.
subject complement
FDLP/*complement*.
subjective
DLDC; FDLP/*subject*; HL.
subjective camera
HL.
subjective complement
ME/*441*.
subjectivist critic
DLDC/*criticism*.
subjectivity
DLTC; DLTS.
subjectivity and objectivity
PEPP.
subject, logical
EDSL/*269*.
subject matter
EDSL/*118*.
subject, psychological
EDSL/*271*.
subject-raising
FDLP/*raising*.
subject-verb-complement
FDLP/*complement*.
subject-verb-object
FDLP/*complement*.
subjunct
GLT.
subjunctive
FDLP.

subjunctive mood
ME/*441*.
sublime
DLTC; HL; PEPP.
sublimity
DLTS.
sublogic
EDSL/*114*.
submerged metaphor
DLDC/*figurative language*.
sub-minimal pairs
GLT.
subordinate
FDLP/*subordination*.
subordinate clause
FDLP/*clause*; ME/*441*.
subordinate clauses
FDLP/*subordination*.
subordinating conjunction
FDLP/*subordination*.
subordinating language
GLT.
subordination
DLTS; FDLP; ME/*289*; ME/*441*.
subordinative construction
GLT.
subordinator
FDLP/*subordination*; GLT; ME/*442*.
subphonemic
GLT.
subplot
DLDC/*plot*; DLTC; DLTS; HL.
subrelationship
GLT.
subset
GLT.
substance
EDSL/*20*; FDLP.
sub-standard
FDLP/*standard*.
substandard
GLT.

substantial universals
EDSL/*136*.
substantival
FDLP/*substantive*.
substantival adjunct
GLT.
substantive
EDSL/*252*; FDLP; GLT; ME/*442*.
substantive universals
FDLP/*universal*.
substitutability technique
FDLP/*commutation*.
substitute
GLT.
substitute language
GLT.
substitute word
FDLP/*substitution*.
substitution
DLTC; FDLP/*commutation*; FDLP; GLT; HL; PEPP; PH.
substitution class
FDLP/*substitution*; GLT.
substitution drills
FDLP/*substitution*.
substitution frame
FDLP/*frame*; FDLP/*substitution*; GLT.
substrate
FDLP.
substrate language
FDLP/*substrate*.
substratum
FDLP/*substrate*; GLT.
substratum theory
GLT.
substring
FDLP/*string*.
sub-text
DLTC.
subtree
FDLP/*tree*.
succès
DLTC.

succès d'estime
DLTS.
successivity
FDLP/*cycle*.
succubus
DLTS.
suction
FDLP.
suction stop
FDLP/*implosive*; FDLP/*stop*; GLT.
suffix
DLTS; EDSL/*200*; FDLP; GLT; ME/*442*.
suffixation
FDLP/*affix*; FDLP/*suffix*.
suffixing
FDLP/*suffix*.
suggestio falsi
DLTS.
suggestion
DLTC.
Sumerian poetry
PEPP.
summary
DLDC/*plot*; DLTC; DLTS; EDSL/*332*.
Summerfield, Charles
OCAL.
Sunnyside
OCAL.
superego
DLTS.
superfix
FDLP; GLT; ME/*442*.
superimposed language
GLT.
superlative
FDLP.
superlative degree
ME/*442*.
supernaturalism
DLTS.
supernatural story
DLTC.

superstratum
FDLP; GLT.
superstratum theory
GLT.
sup-phonemic variant
FDLP/*allo-*.
supplementary movements
FDLP.
suppletion
FDLP; GLT; ME/*442*.
suppletive
FDLP/*suppletion*; GLT.
support vowel
GLT.
suppositio
EDSL/*249*.
suprafix
FDLP/*superfix*.
supraglottal
FDLP.
suprasegmental
FDLP/*prosody*; FDLP.
suprasegmental elements
EDSL/*176*.
suprasegmental morpheme
GLT.
suprasegmental phoneme
GLT; ME/*443*.
suprasegmental phonology
FDLP/*segment*; FDLP/*phonology*.
sura
DLTC.
surd
GLT.
surface form
FDLP/*deep structure*.
surface grammar
FDLP/*surface structure*.
surface morphology
FDLP/*case*.
surface structure
EDSL/*244*; FDLP; LGEP/*45*; ME/*443*.

surface structure constraints
FDLP/*constraint*.
surface subject
FDLP/*deep structure*.
surface verbs
FDLP/*causative*.
surprise ending
DLTC; DLTS.
Surrealism
DMCT; PEPP; CODEL; DLDC; DLTC; DLTS; HL; ME/*289*; OCEL.
surrogate
HL.
survey
DLTS.
suspended rhyme
DLTC.
suspense
DLDC; DLTC; DLTS; EDSL/*321*; HL.
suspension of disbelief
DLTS; DMCT; HL.
suspension pitch
GLT.
suspicious pairs
GLT.
sustained juncture
FDLP/*juncture*.
sutra
DLTC.
sutra
OCEL.
Swahili
FDLP/*lingua franca*.
Swahili poetry
PEPP/*986*.
Swamp Fox
OCAL.
Swedenborgianism
OCAL.
Swedish
FDLP/*dialect*.
Swedish-Finnish Modernists, The
PEPP.

Swedish poetry
PEPP.
sweeping generalization
ME/*290*.
sweetness and light
DLTC; HL.
Sweet Singer of Michigan
OCAL.
Swiss poetry
PEPP.
switchback
DLTS.
switching
GLT.
sword dance
DLTC.
syllaba anceps
PEPP.
syllaba anceps
DLTC.
syllabaries
EDSL/*195*.
syllabary
GLT.
syllabic
FDLP/*syllable*; GLT.
syllabication
GLT.
syllabic consonant
FDLP/*syllable*; ME/*444*.
syllabic contoid
GLT.
syllabic dissimilation
GLT.
syllabic division
FDLP/*syllable*.
syllabic pattern
GLT.
syllabic peak
GLT.
syllabic sign
GLT.
syllabic stress
GLT.

syllabic verse
DLDC/*versification*; DLTC; DLTS; HL; PH/*metre*.
syllabic writing
GLT.
syllabification
FDLP/*syllable*; GLT.
syllabism
PEPP.
syllable
DLTS; EDSL/*186*; FDLP; GLT; ME/*444*; PEPP.
syllable centre
FDLP/*margin*.
syllable length
LGEP/*108*.
syllable margins
FDLP/*margin*.
syllables
LGEP/*63*; LGEP/*89*.
syllable sign
GLT.
syllable-timed
FDLP; FDLP/*isochrony*; LGEP/*105*.
syllable writing
GLT.
syllabogram
GLT.
syllabus
DLTS; HL.
syllepsis
CODEL; DLTC; DLTS; EDSL/*278*; HL; LGEP/*211*; ME/*292*; OCEL; PEPP.
syllogism
CR/*Index*; DLTC; DLTS; HL; ME/*292*.
symbiosis
GLT.
symbol
DLTC; DLTS; DMCT; EDSL/*102*; EDSL/*86*; FDLP/*transcription*; HL; ME/*298*; PEPP; PH.

symbolic action
DLTC; PEPP.
symbolic logic
FDLP/*bracketing*.
symbolic system
GLT.
Symbolism
PEPP; CODEL; DLDC; DLTC; DLTS; GLT; HL; LGEP/*162*; ME/*299*; OCEL; PH/*symbol*.
symbolist
PH/*symbol*.
Symbolist Movement
DLDC.
symbolists, symbolistes
ME/*300*.
symbolization
EDSL/*102*.
symbols
FDLP/*sign*.
symbols, prosodic
PEPP.
symmetry
DLTS; EDSL/*186*; GLT.
symmetry of pattern
GLT.
sympathy
DLDC/*empathy*; DLTC; DLTS; PEPP.
symploce
PEPP.
symploce
HL.
symposium
DLTC; DLTS; HL.
symptom
EDSL/*103*.
symptoms
FDLP/*sign*.
synaeresis
CODEL; DLTC; OCEL; PEPP.
synaesthesia
DLTC; FDLP; HL; PEPP.
synalepha
PH/*elision*.

synaloepha
PEPP.
synaloepha
DLTC.
synaxarion
DLTC.
synchronic
EDSL/*137*; FDLP; GLT; ME/*444*.
synchronic grammar
GLT.
synchronic linguistics
FDLP/*linguistics*; FDLP/*synchronic*; GLT.
synchronic phonemics and phonetics
GLT.
syncopation
DLTC; DLTS; GLT/*syncope*; HL; ME/*444*; PEPP; PH/*metre*.
syncope
DLTC; DLTS; HL; LGEP/*18*; ME/*300*; PEPP.
syncretic form
GLT.
syncretise
FDLP/*syncretism*.
syncretism
FDLP; GLT.
synecdoche
CODEL; DLDC/*figurative language*; DLTC; DLTS; EDSL/*278*; HL; LGEP/*150*; ME/*300*; OCEL; PEPP.
syneciosis
DLTC.
syneresis
DLTS; GLT.
synesis
DLTS.
synesthesia
DLDC/*figurative language*; ME/*300*; PH.
synkrisis
CR/*Index*.

synods
  CR/*Index*.
synonym
  CODEL; DLTC; DLTS; DMCT; FDLP; GLT; OCEL.
synonymic attraction
  GLT.
synonymous
  EDSL/*236*; FDLP/*synonym*.
synonymous parallelism
  DLTC.
synonyms
  HL.
synonymy
  FDLP/*synonym*; LGEP/*38*.
synopsis
  DLTC; HL; ME/*300*.
synoptic
  DLTS.
syntactic aspect
  EDSL/*295*.
syntactic blends
  FDLP/*blend*.
syntactic category
  FDLP/*syntax*; GLT.
syntactic class
  FDLP/*syntax*.
syntactic component
  FDLP/*syntax*.
syntactic compound
  GLT.
syntactic construction
  GLT; ME/*445*.
syntactic coordination
  EDSL/*211*.
syntactic description
  EDSL/*39*.
syntactic doublets
  GLT.
syntactic feature
  FDLP/*category*.
syntactic frame
  FDLP/*frame*.

syntactic function
  EDSL/*214*; EDSL/*209*.
syntactic functions
  FDLP/*function*.
syntactic molecule
  GLT.
syntactic order
  GLT.
syntactic phonology
  GLT.
syntactic relations
  FDLP/*function*.
syntactic relationship
  FDLP/*syntax*.
syntactics
  FDLP/*syntax*; FDLP/*tactics*.
syntactic structure
  FDLP/*syntax*.
Syntactic Structures model
  FDLP/*model*.
syntagm
  FDLP/*syntagmatic*; GLT.
syntagma
  EDSL/*106*; FDLP/*syntagmatic*; GLT.
syntagmatic
  FDLP/*syntagmatic*; FDLP; GLT.
syntagmatic/paradigmatic shift
  FDLP/*syntagmatic*.
syntagmatic axis
  FDLP/*axis*.
syntagmatic economy
  GLT.
syntagmatic relationship
  EDSL/*106*.
syntagmatic rules
  EDSL/*227*.
syntagmatic sound change
  GLT.
syntagmeme
  FDLP/*tagmemics*; FDLP/*syntagmatic*.

syntax
DLTC; DLTS; DMCT; EDSL/*183*; EDSL/*53*; EDSL/*338*; EDSL/*51*; EDSL/*54*; FDLP; FDLP/*axiomatic*; GLT; ME/*445*.

syntax language
GLT.

synthesis
DLTC; DLTS; FDLP/*synthetic*; GLT; ME/*300*; PEPP.

synthetic
FDLP.

synthetic compound
GLT.

synthetic index
GLT.

synthetic language
FDLP/*synthetic*; GLT; ME/*446*.

synthetic proposition
FDLP/*synthetic*.

synthetic rhyme
DLTC; PEPP.

synthetic rhythm
DLTC; PEPP.

synthetic sentence
FDLP/*synthetic*.

Syracuse
CR/*Index*.

system
DLTC; EDSL/*125*; EDSL/*16*; EDSL/*126*; FDLP; GLT; PEPP.

systematic
FDLP/*system*.

systematic phoneme
FDLP/*systematic phonemics*.

systematic phonemics
FDLP.

systematic phonetics
FDLP.

systemic grammar
FDLP/*Hallidayan*; FDLP/*system*.

system-structure theory
FDLP/*Hallidayan*.

systrophe
DLTC.

syzygy
DLTC; HL; PEPP.

T

T
 FDLP; FDLP/*trace*.
tableau
 DLTC; DLTS; HL.
table-talk
 DLTC.
taboo
 DLTS; GLT.
tabulation
 GLT.
Tachtigers
 PEPP.
tacit
 FDLP.
tacit knowledge
 FDLP/*intuition*; FDLP/*tacit*.
tactic behaviour
 FDLP/*phonotactics*.
tactic form
 FDLP/*taxeme*; GLT.
tactics
 FDLP.
tactile sensation
 GLT.
Tafelspel
 DLTC.
tag
 DLTC; FDLP.
Tagelied
 DLTC; PEPP.

tagma
 FDLP/*tagmemics*.
tagmatics
 FDLP/*tagmemics*.
tagmeme
 FDLP/*tagmemics*; GLT; ME/*447*.
tagmemic analysis
 FDLP/*tagmemics*.
tagmemics
 EDSL/*36*; FDLP.
tag question
 FDLP/*tag*; ME/*447*.
tags
 DLTS.
tag statement
 FDLP/*tag*.
tail
 FDLP/*tone group*.
tailed sonnet
 PH/*sonnet*.
tail-rhyme
 DLTC; PEPP.
tail-rhyme romance
 HL.
tail-rhyme stanza
 HL; OCEL; PH/*stanza*.
tainting (of suffuxes)
 GLT.

tale
DLDC/*short story*; DLTC; DLTS; HL; ME/*301*.

tall story
DLTC.

tall tale
DLTS; HL; OCAL.

tamber
FDLP/*timbre*.

tambre
FDLP/*timbre*.

Tamil
FDLP/*flap*.

Tamil poetry
PEPP.

tamizdat
DLTC.

tanka
DLTC; DLTS; PEPP.

tanka
HL; ME/*301*; PH/*haiku*.

Taos, New Mexico
OCAL.

tap
FDLP; GLT.

tapinosis
DLTC; PEPP.

tapped *r*
ME/*447*.

target
FDLP.

target articulation
FDLP/*target*.

target language
FDLP/*target*; GLT.

taste
CR/*Index*; DLTC; DLTS; DMCT; FDLP/*allo*-; HL; PEPP.

ta-ta theory
GLT.

tautological argument
ME/*301*.

tautological utterance
EDSL/*288*.

tautology
DLTC; DLTS; HL; LGEP/*132*; LGEP/*137*; ME/*301*.

tautonym
OO.

taxeme
EDSL/*23*; FDLP; GLT; ME/*447*.

taxeme of expression
GLT.

taxis
FDLP/*tactics*.

taxonomic
FDLP.

taxonomic linguistics
FDLP/*linguistics*.

taxonomy
EDSL/*38*; FDLP/*taxonomic*.

teaching grammar
FDLP/*grammar*.

technai
CR/*Index*.

technical criticism
PEPP.

technique
DLTS; DMCT; HL; ME/*301*.

tecnonym
OO.

teeth
FDLP/*articulation*.

teknonym
OO.

teknonymy
GLT.

telegraphese
DLTS.

telegraphic style
DLTS.

telepathy
DLTS.

telescoped metaphor
DLTC.

telescoped word
GLT.

telescope word
DLTC.
telesilleum
PEPP.
telestich
DLTC; DLTS; HL; PEPP.
teliambos
PEPP.
Telugu poetry
PEPP.
tema con variazioni
DLTC.
tempo
DLTS; FDLP; GLT.
temporal dialect
FDLP/*dialect*.
tençons
OCEL/*tensons*.
tenor
DLDC/*figurative language*; DLTC; DLTS; DMCT; FDLP; HL; LGEP/*151*; LGEP/*154*; PH/*metaphor*.
tenor and vehicle
PEPP.
tenor of discourse
FDLP/*tenor*.
Tensas, Madison, M.D.
OCAL.
tense
FDLP/*lax*; FDLP; FDLP/*tension*; GLT; ME/*447*.
tense vowel
ME/*448*.
tensile
DLTS.
tension
DLDC/*form*; DLTC; DLTS; DMCT; FDLP; HL; ME/*302*; PEPP.
tenson
DLTC.
tenso(n)
PEPP.

tensons
OCEL.
tenuis
GLT.
ten-year test
DLTC.
tenzi
PEPP/*987*.
tenzone
PEPP.
tercet
DLDC/*versification*; DLTC; DLTS; HL; PEPP; PH.
term
ME/*302*.
term, emotive
EDSL/*324*.
term, evaluative
EDSL/*324*.
terminal
FDLP; FDLP/*juncture*; GLT.
terminal contour
GLT.
terminal element
FDLP/*terminal*.
terminal juncture
ME/*448*.
terminal rhyme
DLTS; HL.
terminal-rhyme
DLDC/*versification*.
terminal stress
GLT.
terminal string
EDSL/*226*; FDLP/*terminal*; ME/*448*.
terminal symbol
EDSL/*229*; FDLP/*terminal*.
terminative
EDSL/*311*.
terminology
FDLP/*adultomorphic*.
term paper
ME/*302*.

tern □ 278

tern
 DLTC.
ternaire
 DLTC.
territorial
 FDLP/*dialect*.
tertiary language
 GLT.
tertiary response
 FDLP.
tertiary stress
 GLT.
terza rima
 HL.
terza rima
 CODEL; DLDC/*versification*;
 DLTC; DLTS; ME/*302*; OCEL;
 PEPP; PH.
terza rima sonnet
 DLTC; PEPP.
terzina
 DLTC.
tessitura
 FDLP.
testament
 DLTC; DLTS; HL.
Testament of Man
 OCAL.
testimonial
 ME/*302*.
tetralogy
 DLTC; DLTS; HL; PEPP.
tetrameter
 DLDC/*versification*; DLTC;
 DLTS; HL; ME/*302*; PEPP; PH/
 metre.
tétramètre
 DLTC; PEPP.
tetrapody
 DLTC; PEPP.
tetrastich
 DLTC; DLTS; PEPP.
tetronym
 OO.

text
 CR/*Index*; DMCT; EDSL/*294*;
 EDSL/*356*; FDLP; ME/*303*.
text blindness
 EDSL/*164*.
textbook
 DLTS.
textual
 DLTS.
textual analysis
 EDSL/*295*.
textual critic
 DLDC/*criticism*.
textual criticism
 DLTC; HL; PEPP.
textual meaning
 FDLP/*text*.
textual studies, literary
 FDLP/*computational linguistics*.
texture
 DLDC/*form*; DLTC; DLTS;
 DMCT; HL; ME/*303*; PEPP;
 PH.
T forms
 FDLP.
TG
 FDLP.
Thai poetry
 PEPP.
that-clause
 FDLP.
that-clause
 ME/*449*.
theater
 DLTS.
theater-in-the-round
 DLTS; HL.
Theater in the U.S.
 OCAL.
theater of cruelty
 HL.
Theater of the Absurd
 DLTS; ME/*304*; HL.
theatre
 CODEL.

Theatre Guild, The
OCAL.
theatre-in-the-round
DLTC.
theatre of cruelty
DLTC.
theatre of panic
DLTC.
theatre of silence
DLTC.
Theatre of the Absurd
DLTC.
theatricalism
DLTC.
thematic
FDLP/*theme*; GLT.
thematic aspects
FDLP/*communication*.
thematic flection
GLT.
thematic morpheme
GLT.
thematic structure
FDLP/*theme*.
thematic textual analysis
EDSL/*295*.
thematic vowel
GLT.
thematisation
FDLP/*theme*.
theme
DLTC; DLTS; DMCT; FDLP; GLT; HL; ME/*304*; PEPP/*987*.
theogony
DLTC.
Theophrastan characters
ME/*305*.
theorems
FDLP/*axiomatic*.
theoretical base form
GLT.
theoretical critic
DLDC/*criticism*.

theoretical criticism
HL; PEPP.
theoretical grammar
FDLP/*grammar*.
theoretical knowledge
CR/*Index*.
theoretical linguistics
FDLP/*counter-intuitive*.
there transformation
ME/*449*.
thesaurus
DLTC; DLTS.
thesis
CR/*Index*.
thesis
DLTC; DLTS; HL; ME/*305*; PEPP; PH.
thesis novel
DLTC; HL.
thesis play
DLTC; HL.
thesis question
ME/*306*.
thesis statement
ME/*306*.
thing
FDLP/*noun*.
third person
FDLP/*person*.
thorn
ME/*449*; ME/*449*.
Three Unities
DLDC/*unity*; DLTS.
threnody
DLDC/*elegy*; DLTC; DLTS; DMCT; HL; PEPP; PH/*elegy*.
thriller
DLTC.
thyroid cartilage
FDLP/*vocal cords*.
Tibetan poetry
PEPP.
til(de)
GLT.

timbre
DLTS; EDSL/*177*; FDLP; GLT.
time
EDSL/*305*; FDLP/*adverb*.
time-depth
GLT.
time, discursive
EDSL/*318*.
time, external
EDSL/*319*.
time, historical
EDSL/*319*.
time, internal
EDSL/*319*.
time novels
DLTC.
time, reader's
EDSL/*319*.
time, reading
EDSL/*319*.
time, story
EDSL/*319*.
time, writer's
EDSL/*319*.
time, writing
EDSL/*319*.
timing
FDLP.
Tin Pan Alley
OCAL.
tip
FDLP.
tip-of-the-tongue
FDLP/*accessibility*.
tip-of-the-tongue phenomenon
FDLP.
tirade
DLTC; DLTS.
title
HL; ME/*306*.
titles
FDLP/*address*; FDLP/*apposition*.
tmesis
DLTC; DLTS; PEPP.

token
EDSL/*105*.
tome
DLTS.
tonal configuration
FDLP/*configuration*.
tonal quality
FDLP/*timbre*.
tone
DLDC; DLTC; DLTS; EDSL/*179*; FDLP; GLT; HL; LGEP/*9*; ME/*307*; PEPP; PH.
tone color
HL; PH/*texture*.
tone-color
PEPP.
tone colour
DLTC.
tone group
FDLP.
tone groups
FDLP/*intonation*.
tone language
FDLP/*tone*; GLT.
toneme
FDLP/*tone*; GLT.
tonemics
FDLP/*tone*.
tone registers
GLT.
tone sandhi
FDLP/*tone*.
tonetics
FDLP/*tone*.
tone unit
FDLP/*information*; FDLP/*tone group*.
tongue
FDLP.
tongue advancement
GLT.
tongue-body feature
FDLP/*tongue*.
tongue height
GLT.

281 □ **Tractarian Movement**

tongue-slip
FDLP.

tongue twister
DLTC; DLTS.

tongue-twisters
FDLP/*dissimilation*.

tonic
FDLP.

tonic accent
GLT.

tonicity
FDLP/*tonic*.

tonic syllable
FDLP/*tonic*; GLT.

topic
DLDC; EDSL/*271*; FDLP/*topicalisation*; GLT.

topic/comment contrast
FDLP/*topicalisation*.

topicalisation
FDLP.

topic-changing
FDLP/*adjacency pair*.

topic outline
ME/*307*.

topics: dialectical and rhetorical
CR/*Index*.

topic sentence
FDLP/*topicalisation*; ME/*307*.

topographical poem
PEPP.

topographical poetry
DLTC; HL.

topoi
DLDC/*topic*.

toponomasiology
GLT.

toponomastics
GLT.

toponomatology
GLT.

toponym
OO.

toponymic
GLT.

toponymy
DLTS.

topos
DLDC/*topic*.

topos
DMCT; EDSL/*220*; HL; PEPP/*989*.

tornada
PEPP.

tornada
DLTC.

torture
CR/*Index*.

total accountability
FDLP.

total significance
LGEP/*40*.

total synonymy
FDLP/*synonym*.

total theatre
DLTC.

touchstone
DLTC; DLTS; HL; PEPP.

tough literature
ME/*307*.

tough movement
FDLP.

tour de force
DLTC; DLTS; HL; ME/*308*.

trace
EDSL/*350*; FDLP.

trace theory
FDLP/*trace*.

trachea
FDLP/*larynx*.

tract
DLTC; DLTS; HL.

tractarianism
HL.

Tractarian Movement
CODEL; DLTC; ME/*308*; OCEL.

trade language
FDLP/*language*; GLT.
tradition
DLTC; DMCT; HL; PEPP.
traditional
FDLP.
traditional ballad
DLDC/*ballad*; HL.
traditional grammar
FDLP/*traditional*; FDLP/*grammar*; ME/*449*.
traductio
PEPP.
tragedy
CODEL; DLDC; DLTC; DLTS; DMCT; HL; ME/*308*; OCEL; PEPP.
tragedy of blood
DLTC; HL.
tragic
EDSL/*154*.
tragic flaw
DLTC; DLTS; HL; ME/*308*; PEPP.
tragic force
HL.
tragic irony
DLDC/*irony*; DLTC; HL; ME/*308*; PH/*irony*.
tragicomedy
DLDC; DLTC; DLTS; HL; PEPP.
tranche de vie
DLDC/*naturalism*; DLTC.
tranche de vie
DLTS.
Transcendental Club
CODEL; HL; OCAL; OCEL.
Transcendentalism
HL; OCAL; DLTC; DLTS; ME/*309*.
transcendental linguistics
GLT.
transcribe
FDLP/*transcription*.

transcription
FDLP; GLT; ME/*450*.
transcription, phonemic
EDSL/*172*.
transcription, phonetic
EDSL/*172*.
transfer
FDLP.
transference of meaning
LGEP/*49*; LGEP/*148*.
transference, rules of
LGEP/*148*.
transferend
EDSL/*240*.
transfer features
EDSL/*130*.
transfer grammar
GLT.
transferred epithet
DLDC/*figurative language*; DLTC; HL; ME/*310*.
transferred meaning
GLT.
transform
FDLP; ME/*451*.
transformation
EDSL/*289*; EDSL/*242*; EDSL/*241*; FDLP; FDLP/*a-over-a*; GLT; ME/*452*.
transformation(al)
GLT.
transformational analysis
GLT.
transformational component
FDLP/*component*.
transformational cycle
EDSL/*234*; FDLP/*cycle*.
transformational derivation
FDLP.
transformational grammar
FDLP; ME/*452*.
transformational history
FDLP.

283 □ transposition

transformational rule
EDSL/*231*; FDLP/*axiomatic*; FDLP; ME/*453*.

transformation, generalized
EDSL/*243*.

transformation, nominalization
EDSL/*208*.

transformation, obligatory
EDSL/*243*.

transformation, optional
EDSL/*243*.

transformation, reflexivization
EDSL/*243*.

transformation, singulary
EDSL/*243*.

transformations of appearance
EDSL/*292*.

transformations of aspect
EDSL/*291*.

transformations of attitude
EDSL/*293*.

transformations of description
EDSL/*292*.

transformations of intent
EDSL/*291*.

transformations of knowledge
EDSL/*292*.

transformations of manner
EDSL/*291*.

transformations of mode
EDSL/*291*.

transformations of result
EDSL/*291*.

transformations of status
EDSL/*292*.

transformations of subjectivization
EDSL/*293*.

transformations of supposition
EDSL/*293*.

transformation, syntactic
EDSL/*239*.

transform grammar
GLT.

transient
FDLP/*transition*.

transition
DLTS; FDLP; GLT; ME/*310*.

transitional
FDLP/*transition*.

transitional areas
FDLP/*area*.

transitional sound
GLT.

transitional writing
GLT.

transition area
GLT.

transitive
FDLP/*transitivity*.

transitive relationship
EDSL/*268*.

transitive verb
ME/*453*.

transitivity
FDLP.

translaation
EDSL/*239*.

translatio
CR/*Index*.

translation
DLTC; DLTS; FDLP/*applied linguistics*; FDLP/*computational linguistics*; FDLP/*application*; FDLP/*contrast*; HL; PEPP.

translation loan word
GLT.

translations
DMCT.

translative
EDSL/*240*.

transliteration
GLT.

transmission
GLT.

transmutation
GLT.

transposition
EDSL/*239*; GLT; ME/*453*.

transpositive
EDSL/5.
travel book
DLTC.
Traven, B.
OCAL.
travesty
DLDC/*burlesque*; DLTC; DLTS; DMCT; HL.
treatise
DLTC; DLTS.
tree
EDSL/228; FDLP.
tree diagram
FDLP/*tree*; ME/453.
tree-pruning rule
EDSL/233.
tree stem theory
GLT.
triad
DLTC; DLTS; PEPP.
triadic
FDLP.
triads
CODEL; OCEL.
trial
GLT.
tribe
CR/*Index*.
Tribe of Ben
DLTC; HL; PEPP.
tribrach
CODEL; DLTC; DLTS; EDSL/187; HL; ME/311; OCEL; PEPP.
trick ending
DLTS.
tricolon
CR/*Index*.
triconsonantal root
GLT.
trigraph
GLT.
trihemimeral
PEPP.

trilingualism
GLT.
triliteral root
GLT.
triliteral theory
GLT.
trill
FDLP; GLT.
trilled
FDLP/*trill*.
trilled *r*
ME/453.
trilogy
CODEL; DLTC; DLTS; HL; ME/311; OCEL; PEPP.
trimeter
CODEL; DLDC/*versification*; DLTC; DLTS; HL; ME/311; OCEL; PEPP; PH/*metre*.
trimètre
DLTC; PEPP.
triolet
PEPP.
triolet
CODEL; DLTC; DLTS; EDSL/192; HL; OCEL; PH/*rondeau*.
trionym
OO.
tripartite
GLT.
triphthong
FDLP; GLT.
triple meter
DLTC; HL; PEPP.
triple rhyme
DLTC; HL; PEPP; PH/*rhyme*.
triple-rhyme
DLDC/*versification*.
triple rhythm
DLTC; PH.
triplet
CODEL; DLDC/*versification*; DLTC; DLTS; EDSL/192; HL; OCEL; PEPP.

285 □ tumbling verse

triplets
GLT.
tripody
DLTC; PEPP.
trisemic
DLTC; PEPP.
tristich
DLTC; DLTS; HL.
trisyllabic
DLTS; FDLP/*disyllable*; PH/*metre*.
tritagonist
DLTC; DLTS; HL.
trite expression
HL.
triteness
DLTS; ME/*311*.
trivium
CODEL; CR/*Index*; DLTC; DLTS; HL; OCEL.
trobar
DLTC.
trobar clus
DLTC; PEPP.
trochaic
DLDC/*versification*; FDLP/*foot*; PH/*metre*.
trochee
CODEL; DLDC/*versification*; DLTC; DLTS; EDSL/*187*; HL; LGEP/*112*; ME/*311*; OCEL; PEPP.
Troilus stanza
DLTC; PH/*stanza*.
trope
DLDC; DLTC; DLTS; EDSL/*275*; HL; ME/*311*; PEPP; PH/*figurative language*.
tropes
CR/*Index*; DLDC/*figurative language*; LGEP/*74*.
tropism
DLTS.

tropological interpretation of Scripture
CR/*Index*.
troubadour
DLTC; DLTS; HL; PEPP; PH.
troubadours
ME/*312*; OCEL.
trough
GLT.
trouvère
DLTC; HL; PEPP.
trouvères
OCEL.
trouvères
CODEL; PH/*troubadour*.
truism
DLTS; ME/*312*.
T rule
FDLP.
truncated
PH/*catalectic*.
truncation
DLTC; HL; PEPP; PH/*catalectic*.
truth
FDLP/*correspond*.
truth and poetry
PEPP.
truth-conditional
FDLP.
truth-conditional semantics
FDLP.
truth-value
FDLP/*connotation*.
Tudor
DLTS; HL.
Tudor Period
DLTC.
Tuesday Club of Annapolis
OCAL.
Tuesday Club of Philadelphia
OCAL.
tumbling verse
DLTC; HL; PEPP; PH/*Skeltonic verse*.

T-unit
   ME/*447*.
tupos
   DLDC/*type*.
tu quoque
   ME/*312*.
turbulence
   FDLP/*abrupt*.
Turkish
   FDLP/*agglutinative*.
Turkish poetry
   PEPP.
turn
   FDLP; GLT.
turning point
   DLTC.
turn-taking
   FDLP/*turn*.
Twain, Mark
   OCAL.
twang
   FDLP/*articulatory setting*.
two-syllable rhyme
   LGEP/*91*.
two-way classification
   FDLP/*closed*.

type
   DLDC; DLTS; EDSL/*105*; HL.
type of activity
   FDLP/*aspect*.
types
   EDSL/*149*.
typography
   FDLP/*graphetics*.
typological
   DLTC.
typological classification
   GLT.
typological comparison
   FDLP/*typological linguistics*.
typological linguistics
   FDLP/*linguistics*; FDLP.
typologies
   EDSL/*152*.
typology
   EDSL/*81*; FDLP/*typological linguistics*; GLT.
typonym
   OO.
tz'u
   DLTC.

U

ubi sunt
   DLDC/*type*; DLTC; ME/*313*; PEPP.

ubi sunt formula
   HL.

ubi sunt theme
   DLTS.

UC
   FDLP.

Ukrainian poetry
   PEPP.

ultimate constituent
   FDLP; ME/*454*.

ultimate constituents
   FDLP/*constituent*; GLT.

ultima Thule
   HL.

ultima Thule
   CODEL; DLTS; OCEL.

ultraism
   DLTC; PEPP.

Umgangssprache
   GLT.

umgekehrte Schreibung
   GLT.

umlaut
   DLTS; GLT; ME/*454*.

unabridged
   DLTS.

unacceptable
   FDLP/*acceptability*.

unanalysable
   FDLP/*analysable*.

Unanimism
   PEPP; DLTC.

unbounded noun
   GLT.

unchecked
   FDLP/*checked*.

Uncle Sam
   OCAL.

uncompleted aspect
   EDSL/*309*.

unconditioned
   GLT.

unconscious, the
   DLTC.

uncountable nouns
   FDLP/*countable*.

under-differentiation
   GLT.

under-extension
   FDLP.

underground press
   HL.

underlying
   FDLP.

underlying form
   FDLP/*underlying*; GLT.

underlying phrase-marker
FDLP/*underlying*.

underlying string
FDLP/*underlying*.

underlying structure
FDLP/*surface structure*; FDLP/*underlying*.

underplot
DLDC/*plot*.

understatement
DLDC/*figurative language*; DLTC; DLTS; HL; LGEP/*168*; ME/*314*; PEPP.

understood
FDLP/*ellipsis*.

undistributed middle
ME/*315*.

ungoverned
FDLP/*govern*.

ungradable
FDLP/*gradability*.

ungraded antonyms
FDLP/*antonym*.

ungrammatical
EDSL/*127*; FDLP/*grammaticality*.

unidirectional
FDLP/*co-occur*.

unilateral
FDLP/*lateral*.

uninterruptability
FDLP/*cohesion*; FDLP/*interruptability*.

uninterruptibility
FDLP/*word*.

unintrusive narrator
HL.

unique constituent
GLT.

unique morpheme
GLT.

unit
EDSL/*216*; FDLP.

Unitarianism
HL; OCAL.

Unities
CODEL; DLTC; HL; ME/*315*.

unities, the
OCEL.

unities, three
DLTS.

unit noun
FDLP/*unit*.

units of information
FDLP/*information*.

unity
CR/*Index*; DLDC; DLTC; DLTS; HL; ME/*315*; PEPP.

universal
DLDC/*concrete*; FDLP.

universal base
FDLP/*universal*.

universal combination
GLT.

universal grammar
FDLP/*grammar*; FDLP/*universal*; GLT.

Universalism
OCAL.

universality
DLTC; DLTS; HL.

universal language
GLT.

universal quantification
FDLP/*quantifier*.

universe of discourse
FDLP/*discourse*.

universities, medieval
CR/*Index*.

universities, Renaissance
CR/*Index*.

university plays
HL.

University Wits
CODEL; DLTC; ME/*315*; OCEL; HL.

unmarked
EDSL/*112*; FDLP/*markedness*.

unmarked member
GLT.

unmarked sequence
FDLP/*actor-action-goal.*
unproductive
FDLP/*productivity*; GLT.
unproductive suffix
GLT.
unreliable narrator
HL.
unrounded
FDLP/*flat*; FDLP/*rounding.*
unrounding
GLT.
unstable
GLT.
unstressed
FDLP/*stress*; GLT.
untranslatableness
DLTC.
unvoiced
FDLP/*voice*; GLT.
unvoicing
GLT.
unwritten languages
FDLP/*dialect.*
upajati
PEPP.
ur-
GLT.
urban dialects
FDLP/*dialect.*
urbanity
DLTS.
Urdu poetry
PEPP.
Uruguayan poetry
PEPP.
usage
DLTC; DLTS; EDSL/*126*; FDLP; ME/*454.*
usage doctrine (doctrine of usage)
GLT.
usage label
FDLP/*usage*; ME/*455.*
uta
PEPP.
utilitarianism
DLTS.
utilitarian writing
ME/*315.*
utilitarinism
HL.
Utopia
DLDC; DLTC; HL; ME/*316.*
utopian
DLTS.
Utopian literature
DLDC/*Utopia.*
ut pictura poesis
DLTC; PEPP.
utterance
EDSL/*323*; FDLP; GLT.
uvular
FDLP; GLT.

V

V
  FDLP/*analysable*; FDLP/*arc*.
vade mecum
  DLTC; HL.
vade mecum
  DLTS.
vagueness
  EDSL/*237*; FDLP/*ambiguity*; ME/*317*.
vague sentence
  FDLP/*ambiguity*.
vague set
  EDSL/*237*.
Vaison, Second Council of
  CR/*Index*.
valency
  FDLP.
valency grammar
  FDLP/*valency*.
valeur
  FDLP/*value*.
value
  DMCT; EDSL/*16*; FDLP; PEPP.
value judgements
  FDLP/*correct*.
vaporous
  DLTS.
vapors
  DLTS.

vapours
  HL.
variability
  EDSL/*145*.
variable
  FDLP; GLT.
variable rule
  FDLP/*variable*.
variable syllable
  DLTC; PH.
variant
  FDLP; PH/*cesura*.
variants
  FDLP/*conditioned*; GLT.
variants, phonetic
  GLT.
variant units
  FDLP/*allo-*.
variation
  DMCT.
variety
  FDLP.
variorum
  CODEL; DLTC; DLTS; OCEL.
variorum edition
  CODEL; HL; OCEL.
Varronian satire
  HL.
vates
  DLTC.

vatic ☐ **292**

vatic
  HL.
vaudeville
  CODEL; DLTC; DLTS; HL; OCAL; OCEL.
vehicle
  DLDC/*figurative language*; DLTC; DLTS; DMCT; HL; LGEP/*151*; LGEP/*154*; PEPP; PH/*metaphor*.
vehicular language
  GLT.
velar
  FDLP/*velar*; FDLP; GLT.
velaric
  FDLP/*air-stream mechanism*; FDLP/*velar*.
velarisation
  FDLP/*articulation*; FDLP/*velar*.
velarised
  FDLP/*dark*.
velarized
  GLT.
velar stop
  ME/*456*.
velar vowel
  GLT.
velic closure
  FDLP/*velar*.
velum
  FDLP/*air-stream mechanism*; FDLP/*velar*.
venedotian code
  DLTC.
Venezuelan poetry
  PEPP.
Venice
  CR/*Index*.
ventricular
  FDLP.
Venus and Adonis stanza
  DLTC; PEPP.
verb
  FDLP; ME/*456*.

verbal
  FDLP/*verb*; GLT; ME/*457*.
verbal adjective
  FDLP/*verb*.
verbal aspect
  EDSL/*294*.
verbal clusters
  FDLP/*verb*.
verbal group
  FDLP/*verb*.
verbal irony
  DLDC/*irony*; DMCT.
verbal language
  EDSL/*103*.
verbal noun
  FDLP/*verb*.
verbal-noun
  FDLP/*-ing* form.
verbal pause
  EDSL/*187*.
verbal repetition
  LGEP/*73*.
verbal response
  EDSL/*69*.
verbal texture
  PH/*texture*.
verb cluster
  GLT.
verb-headed construction
  ME/*456*.
verbiage
  DLTS; ME/*317*.
verbid
  GLT.
verbless
  FDLP.
verbless poetry
  PEPP/*989*.
verbocrap
  DLTC.
verbosity
  DLTS; ME/*317*.

Verb Phrase
FDLP/*assign*; FDLP/*verb*; ME/*456*.
Verfremdung
DLTC.
verisimilitude
DLTC; DLTS; DMCT; HL; ME/*317*; PEPP.
verism
DLTC.
verist
DLTS.
vernacular
DLTC; DLTS; FDLP; GLT.
vernacular languages
CR/*Index*.
Verner's Law
ME/*457*; GLT.
Verona
CR/*Index*.
vers
PEPP.
vers
DLTC.
vers de société
DLDC/*light verse*; DLTC; HL; ME/*318*; PEPP.
vers de société
DLTS; PH/*light verse*.
verse
DLDC/*versification*; DLDC/*literature*; DLTC; DLTS; DMCT; HL; ME/*318*; PH.
verse and prose
PEPP.
verse design
EDSL/*188*.
verse drama
PEPP.
verse epistle
DMCT.
verse instance
EDSL/*188*.
verse lineation
LGEP/*47*.

verse paragraph
DLDC/*versification*; DLTC; HL; LGEP/*125*; PEPP; PH.
verse structure
FDLP/*foot*.
verset
DLTC; PEPP.
versicle
DLTC.
versification
DLDC; DLTC; DLTS; HL; PEPP; PH.
versi sciolti
PEPP.
vers libérés
DLTC.
vers libre
DLDC/*versification*; HL; ME/*318*; OCAL/*free verse*; PEPP.
vers libre
DLTS; DMCT.
vers libres
DLTC; OCEL.
vers libres
CODEL.
verso
DLTS.
verso piano
DLTC.
verso piano
PEPP.
verso sciolto
DLTC.
verso sdrucciolo
DLTC; PEPP.
verso tronco
DLTC; PEPP.
versus politicus
PEPP.
versus pythius
PEPP.
versus spondaicus
PEPP.
V forms
FDLP.

vibrant
   GLT.
vibratory feedback
   GLT.
vibratory phonetics
   GLT.
vice
   HL.
Vicenza
   CR/*Index*.
Vice, the
   DLTC.
Victorian
   CODEL; DLDC; DLTS; HL; OCEL; ME/*318*.
Victorian Period
   DLTC.
Vietnamese
   FDLP/*isolating*; FDLP/*class*.
Vietnamese poetry
   PEPP.
viewpoint
   DLTC; DLTS.
vigilantes
   OCAL.
vignette
   CODEL; DLTC; DLTS; HL; OCEL.
villain
   DLTC; DLTS; HL.
villancico
   DLTC; PEPP.
villanelle
   PEPP.
villanelle
   CODEL; DLTC; DLTS; HL; ME/*319*; OCEL; PH.
virelai
   PEPP.
virelay
   CODEL; DLTS; HL; OCEL; PH.
vireli
   DLTC.
Virgin play
   HL.

virgule
   DLTC; HL; ME/*319*; PH.
virtualités
   GLT.
virtuemes
   EDSL/*334*.
virtues of style
   CR/*Index*.
visa
   DLTC.
visible speech
   EDSL/*189*.
vision
   PEPP/*990*.
vision, angle of
   EDSL/*332*.
vision of life
   ME/*320*.
visual patterning
   LGEP/*47*.
vivacity
   CR/*Index*.
vocable
   GLT; PH.
vocabulary
   FDLP; GLT.
vocabulary change
   GLT.
vocabulary word
   GLT.
vocal apparatus
   FDLP/*articulation*.
vocal-auditory channel
   FDLP.
vocal bands
   FDLP/*vocal cords*.
vocal characterizers
   GLT.
vocal cords
   FDLP.
vocal folds
   FDLP/*vocal cords*.
vocalic
   FDLP; GLT.

vocalic assonance
DLTC; PH/*rhyme*.
vocalic consonant
GLT.
vocalic off-glide
GLT.
vocalisation
FDLP.
vocalism
GLT.
vocalization
GLT.
vocal lip control
GLT.
vocal lips
FDLP/*vocal cords*.
vocal organs
FDLP.
vocal qualifier
FDLP; GLT.
vocal segregates
GLT.
vocal tract
FDLP/*air-stream mechanism*; FDLP.
vocal tract articulation
GLT.
vocative
FDLP.
vocative case
ME/*457*.
vocoid
FDLP; GLT.
voice
DLDC/*persona*; FDLP/*air-stream mechanism*; FDLP; GLT; ME/*320*; PEPP/*991*.
voice box
FDLP/*larynx*.
voiced
FDLP/*voice*.
voiced sounds
GLT.
voiced stops
FDLP/*aspiration*.

voiced voiceless [*sic*]
ME/*458*.
voice dynamics
FDLP.
voiceless
FDLP/*voice*.
voiceless plosive
FDLP/*alpha notation*.
voiceless sounds
GLT.
voiceless stops
FDLP/*aspiration*.
voiceless vowel
FDLP/*vowel*.
voice of verbs
ME/*458*.
voice onset time
FDLP/*voice*.
voice-over
HL.
voice-print
FDLP.
voice qualifier
FDLP/*vocal qualifier*; GLT.
voice quality
FDLP; FDLP/*creak*.
voice set
FDLP/*voice quality*.
voicing
GLT.
voicing lag
FDLP/*lag*; FDLP.
voicing lead
FDLP/*lag*; FDLP.
Volapük
DLTC.
Volgare
GLT.
Volksmärchen
DLTC.
volta
ME/*321*.
volta
DLTC; DLTS; HL; PEPP.

volume
    FDLP/*loudness*.
vorticism
    DLTC; DLTS; HL; OCEL; PEPP.
VOT
    FDLP/*voice*; FDLP.
vowel
    FDLP; GLT; ME/*458*.
vowel cluster
    GLT.
vowel fracture
    GLT.
vowel gradation
    GLT.
vowel harmony
    FDLP/*vowel*; GLT.
vowel length
    FDLP/*chroneme*.
vowel mutation
    GLT.
vowel quadrilateral
    FDLP/*vowel*.
vowel quality
    FDLP/*vowel*; GLT.
vowel quantity
    GLT.
vowel rhyme
    DLTC; DLTS; PEPP; PH/*rhyme*.
vowel shift
    GLT.

vowel system
    FDLP/*vowel*.
vowel triangle
    FDLP/*vowel*.
vox nihili
    GLT.
voyelle d'appui
    GLT.
VP
    FDLP.
vraisemblance
    DLTC.
vuelta
    DLTC.
vulgar
    GLT.
vulgarism
    DLTS; GLT.
vulgarity
    DLTC; DLTS.
Vulgar Latin
    GLT.
Vulgate
    CODEL; DLTS; HL; ME/*321*.
vulgate English
    GLT.
Vulgate, The
    OCEL.

W

'wabbit' phenomenon
  FDLP/*'fis' phenomenon*.
wails
  EDSL/*156*.
waka
  PEPP.
Wall Street
  OCAL.
Walpole Literary Club
  OCAL.
wants
  FDLP/*desiderative*.
Ward, Artemus
  OCAL.
Wardour-Street English
  CODEL; HL; OCEL.
War of 1812
  OCAL.
War of Independence
  OCAL/*Revolutionary War*.
war of the theaters
  HL.
Washington, District of Columbia
  OCAL.
Washington Square Players
  OCAL.
wave
  FDLP.
wave mode
  FDLP/*wave*.

wave theory
  FDLP/*wave*; GLT; ME/*459*.
Wayside Inn
  OCAL.
weak
  FDLP/*lenis*; FDLP/*fortis*; GLT.
weak ending
  CODEL; DLDC/*versification*; DLTC; DLTS; HL; OCEL; PEPP; PH.
weakening
  GLT.
weak form
  FDLP.
weak generative capacity
  FDLP/*capacity*.
weak grade
  GLT.
weakly adequate
  FDLP/*adequacy*.
weak stress
  GLT.
wedge verse
  PEPP.
weight
  FDLP/*accent*; PH.
Wellentheorie
  GLT.
well-formed
  FDLP.

well-formedness
FDLP/*global*; FDLP/*well-formed*.
well-made novel
HL.
well-made play
DLDC/*pièce bien faite*; DLTC; HL.
Welsh
FDLP/*fricative*; FDLP/*lateral*; FDLP/*bilabial*; FDLP/*fixed*; FDLP/*mutation*; FDLP/*discontinuous*; FDLP/*code*.
Welsh forms
PH.
Welsh literature
HL.
Welsh poetry
PEPP.
Welsh prosody
PEPP.
Weltanschauung
DLTC; ME/*322*.
Weltanschauung
DLTS.
Weltliteratur
DLTC.
Weltschmerz
DLTC; ME/*322*.
Weltschmerz
DLTS.
wên and wu
DLTC.
West African languages
FDLP/*covered*; FDLP/*coarticulation*.
Westchester Farmer
OCAL.
westerns
HL.
Western story
DLTS.
West Point
OCAL.
Wetherell, Elizabeth
OCAL.

Wharf Theater
OCAL/*Provincetown Players*.
wh-clause
ME/*459*.
wheel
DLTC; PEPP.
whichmire
ME/*322*.
whimsical
HL.
whimsy
DLTS.
whisper
FDLP/*larynx*; GLT.
whispered speech
FDLP/*glottal*.
whistle-speech
FDLP.
whiz-**deletion**
FDLP.
whodunit
DLTC; DLTS.
Whorfian
FDLP.
Whorfian hypothesis
FDLP/*Whorfian*.
wh-**question**
FDLP.
wh-question
ME/*460*.
wh-word
ME/*460*.
wide
FDLP/*diphthong*.
widened meaning
GLT.
wide vowel
GLT.
widow
HL.
Widow Bedott
OCAL.
Wilderness Road
OCAL.

Williamsburg
OCAL.
willing suspension of disbelief
DLTC.
windpipe
FDLP/*larynx*.
wisdom and eloquence
CR/*Index*.
wisdom literature
CR/*Index*.
wit
DLDC/*comedy*; DLDC; DLTC; DLTS; DMCT; ME/*322*; PEPP; PH.
wit and humor
HL.
witness
EDSL/*331*.
witnesses
CR/*Index*.
women as actors
HL.
word
DLTS; FDLP; GLT; ME/*460*.
word accent
FDLP/*accent*; HL; PEPP.
word and paradigm
FDLP.
word-blend
LGEP/*61*.
word choice
CR/*Index*.
word class
FDLP/*word*; GLT.
word-class
FDLP/*adverb*.
word classes
FDLP/*invariable*.
word-classes
FDLP/*adverb*.
word-crossing
GLT.
word-final
FDLP/*assimilation*.

word-form
FDLP/*word*.
word formation
GLT.
word-formation
FDLP.
word-identification
FDLP/*congruence*.
wordiness
ME/*323*.
word order
FDLP; FDLP/*word*; GLT; ME/*460*.
word-play
LGEP/*209*.
words and things, relationship
FDLP/*correspond*.
word sign
GLT.
word stress
FDLP/*stress*; FDLP/*accent*; GLT.
working hypothesis
FDLP/*heuristic*.
World War, The First
OCAL.
World War, The Second
OCAL.
WP
FDLP/*word and paradigm*.
wrenched accent
DLTC; GLT; HL; PEPP; PH.
wrenched rhyme
ME/*323*.
writing
CR/*Index*; EDSL/*193*; GLT.
writing system
FDLP/*graphology*.
wrong
FDLP/*correct*.
wugs
FDLP.
wynn
ME/*460*; ME/*460*.

X

Xanaduism
  DLTC.
Xenophanic
  DLTC.

Xhosa
  FDLP/*click*.

Y

Yale Series of Younger Poets
  OCAL.
Yankee
  OCAL.
yarn
  DLTC; DLTS.
Yazoo frauds
  OCAL.
year book
  DLTC.
yellow-backs
  CODEL; DLTC; OCEL.
Yellow Book, The
  DLTC.
yellow journalism
  CODEL; DLTC; DLTS; OCEL.
yellow press
  OCAL.
yes/no question
  ME/*461*.
yes-no question
  FDLP.
Yiddish poetry
  PEPP.

yield
  GLT.
yod
  GLT.
yodization
  GLT.
yogh
  ME/*461*; ME/*461*.
yo-he-ho theory
  GLT.
Yoruba poetry
  PEPP/*992*.
Young Grammarians
  GLT.
young man from the provinces
  HL.
Young Vienna
  PEPP.
yüeh-fu
  DLTC.
Yugoslav poetry
  PEPP.

Z

zany
CODEL; DLTC; OCEL.
zarzuela
DLTC.
Zeichensetzen
EDSL/*340*.
Zeitgeist
DLTC; OCEL.
Zeitgeist
CODEL; DLTS.
zéjel
DLTC; PEPP.
Zen
ME/*324*.
ženske pesme
DLTC.
zero
FDLP; GLT.
zero allomorph
GLT; ME/*462*; ME/*462*.
zero anaphora
FDLP/*zero*; GLT.
zero-article
FDLP/*zero*.
zero change
GLT.

zero connector
GLT.
zero-connector
FDLP/*zero*.
zero ending
GLT.
zero grade
GLT.
zero morph
FDLP/*morpheme*; FDLP/*zero*.
zero operation
FDLP/*zero*.
zero phoneme
FDLP/*zero*.
zeugma
CODEL; DLDC; DLTC; DLTS; EDSL/*279*; HL; ME/*324*; OCEL; PEPP.
Zoar
OCAL.
zoom shot
HL.
zoösemiotics
FDLP.
Zulu
FDLP/*click*.